Consciousness and Physicalism

Consciousness and Physicalism: A Defense of a Research Program explores the nature of consciousness and its place in the world, offering a revisionist account of what it means to say that consciousness is nothing over and above the physical. By synthesizing work in the philosophy of mind, metaphysics, and philosophy of science from the last 20 years and forging a dialogue with contemporary research in the empirical sciences of the mind, Andreas Elpidorou and Guy Dove advance and defend a novel formulation of physicalism. Although physicalism has been traditionally understood to be a metaphysical thesis, Elpidorou and Dove argue that there is an alternative and indeed preferable understanding of physicalism that both renders physicalism a scientifically informed explanatory project and allows us to make important progress in addressing the ontological problem of consciousness. Physicalism, Elpidorou and Dove hold, is best viewed not as a thesis (metaphysical or otherwise) but as an interdisciplinary research program that aims to explain compositionally all natural phenomena that are central to our understanding of our place in nature. *Consciousness and Physicalism* is replete with philosophical arguments and informed, through and through, by findings in many areas of scientific research. It advances the debate regarding the ontological status of consciousness. It will interest students and scholars in philosophy of mind, metaphysics, philosophy of cognitive science, and philosophy of science. And it will challenge both foes and friends of physicalism.

Andreas Elpidorou is an Assistant Professor in the Department of Philosophy at the University of Louisville. He specializes in the philosophical study of the mind and has written extensively on the character of consciousness, cognition, and emotions.

Guy Dove is an Associate Professor in the Department of Philosophy at the University of Louisville. He specializes in philosophy of cognitive science and has published articles on concepts, embodied cognition, language development, and physicalism.

Routledge Studies in Contemporary Philosophy

Nature and Normativity
Biology, Teleology, and Meaning
Mark Okrent

Formal Epistemology and Cartesian Skepticism
In Defense of Belief in the Natural World
Tomoji Shogenji

Epistemic Rationality and Epistemic Normativity
Patrick Bondy

From Rules to Meanings
New Essays on Inferentialism
Edited by Ondřej Beran, Vojtěch Kolman, and Ladislav Koreň

Toleration and Freedom from Harm
Liberalism Reconceived
Andrew Jason Cohen

Voicing Dissent
The Ethics and Epistemology of Making Disagreement Public
Edited by Casey Rebecca Johnson

New Directions in the Philosophy of Memory
Edited by Kourken Michaelian, Dorothea Debus, and Denis Perrin

A Pragmatic Approach to Libertarian Free Will
John Lemos

Consciousness and Physicalism
A Defense of a Research Program
Andreas Elpidorou and Guy Dove

For more information about this series, please visit: https://www.routledge.com/Routledge-Studies-in-Contemporary-Philosophy/book-series/RSCP

Consciousness and Physicalism

A Defense of a Research Program

Andreas Elpidorou and Guy Dove

Routledge
Taylor & Francis Group
NEW YORK AND LONDON

First published 2018
by Routledge
711 Third Avenue, New York, NY 10017

and by Routledge
2 Park Square, Milton Park, Abingdon, Oxon OX14 4RN

Routledge is an imprint of the Taylor & Francis Group, an informa business

Library of Congress Cataloging-in-Publication Data
Names: Elpidorou, Andreas, author.
Title: Consciousness and physicalism : a defense of a research program / by Andreas Elpidorou and Guy Dove.
Description: 1 [edition]. | New York : Taylor & Francis, 2018. | Series: Routledge studies in contemporary philosophy ; 108 | Includes bibliographical references and index.
Identifiers: LCCN 2018004860 | ISBN 9781138928053 (hardback)
Subjects: LCSH: Consciousness. | Materialism.
Classification: LCC B808.9 .E47 2018 | DDC 128/.2—dc23
LC record available at https://lccn.loc.gov/2018004860

ISBN: 978-1-138-92805-3 (hbk)
ISBN: 978-1-315-68207-5 (ebk)

Typeset in Sabon
by Apex CoVantage, LLC

Contents

Figures

Acknowledgments

Andreas Elpidorou

This book has been a long time in the making. The intention of writing a book on consciousness and physicalism was formed in early 2012, more or less simultaneously with the completion of my doctoral dissertation. Although the desire to write the book never wavered the slightest, the years between the initial intention and the publication of the book were marked by a tide of changes in my intellectual preferences. I have gone from physicalism to neutral monism, from neutral monism to naturalism, and then back to physicalism at least twice. And even when I settled on physicalism, there was vacillation about the exact form of physicalism that ought to be accepted. Determining where one stands with the issue of consciousness is no trivial matter; defending one's preferred view is an order of difficulty greater. Whoever says otherwise has not, I believe, thought about consciousness hard enough. The idea for a book might have originated in me, yet the final product is a true collaborative effort with Guy. Despite differences in our philosophical sensibilities, we agree on a contention that proved to be of utmost importance: whatever physicalism is, we think, it must be realistic, useful, and grounded in scientific practice. The pages that follow are an expression and defense of this agreement.

I am grateful to a great number of individuals—too many indeed that I am afraid that I will inevitably and unfortunately leave someone out. My greatest debt goes to Lauren Freeman for her unwavering support, Herculean patience, and love. I thank Dan Dahlstrom, Walter Hopp, Charles Griswold, and Alex Byrne for their generous feedback on my early work on consciousness and physicalism. Dan, Walter, and Charles ought to be thanked twice. They were, and continue to be, my mentors. I thank Esa Diaz-Leon for being a source of philosophical inspiration and an exemplar. I thank Daniel Stoljar and Philip Goff for their kindness and willingness to read and comment on work that I, without asking, sent their way. I thank Lauren Freeman, John Gibson, Stephen Hanson, and Avery Kolers for conversations on topics related to the book. I thank Philippe Chuard, Alex Grzankowski, Kevin Morris, Adam Podlaskowski, William Robinson, and Gene Witmer for their commentaries on papers on consciousness and physicalism. I thank Andrew Melnyk, Barbara Montero, and Jessica Wilson for conversations (either in person or over email) about physicalism. I thank audiences and the philosophy faculty at the University of Denver, Lehigh University, and the University of New Mexico. I am especially thankful to Gordon Bearn, Kelly Becker, Mark Bickhard, Robin Dillon, Paul Livingston, Marco Nathan, Naomi Reshotko, Jere Surber, Iain Thomson, and Roslyn Weiss for their questions. I also thank audiences at the following conferences: the 2011 meeting of the Central division of the APA, the 73rd annual meeting of the Southwestern Philosophical Society, the 2011 meeting of the Society for Exact Philosophy, the 2012 meeting of the Central division of the APA, the 2014 meeting of the Pacific division of the APA, the first annual meeting of the Society for the Metaphysics of Science, and the Cognition, Consciousness, and Behavior conference at the University of Louisville. I thank John Gibson and the *Commonwealth Center for the Humanities and Society* for a fellowship and a course release during the 2016–17 academic year. In the Spring semester of 2015, I had the pleasure of teaching a seminar on consciousness. I am grateful to all the students for their participation. I thank Kelly Trogdon for extensive comments on Chapter 2, and Karen Bennett and Louis deRosset for their help and patience with my questions on grounding. I thank Margo Irvin for first commissioning the project and our editor, Andrew Weckenmann, for his support and belief in the project. I thank Springer for permission to reuse a version of "Introduction: The Character of Physicalism" (originally published in *Topoi*) as Chapter 2 and John Wiley and Sons for permission to reuse parts of "Embodied Conceivability: How to Keep the Phenomenal Concept Strategy Grounded" (originally published in *Ming & Language*) as Chapter 7. And, of course, I thank Guy for being a friend and an ideal collaborator.

Finally, I thank Rafa and Penelope: for their existence, smiles, and tantrums. Φύσις κρύπτεσθαι φιλεῖ. Yet, it is hard not to keep looking.

Acknowledgments

Guy Dove

Philosophy is an inherently social activity. This book never would have happened without the help of a large number of people. Although I am almost sure to miss someone, I want to acknowledge the many concrete ways that other people have provided assistance. First and foremost, I need to thank Jennifer Catlett for her unconditional support and physician's eye for philosophical BS. I also need to thank Bill Wimsatt for making me see that philosophy could be a scientifically informed enterprise. I thank all of the philosophers that I have pestered over the years about physicalism; many ideas have been floated and way too many questions asked. For their patience and critical acumen, I am indebted to Fred Adams, Ken Aizawa, Colin Allen, Clare Batty, Dylan Black, Tony Chemero, Julianne Chung, Sean Hermanson, Barbara Montero, Brian McLaughlin, Alyssa Ney, Tom Polger, Jesse Prinz, Elizabeth Schechter, Larry Shapiro, Kari Theurer, and Josh Weisberg. I also want to thank several researchers in the psychological and brain sciences for what has to be an even greater imposition—in particular, Michael Arbib, Anna Borghi, Cara Cashon, Arthur Glenberg, David Landy, Martin Pickering, Friedemann Pulvermüller, and Gabriella Vigliocco. I thank Springer for permission to reuse a substantial portion of "Redefining Physicalism" (originally published in *Topoi*) as Chapter 3. An early version of this paper was presented at Florida International University in 2016, and I am grateful for the useful feedback provided by the remarkably engaged students in attendance. Jessica Wilson graciously responded to the *Topoi* article through email and the current version is better as a result. I also thank John Wiley and Sons for permission to reuse parts of "Embodied Conceivability: How to Keep the Phenomenal Concept Strategy Grounded" (originally published in *Ming & Language*) as Chapter 7. Versions of this paper were presented at the Consciousness, Cognition, and Behavior Conference held at the University of Louisville in 2015 and at the 2015 Annual Meeting of the Society for Philosophy and Psychology (SPP). Andreas and I are grateful for the penetrating questions asked by both audiences. A version of a new manuscript on Hempel's Dilemma was presented at the 2017 Annual Meeting of the Southern Society for Philosophy and Psychology (SSPP). I thank Kevin Morris for his insightful commentary and the audience for their thoughtful responses.

Naturally, I also need to thank Andreas for the opportunity to collaborate on this project. Although we approach these issues from different perspectives, we have managed to come together and have arrived at a place neither of us expected to be. Much to our families' collective consternation, there is not a question in this book that we haven't actively discussed.

Finally, I would like to dedicate this book to my children, Isabelle and William, who have given me so much.

1 Introduction

Let's Get Physical

1. Impetus

Very early on in his monumental *The Mind and Its Place in Nature*, C. D. Broad comments that as the second speaker for the Tarner lectures he will take care not to revisit ground covered by his predecessor, Alfred North Whitehead. To do so, he writes, "would be to expose myself to the most unflattering comparisons" (1925, p. 3). Today, anyone who writes a book on consciousness' place in the world has to confront and indeed withstand all sorts of unflattering comparisons.

In the last 30 years or so, a whole coterie of philosophical works on consciousness has been penned, typed, or printed. Some of them are works of remarkable clarity, philosophical rigor, and ingenuity, and they have rightly served as paradigms to many philosophical works that postdate them; the current work is no exception to the trend of works that follow in their footsteps. But if philosophers' productive engagement with consciousness and the mind were not enough, the sciences of the mind are progressing at such a rate that any state-of-the-art compendium runs the risk of being outdated the very moment that it is completed. Indeed, it is often said that in the last two decades, we have learned more about the workings of the brain than we were able to gather in all of previous human history. But even if such an assertion turns out to be an overstatement, its hyperbole is instructive. In recent years researchers have successfully erased, reactivated, and even transferred memories from one brain to another (Berger et al., 2011; Garner et al., 2012; Nabavi et al., 2014); they were able to construct systems that permit primitive brain-to-brain communication (Grau et al., 2014; Rao et al., 2014); they successfully reconstructed videos of entire visual scenes from decoding a person's neural activity in the visual cortex (Nishimoto et al., 2011); and by disrupting electrical activity in the claustrum, they were able to induce a loss of consciousness in a subject who otherwise remained awake (Koubeissi et al., 2014). Although not all the aforementioned empirical work directly pertains to consciousness, it is still exemplary of the progress that we have made in unlocking the mysteries of the mind. In the wake of such philosophical and scientific waves of writings on consciousness, what is then the need for another book on consciousness? The answer is simple: consciousness remains—still—a challenge for a physicalist (or materialist) conception of the world. And just like any challenge, it calls for a response.

2. A Balancing Act

The world consists of a plurality. In it, we find entities that range from the astronomically large to the microscopically small. Some are organic and others inorganic. Some are simple as rocks and others are complex as self-conscious human beings and supercomputers. Some are naturally occurring like stars, deserts, and hydrogen. Others are our creations: there are pens, self-driving cars, and artificial hearts; there are democracies, cultural norms, and rules of etiquette. The exact number of such entities is not to the point. What is important is the undeniable fact that our world is ontologically rich. Ostensibly at least, our world's inventory far surpasses that of physics.

> PLURALITY: The world—our world—contains more things than the things posited to exist by physics or even by our physical sciences.

Most people—philosophers or not—do not deny that the entities mentioned earlier exist. Thus, they accept PLURALITY. Such an attitude is also common amongst physicalists. But whereas individuals who belong in the first group are under no obligation to render PLURALITY consistent with the rest of their beliefs, physicalists cannot shirk that responsibility. That is because physicalists are committed to an additional principle that seems to be at odds with plurality:

> AUSTERITY: In our world, nothing exists but the physical.

AUSTERITY lies at the core of physicalism (Jackson, 2006; Papineau, 2001; Smart, 1963). Not only does it expunge entities that are incompatible with physicalism (e.g., immaterial or supernatural entities) from our world, it also assigns a clear priority to the physical. To paraphrase Wilfrid Sellars only slightly, AUSTERITY renders physics the measure of all things, of what is that it is, and of what is not that it is not (1991, p. 173). If some thing exists, and physicalism is true, then that thing must be physical.

The conjunction of PLURALITY and AUSTERITY makes physicalism attractive. Our world contains all the things that we ordinarily assume to exist and all the things that our special sciences tell us that they exist. Yet, the acceptance of AUSTERITY renders all those things fundamentally similar. Appearances to the contrary notwithstanding, everything that exists obeys the same rules and laws. The world is both incredibly rich and simple at the same time. But can physicalists coherently embrace both PLURALITY and AUSTERITY?

No entity exemplifies the difficulty of rendering consistent both PLURALITY and AUSTERITY better than (phenomenal[1]) consciousness. Thinking philosophically about consciousness often feels like a balancing act. There is, first, the pull of consciousness' uniqueness. Just think of what it feels like to accidentally touch a hot stove or to bite your own tongue. Consider the smell of fresh rain, the weightlessness of falling asleep, or the nauseating smell of having your teeth drilled at the dentist. What it is like to undergo all of these experiences, indeed what it is like to be conscious of the world, your self, and others, has an elusive nature. Consciousness might be a most personal phenomenon, one with which we are intimately acquainted, yet it does not cease to appear extraordinary. Pre-theoretically at least, consciousness defies assimilation to the natural world order; it is strikingly dissimilar to the world of physical or material entities.

The pull of consciousness' uniqueness is strong, but one cannot be left unimpressed by a preponderance of evidence, both everyday and scientific, that points to the view that whatever consciousness is, it is intimately related to our biological makeup. One too many drinks and consciousness is affected; a blow to the head and consciousness might be gone. Bilateral damage to central thalamus and thalamic manipulations (such as reduction of thalamic metabolism and blood flow) can make consciousness disappear (Alkire & Miller, 2005; Bogen, 1995; Churchland, 2013; Laureys, 2005; Posner, Saper, Schiff, & Plum, 2007); fusiform lesions lead to prosopagnosia (Barton, Press, Keenan, & O'Connor, 2002; Kanwisher & Yovel, 2006); lesions in V1 (primary visual cortex) can cause blindness or severe loss of vision (Leopold, 2012); and middle temporal lesions can result in the loss of the visual experience of motion (Churchland, 2013; Ramachandran & Blakeslee, 1998). We know that consciousness is either lost or severely affected during generalized absence seizures (i.e., the abnormal and hypersynchronous discharge of neurons; Blumenfeld, 2011) and that the areas most affected by such seizures correspond to the ones that are altered in sleep and anesthesia (Tononi & Koch, 2008). Consciousness may have its own spectral allure, but the predictive and manipulative power of our brain sciences is a constant reminder that consciousness is not a free-floating, ungrounded phenomenon.

The combination of those two attitudes about consciousness gives rise to a puzzle: How does consciousness arise out of our biology? Consciousness' existence calls for an explanation, but such an explanation is one that currently escapes us. Consciousness is at the same time real (its presence makes a difference), biologically grounded, and elusive. There remains a gap between, on the one hand, what we know about physics, chemistry, neurobiology, and psychology, and, what we think we know about consciousness. When we put all available pieces together in an attempt to explain how something that is not conscious (physical, biological, neural, or otherwise) can be conscious, we are faced with a difficulty. How is it exactly that this entity is bestowed with sentience whereas a different one is not? Why should the activation of this neurological structure give rise to the experience of blue whereas the activation of a different structure feels like pain? We were able to figure out the grounds of solidity, photosynthesis, combustion, digestion, cell mutation, and countless others. We have shown that even though they are qualitatively different from their components, such phenomena are nothing over and above their components. When it comes to consciousness, there is a wide consensus that consciousness' components are areas of the brain (Schiff, 2008; Churchland, 2013), although one should not preclude the possibility of an externalist, embodied, or enactive extension to the current approaches to consciousness. Furthermore, consciousness appears to require at the very least a certain type of interconnection, either in the form of functional unity or synchronization (Dehaene & Changeux, 2011; Tononi, Boly, Massimini, & Koch, 2016). All the same, a theory that renders its presence and workings intelligent in terms of its non-conscious (physical) components is not currently available.

That much is readily admitted both by the optimists and the skeptics. The optimists see our current predicament as a call for further research. Our knowledge is not complete, they hold, but it will be, or at least we will learn enough about consciousness' physical grounds that its existence will cease to appear puzzling. The skeptics disagree. Whereas the optimists see an opportunity and an attainable goal, the skeptics see an insurmountable gulf. Consciousness might not be the only currently unexplained phenomenon, but the challenge that consciousness poses is, according to them, of a distinct kind. The skeptics are not united. Some of them hold that there is and will be no explanation for consciousness, period. Given our cognitive abilities, we are simply incapable of understanding it (Huxley, 1902; McGinn, 1989; Nagel, 1974; see for discussion Flanagan, 1991). For others, however, the problem of consciousness is a problem that arises only due to one's commitment to a purely physicalist ontology. Once we give up our physicalist ontology, or at least relax it in certain respects, the problem of consciousness becomes tractable (Descartes, 1642/2008; Chalmers, 1996; Nagel, 1979; Strawson, 2008).

This book is an expression of mitigated optimism with regard to consciousness. In it, we explore the prospects of a view about the world and consciousness that, on the one hand, is physicalistic insofar as it holds that all that exists in the world, consciousness included, is physical, but, on the other hand, is importantly different from traditional metaphysical or conceptual formulations of physicalism. We offer a revisionist account of what it means to say that consciousness is nothing over and above the physical and with it an alternative formulation of physicalism. Physicalism, we argue, should be understood as an interdisciplinary research program that aims to compositionally explain all natural phenomena that are central to our understanding of our place in nature. It is thus scientific (compositional) explanation, not metaphysics or conceptual analysis, that renders consistent the joint acceptance of PLURALITY and AUSTERITY. Our proposed reconstructive take on physicalism (what we call "research program physicalism"[2]) is optimistic insofar as it is committed to the claim that consciousness will eventually be captured by a physically grounded compositional explanation. The optimism is mitigated, however, by the fact that physicalism *qua* research program is an empirical enterprise. Its success cannot be assumed nor a priori established via philosophical arguments or conceptual analyses. Research program physicalism is a bet: It is the expectation that consciousness will be compositionally explained. Its success or fulfillment, we deem, is probable, but by no means certain.

There are views in the literature that share important aspects of our position. Patricia Churchland takes physicalism to be an empirical issue and finds the contention that consciousness will be physically explained to be a "highly probable hypothesis" (1994, p. 23). Barbara Montero (2013) denies (overly) metaphysical characterizations of physicalism. In fact, she argues that physicalism is not committed to the claim that the non-physical supervenes on the physical. By utilizing the notion of grounding, Shamik Dasgupta (2014) offers an explanatory characterization of physicalism. And Bas van Fraassen (2002), Jeffrey Poland (1994, 2003), and Alyssa Ney (2008), among others, deny that physicalism should be understood as a metaphysical *thesis*. Although these positions are similar to our proposed account, they are also importantly different. Unlike Churchland, we take our everyday experience of consciousness seriously and we strive to show how physicalism can explain it. Unlike Montero, we do not merely reject physicalism's metaphysical commitments, we replace them with strong explanatory ones. Unlike Dasgupta, we do not think that the relevant notion of explanation is a metaphysical one—explanation we argue is a scientific matter and thus our notions of explanation should be guided by actual and successful scientific practices. We agree with van Fraassen, Poland, and Ney that physicalism should not be viewed as a metaphysical thesis. However, our resulting reconceptualization of physicalism (as an interdisciplinary program) is not only markedly different from theirs, but also one that avoids difficulties that they face.

3. What Does a Science of Consciousness Look Like?

If one focuses primarily on those aspects of consciousness that seem to defy, in their very conception, scientific explanation, then one might get the impression that interdisciplinary research on consciousness is hopeless and that we have not learned anything significant in the last few decades. This impression is, of course, misleading at best. Researchers in cognitive neuroscience, neuropsychology, perception science, and other fields are actively investigating consciousness and have uncovered important findings concerning the cognitive features of consciousness and the underlying biological mechanisms that support it. Indeed, any attempt to summarize this activity would be overwhelming and well beyond the purview of this monograph. We propose instead to just highlight a sliver of this activity in order to counterbalance this false impression and give a hint of the promise of an interdisciplinary approach. We are going to focus on conscious visual perception for several reasons: vision science is arguably the most fully developed area of neurobiology and cognitive neuroscience; visual experience is often cited in philosophical discussions of consciousness; and visual perception is a variety of conscious experience that involves consciousness of something rather than a general state of awareness.

Research on consciousness has undergone the sort of intuitive upheaval that is typical in the sciences but often overlooked in philosophical discussions of the limits of science. Consider, for instance, the basic distinction between unconscious and conscious mental activity. At the beginning of the nineteenth century, it was generally presumed that thinking and reasoning were conscious activities full stop. The very idea that there could be unconscious thinking and reasoning was rarely even recognized as a meaningful possibility. Breaking with this received view, Hermann von Helmholtz (1866/2005) proposed that conscious perception relies on "unconscious inferences." He offered this theoretical proposal because he inferred from his measurement of the velocity of peripheral nerve impulses and the slowness of reaction times in psychophysical experiments that a great deal of mental work was being carried out prior to conscious perception. This idea struck many of his contemporaries as outrageous and possibly incoherent.

At the dawn of the twentieth century, Sigmund Freud (1915/1963) famously proposed that unconscious thinking played a fundamental role in our psychological dynamics. Indeed, while many of the theoretical underpinnings of psychoanalysis have not fared well, Freud's greatest contribution to contemporary psychological theory may well be the distinction between conscious and unconscious mental activity. The notion that a significant proportion of our thinking and reasoning is unconscious has become a central dogma of contemporary cognitive science. In keeping with Helmholtz's insight, perception researchers have been on the front lines of the effort to uncover the relationship between conscious and unconscious processing. It is common in this field to make a conceptual distinction between mere sensitivity to the physical features of a stimulus and the conscious perception of them (as well as the various higher-level properties that they may seem to possess). Researchers have expended a great deal of effort to uncover not only the neural mechanisms involved in conscious perception but also their functional profile. Importantly, this research relies heavily on both behavioral and introspective evidence.

When psychophysical research began in the nineteenth century with the work of Gustav Fechner (1860/1966), there was a general worry that our perceptual judgments were not reliable enough to support physical experimentation because of their inherent subjectivity (Murray, 1993). Fechner's ability to uncover robust formal relationships between physical parameters and perceptual judgments alleviated this concern to some extent. The success of psychophysics then laid the foundation for the use of introspective responses in perception science, and in the intervening years researchers have been able to uncover a great deal about our sensory systems, particularly the visual system.

One particularly dramatic indication of the importance of introspection is the widespread use of visual illusions as test cases in neurobiology. Indeed, we highly recommend that you use Google to see the finalists for *The Best Illusion of the Year Contest* held annually by the Neural Correlate Society. To see how illusions have become a central explanandum in vision science, consider a pair of parade cases: in the late 1800s, Ernst Mach noticed that illusory light and dark grey bands are perceived at the borders between differing shades of grey (Figure 1.1) and Ludimar Hermann (Figure 1.2) noticed that ghost-like grey spots emerge with black grids against a white background (Eagleman, 2001). These illusory perceptions, which have come to be known as Mach bands and the Hermann grid, respectively, are now thought to arise primarily because of lateral inhibition in neural circuits associated with edge-detection. Lateral inhibition is a robust feature of the nervous system and has been implicated in a number of perceptual phenomena, including other visual illusions. Sensory neurons have measurable receptive fields; relevant stimuli that fall within these fields on the receptor surface modulate their activity and stimuli that fall outside of these fields do not. Neurophysiologists have found, though, that the activity of neurons with adjacent and overlapping receptive fields may either inhibit or excite the activity of neighboring neurons. The standard explanation for the Hermann grid builds on the proposal that neurons processing the white centers of the grid are receiving more inhibitory signals than those in the corridors (because the former have more white areas nearby than the latter). Similar circuits involving lateral inhibition have also been implicated in Mach

Figure 1.1 Mach Bands

Figure 1.2 Hermann Grid

bands, although there has been some recent evidence that higher-level vision processes associated with the perception of highlights on curved surfaces may also be at play (Lotto, Williams, & Purves, 1999).

The important point for our purposes is that vision scientists seek to explain the existence, persistence, and phenomenal character of illusions in terms of the underlying biological mechanisms. This effort not only relies on experiments involving introspective reports but also on careful behavioral experiments, single-unit recordings from neurons in living animal models, physical and chemical ablation experiments, clinical studies of patients with lesions, in vivo brain imaging experiments, and many other experimental paradigms. What is ultimately sought from this multifaceted research effort is a detailed and specific compositional explanation of how illusions and other perceptual phenomena arise from neural mechanisms.

It is fair to respond that, while the sort of examples outlined above may show the robustness of an integrated approach to vision science that includes introspective reports, the question of how visual experience becomes conscious remains unanswered. Researchers acknowledge this and are actively employing the same sort of interdisciplinary and multi-level methodology to address this lacuna. One of the ways they do this is by looking to neuropsychological case studies of impaired conscious experience. Damage to areas of the visual system can lead to impairments of conscious visual recognition that do not involve impairments of sensitivity to basic visual features such as color, distance, and motion. These impairments, known as visual agnosias, come in a number of striking varieties. Some patients with damage to the anterior inferior temporal lobe are able to match or accurately copy line drawings of everyday objects that they cannot visually recognize or categorize while others with damage to the posterior inferior temporal cortex are able to label visual objects but are unable to see them as a unified whole (Farah, 1990). Patients with Balint's Syndrome often see the world in a piecemeal fashion (Rafal, 2003). This aspect of the syndrome is known as simultagnosia because patients experience difficulty seeing one object at a time and are often only able to make out pieces of individual objects (Dalrymple, Barton, & Kingstone, 2013). Visual agnosia can also involve specific types of object recognition. Prosopagnosia, which may be congenital or the result of acquired lesions, involves an impairment of the ability to recognize people by their faces (Fox, Iaria, & Barton, 2008; Grüter, Grüter, & Carbon, 2008; Sacks, 2010). Bilateral damage to an area of the cortex associated with visual motion processing can lead to motion agnosia (Zihl, von Cramon, Mai, & Schmid, 1991).

Researchers study these impairments in part to differentiate conscious and unconscious cognitive processes. For instance, there is some evidence that some patients with prosopagnosia can retain an unconscious ability to recognize faces (Eimer, Gosling, & Duchaine, 2012; Rivolta, Palermo, Schmalzl, & Coltheart, 2012; Simon et al., 2011). These patients have been found to have differing autonomic responses to familiar and unfamiliar faces and perform better than chance when asked to guess whether a face is familiar or not. Consider another well-known example: the case of DF. This patient suffered from damage to her lateral occipital complex (James, Culham, Humphrey, Milner, & Goodale, 2003) and was impaired with respect to visual object-form recognition (visual form agnosia). Although she was able to draw objects from memory, she could neither name nor copy simple line drawings. Remarkably, DF was able to use visual form information to handle various grasp movement tasks. Researchers compared DF's ability to perceptually match the orientation of a slot with her ability to insert a card into the slot; while control subjects were able to perform both tasks equally well, DF could not (Goodale, Milner, Jakobson, & Carey, 1991; Milner & Goodale, 2006; for recent qualifications see Schenk, 2012). Given that she is not consciously aware of the orientation of either the card or the slot, it is unsurprising that she had trouble with the orientation-matching task. However, when instructed to "post" the card with a quick motion, DF was able to do so successfully. This seminal study, and those that followed it, suggest that some motor tasks are guided by unconscious visual processing.

Neuropsychological case studies such as these are not determinative in and of themselves. Over and above the fact that one should never rely on individual experiments, these studies face their own specific epistemic challenges. Fortunately, the thesis that some forms of action are under the control of unconscious visual processing is supported by a large body of research involving a number of different levels of grain, including evidence of separate major vision pathways defined at the cellular level, analogous deficits in monkeys with artificial lesions, and similar dissociations between perception and action in neurotypical participants (Goodale, 2004; Goodale & Milner, 1992).

This research fits within a general research strategy that seeks to identify the underlying neural correlates of conscious experience. More specifically, researchers have begun to look for sets of neural factors that are jointly sufficient for a conscious experience in the hopes that this will shed light on the underlying neural mechanisms (Chalmers, 2000; Koch, 2004). It may be helpful to examine a particular example: research on binocular rivalry. When two distinct images are simultaneously presented individually—one image to an eye—a curious thing happens. Rather than merge together to form a single visual percept, the images compete for visual awareness. Perceivers tend to see only one image at a time for a few seconds. Binocular rivalry is thus a form of bistable perception similar to that induced by well-known ambiguous figures such as the Necker cube and the Rabbit/Duck drawing. Because the switch from an awareness of one image to an awareness of the other occurs spontaneously and stochastically despite the constancy of the relevant stimuli, binocular rivalry has been used to explore the dynamics of, and underlying neural mechanisms responsible for, visual awareness. Two early studies have been particularly influential. In the first (Leopold & Logothetis, 1996), the activity of individual neurons in the visual cortex of alert monkeys was recorded while the subjects indicated the perceived orientation of orthogonal gratings. The firing pattern of a number of orientation-selective cells in higher visual areas, particularly V4, correlated with the perceptual dominance of a particular stimulus. In the second (Tong, Nakayama, Vaughan, & Kanwisher, 1998), binocular rivalry was induced in human participants by means of the dichoptic presentation of picture of a face and a picture of a house. Neuroimaging (fMRI) was used to measure the activity of a portion of the fusiform gyrus that responds more to faces than houses and the activity of a portion of the parahippocampal gyrus that responds more to houses than faces. Remarkably, the fMRI responses of these areas were modulated in a time-locked fashion with both the perceptual dominance and suppression of the relevant stimuli: the fusiform area manifested increased activation during the perceptual dominance of the face percept and decreased activation during its suppression while the parahippocampal area manifested the reverse pattern.

A great many functional neuroimaging studies of binocular rivalry have followed in the intervening years (for reviews see Blake & Logothetis, 2002; Miller, 2013; Tong, Meng, & Blake, 2006). One core issue that has emerged in this literature concerns whether the rivalry arises early or late in visual processing. Some evidence indicates that rivalry arises from early competition between monocular processing streams, which Philipp Sterzer (2013) refers to as "eye rivalry." For instance, John-Dylan Haynes and Geraint Rees (2005) demonstrate that it is possible to use eye-based patterns of activity in V1 to predict the fluctuating perception in binocular rivalry. In keeping with eye rivalry, applying transcranial magnetic stimulation (TMS) over early visual areas induces perceptual alterations during binocular rivalry (Pearson, Tadin, & Blake, 2007). Other evidence indicates that rivalry arises from later competition among binocular stages of visual processing, which Sterzer (2013) refers to as "pattern rivalry." In keeping with pattern rivalry, many electrophysiological studies find evidence implicating higher visual areas in rivalry but have failed to implicate V1 (for reviews see Leopold & Logothetis, 1999; Sengpiel, 2013). A number of models of the mechanisms responsible for binocular rivalry often resolve the tension between these two bodies of evidence by treating rivalry as multi-level phenomenon involving both eye and pattern rivalry (Dayan, 1998; Freeman, 2005; Tong et al., 2006).

Binocular rivalry has been referred to as a "real workhorse" in the study of visual awareness (Blake, Brascamp, & Heeger, 2014). While our understanding of this perceptual phenomenon remains incomplete, the extant research provides a preliminary exemplar of how it may be possible to investigate the neural mechanisms underlying consciousness. Some have worried, though, that this exemplar exposes an inherent limitation of this research strategy. Both Steven Miller (2001, 2007) and Antti Revonsuo (2000, 2001) point out that identifying particular forms of neural activity as the correlates of conscious experience does not establish that they are causally relevant constituents of that experience. It is important to note that the difficulty not only arises because it can be difficult to distinguish epiphenomenal correlates from constitutive ones, but also because it can be difficult to screen off precursors and consequences (Chalmers, 2000; Hohwy & Bayne, 2013). While Revonsuo proposes that the limitations associated with brain imaging techniques are an important source of this difficulty, Miller (2007) goes farther and suggests that what he refers to as the "correlation/constitution distinction problem" may be an unavoidable epistemic challenge.

We do not question the fact that consciousness presents serious methodological and theoretical challenges—who would question this? The real issue is whether or not these challenges are so profound that it would be impossible in principle to overcome them. We reject this and deny that the difficulties are substantial enough to curtail the project at its onset. Indeed, we suggest that there are a number of reasons to view this sort of a priori judgment with a skeptical eye. For one, the history of philosophy is littered with failed efforts to demarcate the bounds of science. Certainly we understand far more about the nature of life, the motions of heavenly bodies, and the origin of the cosmos now than many from previous centuries would have ever thought to be possible. Beyond this general inductive worry about the ability of philosophers to take a measure of what can and cannot be explained by science (and perhaps their propensity to rush to judgment), there are a number of reasons to question such a skeptical assessment with respect to the particular phenomenon at hand, visual experience.

For one, the correlation/constitution worry is not specific to consciousness. Indeed, the most prominent discussion of the need to distinguish correlation and constitution within the philosophy of mind concerns the degree to which cognition is embodied or extended (Adams & Aizawa, 2008). Granted, Frederick Adams and Kenneth Aizawa's core claim is that the evidence offered in support of embodied or extended cognition is likely to involve the correlates, not the constituents, of cognition (see also Rupert, 2009). Proponents of embodied and extended cognition, however, would certainly offer a different assessment and would likely argue that a core feature of their approach is the claim that aspects of the body and the environment are the constituents of cognitive processes (Chemero, 2009; Clark & Chalmers, 1998; Clark, 2008). This disagreement highlights at least two things: first, the correlation/constitution problem is a general one for cognitive neuroscience, and, second, debates concerning how to address particular forms of this problem are often theory-driven (for some other issues with the correlation/constitution worry, see Hurley, 2010 and Ross & Ladyman, 2010). In the end, understanding consciousness requires going beyond locating its correlates—behavioral or neural. What we need is an *explanation* (Seth, 2009, 2010). Few supporters of the neural correlates of consciousness (NCC) research would deny this, and some would agree that the identification of NCCs is merely a first step towards providing a physical explanation of conscious experience (e.g., Koch, Massimini, Boly, & Tononi, 2016). Some also recognize that the development of innovative theories of consciousness will also be an important step towards finding an empirically supported explanation (e.g., Tononi & Koch, 2015).

Another important factor to consider is that advances in experimental techniques and paradigms are likely to enable researchers to investigate the causal mechanisms responsible for conscious experience with greater sensitivity and flexibility than is currently possible. Giulio Tononi and Christof Koch (2008, p. 257) note in their update of the NCC strategy (citations in the original):

> The growing ability of neuroscientists to manipulate in a reversible, transient, deliberate, and delicate manner identified populations of neurons using methods from molecular biology combined with optical stimulation (Aravanis et al., 2007; Han & Boyden, 2007) enables the

intrepid neuroengineer to move from correlation—observing that a particular conscious state is associated with some neural or hemodynamic activity—to causation.

New methodologies are coming on line that will allow researchers to interrupt, manipulate, and modulate neural activity at different levels of grain (Silva, Bickle, & Landreth, 2014). This should enhance the ability of researchers to develop and test hypotheses concerning the proper constituents of phenomenal states. An intrepid skeptic might counter: This is all well and good, but it does nothing to overcome the fact that the data ultimately involve mere correlation between underlying physical states and phenomenal experience. This objection, though, reflects a failure to appreciate the abductive nature of scientific reasoning. Solving the problem of the relation of underlying neural mechanisms to phenomenal states is likely to involve an inference to the best explanation, but there is nothing special about this. Indeed, solving the problem of whether cognition is extended or not is going to require similar reasoning. Of course, the success of either of these enterprises is not guaranteed, and both face serious evidentiary and methodological challenges. Figuring out what states and processes are precursors, consequences, and epiphenomenal correlates represents a significant challenge for both efforts. Passively identifying correlations is unlikely to be enough. Intercession and manipulation will likely play an important role. Progress is probably going to depend on the development of new theories. But none of this is unusual or particular to research on consciousness.

The third reason to question a priori assessments of the correlation/constitution problem is that they often rest on the unquestioned presupposition that our subjective reports of phenomenal experience are perspicacious and unassailable. While we agree that attempts to scientifically explain consciousness should take these reports seriously, they should also be examined critically and investigated empirically. In other words, they should be taken with a grain of salt. Vision science provides ample support for this need to question our capacity to observe our own phenomenal states. For instance, patients with Anton's syndrome typically experience what is known as cortical blindness, which involves a significant loss of vision produced by cortical lesions (Aldrich, Alessi, Beck, & Gilman, 1987). Characteristically, they deny their blindness in the face of clear evidence to the contrary (something that is known as visual anosognosia) and often confabulate visual experience. Although one could perhaps argue that, despite the fact that these self-reported experiences are the result of confabulation, they are nevertheless completely accurate and the patients really do see what they say they see, there is at least room for doubt. Of course, one might dismiss this evidence due to the pathological nature of the syndrome. However, evidence from neurotypical subjects also suggests that we can be mistaken about the nature of our visual experience.

Consider research on what has come to be known as change blindness. A robust body of experiments employing different paradigms reveals that we are much worse at detecting changes in the visual scene than we intuitively expect (Simons & Rensink, 2005). In these experiments, large visual changes that should be easy to detect go unnoticed under certain contexts. Initially, research focused on highly specific contexts such as when such changes are introduced during saccades (Grimes, 1996; McConkie & Currie, 1996), eye blinks (O'Regan, Rensink, & Clark, 1997; O'Regan, Deubel, Clark, & Rensink, 2000), so-called "flicker" conditions (when an image of a scene is alternated with an altered image of the same scene with an intervening blank mask; Rensink, O'Regan, & Clark, 1997), and in conjunction with transient distractors in the form of "mud splashes" (O'Regan, Rensink, & Clark, 1996, 1999). But then researchers began to find that cruder manipulations of general expectations could induce similar effects (Simons & Rensink, 2005). A particularly striking example involved the switching of interlocutors in a real world situation; Daniel Simons and Daniel Levin (1998) had experimenters initiate a conversation with a stranger and then surreptitiously replaced that experimenter with a different experimenter who was not visually identical in terms of physical appearance or even attire to the first one. A surprising number of participants failed to notice the change. There is an active and ongoing discussion of how to interpret the various change blindness results, including whether or not they imply that vision is some kind of grand illusion (Noë & O'Regan, 2000; Noë, Pessoa, & Thompson, 2000; O'Regan, 1992). While we do not have the space to weigh in on the larger implications of this research, we do think it is possible to draw a much more minimal and measured conclusion: We can be misled about the character of our visual experience. Our performance on various visual tasks fails to comport with our impression that our visual experience is uniform and continuous. More specifically, the scope of visual attention appears to be much more circumscribed than it appears to be in our subjective experience.

The search for the NCC is one of the few clearly articulated research strategies in the science of consciousness. As such, it has appropriately received a great deal of critical attention. It is important, though, to recognize that it represents an early stage in the development a fully formed theory that integrates research from behavioral neuroscience, cognitive neuroscience, neuropsychology, psychophysics, and other fields. Vision science provides a rough sketch of how an interdisciplinary science of consciousness might proceed. Clearly, many questions remain, and it is way too early to declare any kind of victory over philosophically derived skepticism. Nevertheless, vision science lays the groundwork for a plausible physicalist research program.

4. The Road Ahead

In this book we set out to present and defend a novel formulation of physicalism. Physicalism has been traditionally and overwhelmingly understood as a metaphysical thesis. Yet, it does not have to be understood as such. Indeed, as we argue, there is an alternative understanding of physicalism that renders physicalism a scientifically informed explanatory project: Physicalism, we hold, is best viewed not as a thesis (metaphysical or otherwise) but as an interdisciplinary research program that aims to explain all phenomena that are apt for explanation in a manner that renders them physical. Given that our understanding of physicalism has no exact precedent in the literature, we begin the book by motivating our version of physicalism. This is done in two parts.

First, Chapter 2 makes room for our version of physicalism by highlighting difficulties that beset metaphysical conceptions of physicalism. The difficulties that we consider are not ones that stem from anti-physicalist assumptions or arguments; rather, they are endemic to metaphysical formulations of physicalism. Despite their respective differences, metaphysical conceptions of physicalism are all unified in their contention that the non-physical (mental, social, biological, etc.) is (metaphysically speaking) nothing over and above the physical. In this chapter we examine whether the notions of supervenience, a priori entailment, realization, and Grounding can be used to capture the purported metaphysical relationship between the physical and non-physical that renders the latter nothing over and above the former. We argue that all such attempts face substantial difficulties. We conclude not by denying the possibility of a metaphysical formulation of physicalism, but by presenting a novel way out of these difficulties, one that gives up the supposition that physicalism is necessarily a metaphysical thesis.

Whereas Chapter 2 motivates our version of physicalism by presenting issues with traditional metaphysical formulations of physicalism, Chapter 3 focuses on a different problem for physicalism. This is known as "Hempel's Dilemma" and it threatens to undermine the possibility of defining "physical" in a way that can be used by proponents of physicalism. Our view is that this problem is a serious one: It demands the physicalists' attention and its solution calls for a rethinking of physicalism's relationship to science. We argue that metaphysical understandings of physicalism that aim to define "physical" by appeal to the physical sciences are bound to failure. But we propose an alternative formulation of physicalism that can succeed: physicalism as an interdisciplinary research program. As an interdisciplinary research program, physicalism aims to explicate how physical entities give rise to natural phenomena by offering physical explanations of the latter phenomena. Our physicalism is both rigid and flexible in a way that avoids Hempel's Dilemma. It is restricted by its ontological and explanatory commitments but, ultimately, remains open to theoretical and empirical future developments that are permissible by the mandates of physicalism.

By the end of Chapter 3, we have carved out a space for our version of physicalism: There is a version of physicalism that is first and foremost an explanatory project, that by its very nature need not worry about the problems presented in Chapter 2, and that it escapes the grip of Hempel's Dilemma. But is this alternative understanding of physicalism really a form of physicalism? Chapter 4 undertakes the task of demonstrating how our version of physicalism is not only different from traditional versions of physicalism, but demanding enough to justify its name. In this chapter, our main concern is with making explicit the nature and commitments of the research program. We reject traditional understandings of physicalism that rely on the deductive-nomological model of explanation and instead advance the type of explanation that our version of physicalism aims to offer. We argue that research program physicalism is committed to offering compositional explanations of all natural phenomena that are relevant to our understanding of our place in the world, including consciousness. Compositional explanations are ones that make intelligent how the target phenomenon (the "whole") arises out of the workings of its components ("parts"). Research program physicalism turns out to be nomologically reductive because given the laws of nature the whole is rendered nothing over and above its components. However, and contrary to common views about physicalism, the research program does not require a stronger sense of reduction. The research program is empirical. As such, it follows scientific practice and maintains that successful compositional explanations require no metaphysical or logical connections between the whole and its parts. We expect that some readers will be skeptical of our explanatory approach. But we contend that such a skepticism is rooted in one's (often tacit) acceptance that physicalism *must* be committed to a model of explanation that posits either metaphysical or logical connections between explanans and explananda. In the absence of such an assumption there is no reason to worry about the physicalist credentials of the research program. There is nothing physically untoward with it: It posits no spooky existents; it has no room for nomological danglers; it is hierarchical and privileges the physical; and it tackles the various location problems that physicalists had always sought to solve.

The remaining three chapters all deal with the problem of (phenomenal) consciousness. Chapter 5 has a three-fold aim. First, it presents the explanatory gap and argues that in order for the presence of the explanatory gap to be a threat to the research program the gap has to be a permanent one. Second, it shows how traditional anti-physicalist arguments (the knowledge argument and the conceivability argument) require the permanence of the explanatory gap in order to establish their conclusions. Third, it critically evaluates two arguments in support of the conclusion that the gap is indeed permanent: Both arguments attempt to draw a distinction between truths about phenomenal consciousness and truths about the physical nature of the world and our minds and conclude, on the basis of that distinction, that no explanation of consciousness in terms of its physical nature is possible. We reject both of these arguments and make explicit our reasons for doing so.

Chapter 6 continues our investigation into the various reasons for thinking that the explanatory gap cannot be bridged. It is split into two main parts. In the first part, the chapter considers whether we could be irremediably ignorant about some aspect of the world and if so, whether such ignorance could be precluding us from offering a satisfactory explanation of consciousness. We examine three arguments in support of this view and conclude that they all fall short of establishing their conclusion: even if some parts of the world are forever beyond out comprehension, we do not have a reason to think that consciousness is one of them. Such a conclusion does not of course mean that a physicalist (compositional) explanation of consciousness is guaranteed. What it means is that there are no theoretical reasons that arrest the research program. In the second part of the chapter, we take on what is known as "the argument from structure and dynamics" (Chalmers, 2003/2010). In its simplest form, the argument holds that physical truths are truths about structure and dynamics, whereas truths about consciousness are not *purely* structural or dynamic. Given that one cannot derive the latter truths from the former, the argument concludes that consciousness cannot be physically explained. The argument is important. Not only does it pose a threat to the research program, it also offers important support for traditional anti-physicalist arguments. All the same, after a detailed examination of the various ways in which the notions of structure and dynamics can be rendered explicit, we conclude that the argument does not threaten the research program. At the end, consciousness might appear to be recalcitrant to physical explanations, but the available arguments do not demonstrate the impossibility of a physical explanation.

In the final chapter, Chapter 7, we address head-on consciousness' appearance as something other than physical. We acknowledge both the presence and persistence of this appearance. Nonetheless, by drawing upon a large body of evidence suggesting that our concepts are often embodied, we offer an explanation for the apparent uniqueness (or otherness) of consciousness that is fully compatible with research program physicalism: the fact that consciousness appears to us to be other than physical is the result of the working of our concepts. We thus do not explain the appearance away; we ground it in our psychology. Lastly, we argue that bridging the explanatory gap by offering a compositional explanation of consciousness does not require that consciousness must cease to appear other than physical. Not every adequate explanation must be such that leaves us with no ambiguity or perplexity about the character of the explained phenomenon. After all, explanation is one thing, whereas our subjective understanding of explanation is another. The goal of a compositional explanation of consciousness is to make explicit how consciousness arises out of the workings of its components. Such an explanation, however, could still give rise to the appearance that consciousness is something more than its parts. But precisely because this appearance is a product of our current psychological makeup, its presence need not perturb us. It carries no real epistemic weight and it is no indication that the explanatory gap is permanent.

We conclude the book by briefly comparing research program physicalism to other existing formulations of physicalism and by discussing how an acceptance of research program physicalism changes the philosophical landscape on consciousness insofar as it views its competitors (dualism, emergentism, Russellian monism) as competing *research programs*. A rethinking of both the character of physicalism and its relationship to competing views opens up avenues for future progress that were previously closed. Research program physicalism is not only importantly different from extant understandings of physicalism; it also carries great promise. In the pages that follow, we tried to capture and convey this promise and optimism for a type of metaphysics that is scientifically informed.

Notes

1. An organism is phenomenally conscious "if there is something that it is like to *be* that organism" (Nagel, 1974, p. 436). Humans, elephants, and bats are conscious in this sense, whereas tables, rocks, and drops of water are assumed to be not. This type of *qualitative* personal, organismic, or system-level consciousness is often used in order to single out a group of mental states, often called "qualitative states" or "phenomenal states" (for differences between the two, see Van Gulick, 2017). These are states that present their subjects (i.e., their possessors) with certain qualitative or experiential characteristics (e.g., the tartness of lemons, the redness of the setting sun) and consequently, there is something that it is like for the subject to undergo such states.
2. The view that physicalism should be understood as a research program is given in Dove (2016). In a recently published article, Duško Prelević also advocates for an understanding of physicalism that treats it as a research program (Prelević, 2017). We encourage the reader to compare our approach to that of Prelević. There are many important differences between the two views. To name just one: Only our account emphasizes compositional explanation and as such, we are able to offer a clear articulation of the conditions under which research program physicalism would succeed.

References

Adams, F., & Aizawa, K. (2008). *The bounds of cognition*. Malden, MA: John Wiley & Sons.

Aldrich, M. S., Alessi, A. G., Beck, R. W., & Gilman, S. (1987). Cortical blindness: Etiology, diagnosis, and prognosis. *Annals of Neurology*, *21*(2), 149–158.

Alkire, M. T., & Miller, J. (2005). General anesthesia and the neural correlates of consciousness. *Progress in Brain Research*, *150*, 229–597.

Aravanis, A. M., Wang, L. P., Zhang, F., Meltzer, L. A., Mogri, M. Z., Schneider, M. B., & Desseroth, K. (2007). An optical neural interface: In vivo control of rodent motor cortex with integrated fiberoptic and optogenetictechnology. *Journal of Neural Engineering*, *4*(3), S143–S156.

Barton, J. J., Press, D. Z., Keenan, J. P., & O'Connor, M. (2002). Lesions of the fusiform face area impair perception of facial configuration in prosopagnosia. *Neurology*, *58*(1), 71–78.

Berger, T. W., Hampson, R. E., Song, D., Goonawardena, A., Marmarelis, V. Z., & Deadwyler, S. A. (2011). A cortical neural prosthesis for restoring and enhancing memory. *Journal of Neural Engineering*, *8*(4), 046017.

Blake, R., Brascamp, J., & Heeger, D. J. (2014). Can binocular rivalry reveal the neural correlates of consciousness. *Philosophical Transactions of the Royal Society B*, *369*, 1–9.

Blake, R., & Logothetis, N. K. (2002). Visual competition. *Nature Reviews Neuroscience*, *3*(1), 13–21.

Blumenfeld, H. (2011). Epilepsy and the consciousness system: Transient vegetative state? *Neurologic Clinics*, *29*(4), 801–823.

Bogen, J. E. (1995). On the neurophysiology of consciousness: 1. An overview. *Consciousness and Cognition*, *4*(1), 52–62.

Broad, C. D. (1925). *The mind and its place in nature*. New York, NY: Harcourt, Brace & Company, INC.

Chalmers, D. J. (1996). *The conscious mind: In search of a fundamental theory*. New York: Oxford University Press.

Chalmers, D. J. (2000). What is a neural correlate of consciousness? In T. Metzinger (ed.), *Neural correlates of consciousness: Empirical and conceptual questions* (pp. 17–39). Cambridge, MA: MIT Press.

Chalmers, D. J. (2003). Consciousness and its place in nature. In S. P. Stich & T. A. Warfield (eds.), *The Blackwell guide to philosophy of mind* (pp. 102–142). Malden, MA: Blackwell Publishing. Revised version in Chalmers, 2010, pp. 103–140.

Chalmers, D. J. (2010). *The character of consciousness*. New York, NY: Oxford University Press.

Chemero, A. (2009). *Radical embodied cognitive science*. Cambridge, MA: MIT Press.

Churchland, P. S. (1994). Can neurobiology teach us anything about consciousness?. In *Proceedings and Addresses of the American Philosophical Association* (Vol. 67, No. 4, pp. 23–40). American Philosophical Association.

Churchland, P. S. (2013). *Touching a nerve: The self as brain*. New York, NY: W. W. Norton & Company Ltd.

Clark, A. (2008). *Supersizing the mind: Embodiment, action, and cognitive extension*. New York, NY: Oxford University Press.

Clark, A., & Chalmers, D. (1998). The extended mind. *Analysis*, *58*(1), 7–19.

Dalrymple, K. A., Barton, J. J. S., & Kingstone, A. (2013). A world unglued: Simultanagnosia as a spatial restriction of attention. *Frontiers in Human Neuroscience*, *7*, 145. http://doi.org/10.3389/fnhum.2013.00145

Dasgupta, S. (2014). The possibility of physicalism. *The Journal of Philosophy*, *111*(9/10), 557–592.

Dayan, P. (1998). A hierarchical model of binocular rivalry. *Neural Computation*, *10*, 1119–1135.

Dehaene, S., & Changeux, J. P. (2011). Experimental and theoretical approaches to conscious processing. *Neuron*, *70*(2), 200–227.

Descartes, R. (1642/2008). *Meditationes de prima philosophia, in quibus Dei existentia & animae humanae à corpore distinctio demonstrantur: his adjunctae sunt variae objectiones doctorum virorum in istas de Deo & anima demonstrationes, cum responsionibus authoris* (2nd edition). Amsterdam: Elzevir; *Meditations on first philosophy: With selections from the objections and replies* (M. Moriarty, Trans.). Oxford, UK: Oxford University Press.

Dove, G. (2016). Redefining physicalism. *Topoi*, 1–10. Advance online publication.

Eagleman, D. M. (2001). Visual illusions and neurobiology. *Nature Reviews Neuroscience*, 2(12), 920–926.

Eimer, M., Gosling, A., & Duchaine, B. (2012). Electrophysiological markers of covert face recognition in developmental prosopagnosia. *Brain, 135*(2), 542–554.
Farah, M. J. (1990). *Visual agnosia: Disorders of object recognition and what they tell us about normal vision*. Cambridge: MIT Press.
Fechner, G. (1860/1966). *Elements of psychophysics* (H. E. Adler, Trans.). New York: Holt, Rinehart, and Winston.
Flanagan, O. (1991). *The science of the mind*. Cambridge, MA: MIT Press.
Fox, C. J., Iaria, G., & Barton, J. (2008). Disconnection in prosopagnosia and face processing. *Cortex, 44*(8), 996–1009.
Freeman, A. W. (2005). Multistage model for binocular rivalry. *Journal of Neurophysiology, 94*, 4412–4420.
Freud, S. (1915/1963). The unconscious. In P. Reiff (ed.), *General psychological theory: Papers on metapsychology* (pp. 110–150). New York, NY: Macmillan.
Garner, A. R., Rowland, D. C., Hwang, S. Y., Baumgaertel, K., Roth, B. L., Kentros, C., & Mayford, M. (2012). Generation of a synthetic memory trace. *Science, 335*(6075), 1513–1516.
Goodale, M. A. (2004). An evolving view of duplex vision: Separate but interacting cortical pathways for perception and action. *Current Opinion in Neurobiology, 14*(2), 203–211. doi: 10.1016/j.conb.2004.03.002
Goodale, M. A., & Milner, A. D. (1992). Separate visual pathways for perception and action. *Trends in Neuroscience, 15*(1), 20–25.
Goodale, M. A., Milner, A. D., Jakobson, L. S., & Carey, D. P. (1991). A neurological dissociation between perceiving objects and grasping them. *Nature, 349*, 154–156.
Grau, C., Ginhoux, R., Riera, A., Nguyen, T. L., Chauvat, H., Berg, M., . . . Ruffini, G. (2014). Conscious brain-to-brain communication in humans using non-invasive technologies. *PLoS One, 9*(8), e105225.
Grimes, J. (1996). On the failure to detect changes in scenes across saccades. In K. Atkins (ed.), *Perception* (pp. 89–110). New York, NY: Oxford University Press.
Grüter, T., Grüter, M., & Carbon, C.-C. (2008). Neural and genetic foundations of face recognition and prosopagnosia. *Journal of Neuropsychology, 2*, 79–97.
Han, X., & Boyden, E. S. (2007). Multiple-color optical activation, silencing, and desynchronization of neural activity, with single-spike temporal resolution. *PLoS ONE*, 2, e299.
Haynes, J. D., & Rees, G. (2005). Predicting the stream of consciousness from activity in human visual cortex. *Current Biology, 15*(14), 1301–1307.
Helmholtz, H. von (1866/2005). Concerning the perceptions in general. In J. P. C. Southall (Trans.), *Treatise on physiological optics* (Vol. 3, Section 26). Reprinted New York, NY: Dover.
Hohwy, J., & Bayne, T. (2013). The neural correlates of consciousness: Causes, confounds, and constituents. In S. M. Miller (ed.), *The constitution of phenomenal consciousness* (pp. 155–176). Amsterdam/Philadelphia: John Benjamins Publishing Company.
Hurley, S. (2010). Varieties of externalism. In R. Menary (ed.), *The extended mind* (pp. 101–154). Cambridge, MA: MIT Press.
Huxley, T. X. (1902). *Lessons in elementary physiology*. New York, NY: Macmillan.
Jackson, F. (2006). On ensuring that physicalism is not a dual attribute theory in sheep's clothing. *Philosophical Studies, 131*(1), 227–249.
James, T. W., Culham, J., Humphrey, G. K., Milner, A. D., & Goodale, M. A. (2003). Ventral occipital lesions impair object recognition but not object-directed grasping: An fMRI study. *Brain, 126*(11), 2463–2475.

Kanwisher, N., & Yovel, G. (2006). The fusiform face area: A cortical region specialized for the perception of faces. *Philosophical Transactions of the Royal Society of London B: Biological Sciences*, *361*(1476), 2109–2128.

Koch, C. (2004). *The quest for consciousness: A neurobiological approach*. Englewood, CO: Roberts & Company.

Koch, C., Massimini, M., Boly, M., & Tononi, G. (2016). Neural correlates of consciousness: progress and problems. *Nature Reviews Neuroscience*, *17*(5), 307–321.

Koubeissi, M. Z., Bartolomei, F., Beltagy, A., & Picard, F. (2014). Electrical stimulation of a small brain area reversibly disrupts consciousness. *Epilepsy & Behavior*, *37*, 32–35.

Laureys, S. (2005). The neural correlate of (un)awareness: Lessons from the vegetative state. *Trends in Cognitive Sciences*, *9*(12), 556–559.

Leopold, D. A. (2012). Primary visual cortex: Awareness and blindsight. *Annual Review of Neuroscience*, *35*, 91–109.

Leopold, D. A., & Logothetis, N. K. (1996). Activity changes in early visual cortex reflect monkeys' percepts during binocular rivalry. *Nature*, *379*, 549–553.

Leopold, D. A., & Logothetis, N. K. (1999). Multistable phenomena: Changing views in perception. *Trends in Cognitive Sciences*, *3*(7), 254–264.

Lotto, R. B., Williams, S. M., & Purves, D. (1999). Mach bands as empirically derived associations. *Proceedings of the National Academy of Sciences*, *96*, 5245–5250.

McConkie, G. W., & Currie, C. B. (1996). Visual stability across saccades while viewing complex patterns. *Journal of Experimental Psychology: Human Perception and Performance*, *22*, 563–581.

McGinn, C. (1989). Can we solve the mind-body problem? *Mind*, *98*(391), 349–366.

Miller, S. M. (2001). Binocular rivalry and the cerebral hemispheres with a note on the correlates and constitution of visual consciousness. *Brain and Mind*, *2*(1), 119–149.

Miller, S. M. (2007). On the correlation/constitution distinction problem (and other hard problems) in the scientific study of consciousness. *Acta Neuropsychiatrica*, *19*(3), 159–176.

Miller, S. M. (2013). Visual consciousness and binocular rivalry: An introduction. In S. M. Miller (ed.), *The constitution of visual consciousness: Lessons from binocular rivalry* (pp. 1–14). Amsterdam/Philadelphia: John Benjamins Publishing Company.

Milner, D., & Goodale, M. (2006). *The visual brain in action* (2nd edition). New York: Oxford University Press.

Montero, B. G. (2013). Must physicalism imply the supervenience of the mental on the physical? *The Journal of Philosophy*, *110*(2), 93–110.

Murray, D. (1993). A perspective for viewing the history of psychophysics. *Behavioral and Brain Sciences*, *16*(1), 115–137.

Nabavi, S., Fox, R., Proulx, C. D., Lin, J. Y., Tsien, R. Y., & Malinow, R. (2014). Engineering a memory with LTD and LTP. *Nature*, *511*, 348–352.

Nagel, T. (1974). What is it like to be a bat? *The Philosophical Review*, *83*(4), 435–450.

Nagel, T. (1979). Panpsychism. In T. Nagel (ed.), *Mortal questions*. Cambridge, UK: Cambridge University Press.

Ney, A. (2008). Physicalism as an attitude. *Philosophical Studies*, *138*, 1–15.

Nishimoto, S., Vu, A. T., Naselaris, T., Benjamini, Y., Yu, B., & Gallant, J. L. (2011). Reconstructing visual experiences from brain activity evoked by natural movies. *Current Biology*, *21*(19), 1641–1646.

Noë, A., & O'Regan, J. K. (2000). Perception, attention and the grand illusion. *Psyche: An Interdisciplinary Journal of Research on Consciousness*, *6*(15), No pagination specified.

Noë, A., Pessoa, L., & E. Thompson (2000). Beyond the grand illusion: What change blindness really teaches us about vision. *Visual Cognition*, 7, 93–106.
O'Regan, J. K. (1992). Solving the "real" mysteries of visual perception: The world as an outside memory. *Canadian Journal of Psychology/Revue Canadienne de Psychologie*, *46*(3), 461–488.
O'Regan, J. K., Deubel, H., Clark, J. J., & Rensink, R. A. (2000). Picture changes during blinks: Looking without seeing and seeing without looking. *Visual Cognition*, *7*, 191–211.
O'Regan, J. K., Rensink, R. A., & Clark, J. J. (1996). "Mud splashes" render picture changes invisible. *Investigative Ophthalmology and Visual Science*, *37*, S213.
O'Regan, J. K., Rensink, R. A., & Clark, J. J. (1997). Picture changes during blinks: Not seeing where you look and seeing where you don't look. *Investigative Ophthalmology and Visual Science*, *38*, S707.
O'Regan, J. K., Rensink, R. A., & Clark, J. J. (1999). Change blindness as a result of "Mud splashes." *Nature*, *398*, 34.
Papineau, D. (2001). The rise of physicalism. In C. Gillett & B. Loewer (eds.), *Physicalism and its discontents* (pp. 3–36). Cambridge, UK: Cambridge University Press.
Pearson, J., Tadin, D., & Blake, R. (2007). The effects of transcranial magnetic stimulation on visual rivalry. *Journal of Vision*, *7*(2), 2.
Poland, J. (1994). *Physicalism: The philosophical foundations*. Oxford, UK: Oxford University Press.
Poland, J. (2003). Chomsky's challenge to physicalism. In L. M. Antony & N. Hornstein (eds.), *Chomsky and his critics* (pp. 29–48). Oxford, UK: Basil Blackwell.
Posner, J. B., Saper, C. B., Schiff, N. D., & Plum, F. (2007). *Plum and Posner's diagnosis of stupor and coma* (4th edition). New York: Oxford University Press.
Prelević, D. (2017). Physicalism as a research programme. *Grazer Philosophische Studien*. Advance online publication. doi: 10.1163/18756735-000023
Rafal, R. (2003). Balint's syndrome: A disorder of visual cognition. In M. D'Esposito (ed.), *Neurological foundations of cognitive neuroscience* (pp. 27–40). Cambridge, MA: MIT Press.
Ramachandran, V. S., & Blakeslee, S. (1998). *Phantoms in the brain: Probing the mysteries of the human mind*. New York: William Morrow.
Rao, R. P., Stocco, A., Bryan, M., Sarma, D., Youngquist, T. M., Wu, J., & Prat, C. S. (2014). A direct brain-to-brain interface in humans. *PloS ONE*, *9*(11), e111332.
Rensink, R. A., O'Regan, J. K., & Clark, J. J. (1997). To see or not to see: The need for attention to perceive change in scenes. *Psychological Science*, *8*(5), 368–373.
Revonsuo, A. (2000). Prospects for a scientific research program on consciousness. In T. Metzinger (ed.), *Neural correlates of consciousness: Empirical and conceptual questions* (pp. 57–75). Cambridge, MA: MIT Press.
Revonsuo, A. (2001). Can functional brain imaging discover consciousness in the brain? *Journal of Consciousness Studies*, *8*(3), 3–23.
Rivolta, D., Palermo, R., Schmalzl, L., & Coltheart, M. (2012). Covert face recognition in congenital prosopagnosia: A group study. *Cortex*, *48*(3), 344–352.
Ross, D., & Ladyman, J. (2010). The alleged coupling-constitution fallacy and the mature sciences. In R. Menary (ed.), *The extended mind* (pp. 155–166). Cambridge, MA: MIT Press.
Rupert, R. D. (2009). *Cognitive systems and the extended mind*. Oxford, UK: Oxford University Press.
Sacks, O. (2010). Face-blind: Why are some of us so terrible at recognizing faces? *New Yorker*, August 30, 36–43.

Schenk, T. (2012). No dissociation between perception and action in patient DF when haptic feedback is withdrawn. *Journal of Neuroscience*, 32(6), 2013–2017.

Schiff, N. D. (2008). Central thalamic contributions to arousal regulation and neurological disorders of consciousness. *Annals of the New York Academy of Sciences*, *1129*(1), 105–118.

Sellars, W. (1991). *Science, perception and reality*. London, UK: Routledge & Kegan Paul Ltd.Sengpiel, F. (2013). The neuron doctrine of binocular rivalry. In S. M. Miller (ed.), *The constitution of visual consciousness: Lessons from binocular rivalry* (pp. 167–186). Amsterdam/Philadelphia: John Benjamins Publishing Company.

Seth, A. K. (2009). Explanatory correlates of consciousness: Theoretical and computational challenges. *Cognitive Computation*, *1*(1), 50–63.

Seth, A. K. (2010). The grand challenge of consciousness. *Frontiers in Psychology*, *1*(5). http://doi.org/10.3389/fpsyg.2010.00005

Silva, A. J., Bickle, J., & Landreth, A. (2014). *Engineering the next revolution in neuroscience: The new science of experiment planning*. New York, NY: Oxford University Press.

Simon, R. S., Khateb, A., Darque, A., Lazeyras, F., Mayer, E., & Pegna, A. J. (2011). When the brain remembers, but the patient doesn't: Converging fMRI and EEG evidence for covert recognition in a case of prosopagnosia. *Cortex*, *47*(7), 825–838.

Simons, D. J., & Levin, D. T. (1998). Failure to detect changes to people during a real-world interaction. *Psychonomic Bulletin & Review*, *5*(4), 644–649.

Simons, D. J., & Rensink, R. A. (2005). Change blindness: Past, present, and future. *Trends in Cognitive Sciences*, *9*, 16–20.

Smart, J. (1963). Materialism. *The Journal of Philosophy*, *60*(22), 651–662. doi: 10.2307/2023512

Sterzer, P. (2013). Functional neuroimaging of binocular rivalry. In S. M. Miller (ed.), *The constitution of visual consciousness: Lessons from binocular rivalry* (pp. 187–210). Amsterdam/Philadelphia: John Benjamins Publishing Company.

Strawson, G. (2008). *Real materialism and other essays*. Oxford, UK: Oxford University Press.

Tong, F., Meng, M., & Blake, R. (2006). Neural bases of binocular rivalry. *Trends in Cognitive Sciences*, *10*(11), 502–511.

Tong, F., Nakayama, K., Vaughan, J. T., & Kanwisher, N. (1998). Binocular rivalry and visual awareness in human extrastriate cortex. *Neuron*, *21*, 753–759.

Tononi, G., Boly, M., Massimini, M., & Koch, C. (2016). Integrated information theory: From consciousness to its physical substrate. *Nature Reviews Neuroscience*, *17*(7), 450–461. doi: 10.1038/nrn.2016.44

Tononi, G., & Koch, C. (2008). The neural correlates of consciousness: An update. *Annals of the New York Academy of Sciences*, *1124*(1), 239–261.

Tononi, G., & Koch, C. (2015). Consciousness: Here, there and everywhere? *Philosophical Transactions of the Royal Society B*, *370*(1668).

van Fraassen, B. (2002). *The empirical stance*. New Haven, CT: Yale University Press.

van Gulick, R. (2017), Consciousness. In E. N. Zalta (ed.), *The Stanford Encyclopedia of Philosophy* (Summer 2017 Edition). https://plato.stanford.edu/archives/sum2017/entries/consciousness/.

Zihl, J., von Cramon, D., Mai, N., & Schmid, C. (1991). Disturbance of movement vision after bilateral posterior brain damage. *Brain*, *114*, 2235–2252.

2 The Metaphysics of Physicalism

Physicalism demands a consistency between AUSTERITY and PLURALITY. It requires that although many different entities exist in the world, they are nothing over and above the physical. The aim of this chapter is to investigate the prospects of articulating a *metaphysical* account of the relationship of nothing over and aboveness that physicalism requires. To that end, we survey different ways in which proponents of physicalism have made explicit the metaphysical dependence that is said to hold between the non-physical and the physical and which renders the former nothing over and above the latter.

1. Physicalism: Ontology and Metaphysics

At the heart of physicalism lies an ontological (or if you prefer, ontic) thesis.[1] To espouse physicalism is to make certain commitments about what types of things (objects, properties, events, states of affairs) exist in *our* world (Quine, 1948; cf. Hellman & Thompson, 1977, p. 310).[2] If physicalism is true, *every thing* that both (contingently and concretely) exists and plays a causal role in our world is, in some sense, physical.[3] Immaterial angels, ectoplasmatic lions, and Cartesian souls are not to be found in our world, whereas leptons, molecules, mountains, desks, minds, and democracies are. For most proponents of physicalism, however, physicalism is not just ontology; it is also, and importantly so, metaphysics (Schaffer, 2009). Physicalists do not aspire to conjure up long lists enumerating what exists (Jackson, 1994, 1998). Physicalism is instead advanced with the hopes of capturing the *underlying structure* of our world. It aims to tell us not only what exists but also *how* it exists: that is, how certain things are because of, arise out of, or hold in virtue of, some other things (Schaffer, 2009; Rosen, 2010). To use Karen Bennett's wonderfully suggestive term, most proponents of physicalism deny "flatworldism" (Bennett, 2011, p. 28). They have long given up the idea that our world is (metaphysically) flat. Not everything according to their picture is metaphysically on a par. Some things (objects, properties, events) are more fundamental than others. Indeed, the physical nature of the world is claimed to be more fundamental than the economic, social, biological, and even mental nature of our world. The former stands as the ground for everything else. The non-physical nature of the world, in other words, holds in virtue of the world's physical nature and precisely because it depends on it in such a fashion, physicalists maintain that the non-physical is *nothing over and above* the physical.[4]

Three clarifications are in order. First, a detailed discussion of the meaning and extension of the term "physical" will have to wait until Chapter 3. For the purposes of this chapter, we shall take "physical" to denote the set of entities mentioned in either current physics or a slightly modified future version of it. "Physical" is not co-extensive with "microphysical"; current physics contains branches of physics that deal with macroscopic phenomena, such as solid-state physics and astrophysics, and it is best to remain neutral as to whether these phenomena can be reduced without remainder to the microphysical. The phrase "physical nature of the world" will refer to the pattern of physical properties, relations, particulars, etc., that according to current (or slightly modified future) physics is instantiated in our world. "Non-physical" does not mean anti-physical, i.e., entities the existence of which is inconsistent with the truth of physicalism. Rather, "non-physical" denotes things or entities that (a) are not found in the descriptions of the current (or slightly modified future) physics and (b) are assumed to exist contingently and concretely in our world. We are aware of the many difficulties that such a proposed articulation of "physical" faces (e.g., Chomsky, 2000; Crane & Mellor, 1990; Hempel, 1969, 1980; Melnyk, 1997) and we will we deal with them in Chapter 3. The aim of the present chapter is not to define "physical" but to explore the metaphysical relationship that is supposed to hold between the physical (assuming that "physical" can be defined in some way) and everything else (the non-physical).[5]

Second, we distinguish between, on the one hand, "grounding" or "ground," and, on the other hand, "Grounding" (Wilson, 2014). The lowercase terms are meant to denote an asymmetric relationship of metaphysical (or ontological) dependence without specifying its exact nature (Raven, 2015).[6] "Grounding" with a capital "G" refers to the primitive account of metaphysical dependence proposed by Kit Fine (2001, 2012), Jonathan Schaffer (2009), and Gideon Rosen (2010) and then developed by many others (e.g., Audi, 2012a, 2012b; Correia, 2010, 2013; Raven, 2012; Trogdon, 2013a, 2013b). Consequently, to say that the non-physical is grounded in the physical is to commit oneself to the claim that the non-physical holds in virtue of the physical without however taking a position on whether this relationship should be understood in terms of, for example, realization, composition, or even Grounding.

Last, most metaphysical articulations of physicalism take physicalism to be a dimensioned view. Given that the purpose of this chapter is to evaluate the prospects of such articulations of physicalism, we shall accept such an assumption. The assumption that physicalism is a dimensioned or non-flat view excludes certain metaphysical views from counting as forms of physicalism. For example, if the mental is identical to the physical, then the latter cannot be more fundamental than the former. Thus, if physicalism is the view according to which the physical is metaphysically privileged with respect to the mental insofar as the latter metaphysically depends on the former but not vice versa, then various identity theses will not be forms of physicalism as understood here. In this chapter, we shall bracket the issue of identity physicalism. We return to the issue of identity physicalism in Chapter 4.

The two facets of physicalism—the ontological and metaphysical—are not unconnected. Many of the existence questions that physicalists ask (Do social institutions exist? Do minds exist? Do macrophysical objects exist?) are often answered through reflection on the metaphysical structure of the world. For any purported existent entity *a*, physicalists have to determine whether *a* holds in virtue of (= is nothing over and above) something else, *b*. If it does, and if *b* is physical, then *a* can be allowed into their physicalist universe. If there is no *b* such that *a* holds in virtue of it, then physicalists have to decide whether *a* is a basic ingredient of the physicalist universe—a fundamental—or not. If the latter, then they would have to deny *a*'s existence. Finally, if *a* holds in virtue of *b* but *b* is not physical, then physicalists have to repeat this process until they discover a physical ground that gives rise to *a* via giving rise to *b* or until they realize that there is no physical ground for *b* and consequently for *a* (because *b* is fundamental[7] or non-existent, or because the in-virtue-of relationship between *b* and what is thought to give rise to *b* never terminates).[8]

The procedure just described is obviously underspecified. Physicalists need to articulate the *dependence* relationship that is assumed to hold between non-fundamental (or derivative) entities and physical entities. What does it mean exactly to say that the non-physical metaphysically depends on the physical and in doing so it is rendered nothing over and above the physical? Is this dependence relationship one of supervenience, a priori entailment, realization, composition, Grounding, truthmaking,[9] or something else? And whatever it is, what is the ontological status of such a relationship? Is it physicalistically unproblematic or not? That is, can physicalists allow it in their world without incurring unbearable ontological costs (Lynch & Glasgow, 2003; Dasgupta, 2014; Sider, 2011)? In what follows, we present and evaluate different ways in which accounts of physicalism have made explicit the metaphysical dependence that is said to hold between the non-physical and the physical.

2. Fixing

A first and well-attested attempt to capture the primacy of the physical with regard to the non-physical finds recourse in the idea of *fixing*. This idea can be captured by the following conditional proposition:

(1) The physical is more fundamental than the non-physical if fixing the physical fixes the non-physical.

What does it mean to fix something or other? Certain characterizations of "fixing" will not do the requisite work. For instance, "fixing" cannot mean *causing*. First, Cartesian-type interactionist accounts of the relationship between mind and body (assuming that they are coherent) postulate causal relata that are not only metaphysically independent of each other but also equally fundamental. Second, causality is typically taken to be a relationship between distinct events, whereas metaphysical dependence holds arguably between indistinct events (or existents) (Rosen, 2010; Schaffer, 2016). Third, even though effects might in some sense *arise out* of (or be produced by) their causes (Hall, 2004, p. 225), typical causal relationships do not establish metaphysical priority. Hemlock caused Socrates's death, but hemlock is not metaphysically prior to Socrates's death.[10]

Fixing could be understood differently. The physical fixes the non-physical insofar as the physical gives rise to the non-physical (or equivalently, the physical fixes the non-physical if the former suffices for the latter). Such an understanding of fixing supports the basic physicalist contention that the physical nature of our world completely determines its entire nature (be it mental, social, economic, biological). God is usually employed in attempts to make this idea vivid (e.g., Kripke, 1980, 153f.; Chalmers, 1996, pp. 35–41). If physicalism is true, in order to create the world, God only had to create its physical nature. Everything else followed.

There is an obvious problem, however, with this characterization of fixing as an explication of the idea that the physical is more fundamental than the non-physical. Fixing, as a pattern of dependence between the physical and the non-physical, remains silent on the precise nature of the metaphysical relationship between the two. In fact, the physical can give rise to the non-physical without necessarily rendering it nothing over and above it. The non-physical can be wholly distinct from the physical even if it is metaphysically necessitated by the physical (e.g., emergentism). Thus, the concession that the non-physical nature of our world is guaranteed by its physical nature fails to show that it is nothing over and above the physical.

Another approach is to treat "fixing" as interchangeable with a type of asymmetric existential dependence (Tahko & Lowe, 2015). The physical nature of the world is more fundamental than the non-physical insofar as the latter existentially depends on the former but the former does not existentially depend on the latter. Accordingly, let us say that a set of properties *P fixes* a set of properties *Q* iff (a) *necessarily*, *Q* is instantiated only if *P* is instantiated and (b) it is not the case that, *necessarily*, *P* is instantiated only if *Q* is instantiated. The physical nature of our world is more fundamental than the non-physical since the non-physical nature could not exist without the physical but the physical could exist without the non-physical.

A problem with such an account of asymmetric existential dependence comes from Fine's well-known criticisms of modal accounts of ontological dependence (Fine, 1994a, 1994b). Indeed, Fine's remarks show that asymmetric existential dependence is neither necessary nor sufficient for the kind of metaphysical dependence addressed here. First, consider the relationship between Socrates and the singleton set {Socrates}. Necessarily, if Socrates exists then Socrates is the member of {Socrates} and, necessarily, if {Socrates} exists, then Socrates exists. An asymmetric existential dependency does not hold between Socrates and {Socrates}, even though an asymmetric *metaphysical* dependence does hold: {Socrates} metaphysically depends on Socrates but not vice versa. Consequently, asymmetric existential dependence is not necessary for metaphysical dependence or priority. But it is not sufficient either. Assuming that numbers are necessary existents, it is true that, necessarily, if Socrates exists then the number 2 exists. Yet, it is *not* the case that, necessarily, if 2 exists Socrates exists. Consequently, Socrates asymmetrically existentially depends on 2, even though Socrates does not *metaphysically* depend upon 2.

A common strategy for characterizing the metaphysical commitments of physicalism—and to render the principles of AUSTERITY and PLURALITY consistent—is to assert that the physical fixes the non-physical. Several interpretations of what fixing entails have been proposed. As we have seen, though, there are good reasons to surmise that these are not up to the task.

3. Supervenience

Matters do not get any better when we move from fixing to supervenience. Attempts to define physicalism in terms of supervenience face serious problems—ones that have been known for at least three decades (e.g., Horgan, 1993; Kim, 1993a, 1993b, 1998a; Schiffer, 1987, pp. 153–154; Wilson, 1999, 2005). Despite their shortcomings, supervenience-based formulations of physicalism have proved both remarkably recalcitrant and popular.

To be fair, advocates of supervenience-based characterizations of physicalism have often been upfront about the limitations of their approach (e.g., Jackson, 1998). And at times, they have been careful to restrict the scope of their accounts to *minimal* physicalism: a supervenience thesis that proponents of physicalism must accept and which can be used to test whether epistemic arguments against physicalism are successful (Chalmers, 1996; Stoljar, 2015; but see also Hill, 2009b for a different and more damning assessment of the prospects of supervenience physicalism). For present purposes, the issue of whether supervenience gets us minimal physicalism will be put aside (see Montero, 2013 and Montero & Brown, 2017). The question at hand is this: "Can supervenience-based characterizations of physicalism capture the metaphysical primacy that the physical enjoys over the non-physical?" The answer to this question is "no." Supervenience by itself is incapable of capturing the metaphysical character of physicalism.

Supervenience is a logical relation that is assumed to hold (typically at least) between two classes of properties: the supervenient properties and the base properties. Roughly put, the non-physical supervenes on the physical if and only if any two situations that are identical with respect to their physical properties are also identical with respect to their non-physical properties. Stated otherwise, non-physical supervenience on the physical guarantees that there cannot be a difference in the non-physical without a difference in the physical (Davidson, 1980; Lewis, 1986). Using supervenience one can offer the following characterization of the primacy of the physical:

(2) The physical is more fundamental than the non-physical if the non-physical supervenes on the physical.

The claim that there cannot be a difference in the non-physical without a difference in the physical can be understood both as a claim about individuals and about possible worlds. The former approach yields an individual supervenience claim whereas the latter yields global supervenience, both of which come in different modal strengths (e.g., Kim, 1984; McLaughlin & Bennett, 2014; Leuenberger, 2008b). Characterizations of physicalism have typically employed global supervenience so we shall restrict our attention to the global variety.

(2.1) The physical is more fundamental than the non-physical if the non-physical *globally supervenes* on the physical. That is, the physical is more fundamental than the non-physical if for any worlds *w1* and *w2*, if *w1* and *w2* have the same worldwide pattern of distribution of physical properties, then they also have the same worldwide pattern of distribution of non-physical properties.[11]

To hold that the non-physical globally supervenes on the physical is to assert the existence of a pattern of property variation. Just like fixing, however, supervenience remains silent on the precise nature of this pattern. The silence of supervenience ultimately leads to three interrelated problems for any attempt that aims to explicate fundamentality using supervenience. Given that we are covering well-trodden ground, we will be succinct.

Supervenience is non-explanatory: The fact that a supervenience relationship holds does not explain *why* it holds. However, physicalism as a metaphysical view demands an explanation as to why the non-physical is related to the physical in such a manner (e.g., Horgan, 1993; Melnyk, 2003; Schiffer, 1987). What is it exactly about the non-physical that renders it nothing over and above the physical?[12]

Supervenience is unsuited for metaphysical priority: Different reasons speak in support of this contention. First, the fact that the non-physical supervenes on the physical does not guarantee that the latter is metaphysically prior to the former. As pointed out in McLaughlin and Bennett (2014), two possible worlds *w1* and *w2* cannot differ with respect to the instantiation of property *P* without also differing with respect to the instantiation of *not-P*. But the relationship between *P* and *not-P* cannot be that of metaphysical priority: in most cases, *P* does not hold in virtue of *not-P*. Second, the logical form of fundamentality (or ontological priority) is unlike that of supervenience. Fundamentality is asymmetric and irreflexive; supervenience is non-symmetric and reflexive (Kim, 1984; McLaughlin & Bennett, 2014; Rosen, 2010; Schaffer, 2009). Finally, fundamentality (or ontological priority) is a hyperintensional notion, but supervenience is not (Fine, 1994a; Schaffer, 2009). Consider the set of properties that any world necessarily has. There are no two possible worlds that have the same worldwide pattern of instantiation of physical properties but that differ somehow with respect to their necessary properties. Yet, the fact that such necessary properties globally supervene on physical properties, does not show that necessary properties metaphysically depend or hold in virtue of physical properties (McLaughlin & Bennett, 2014; Fine, 1994a).

Supervenience is non-discriminatory: Supervenience-based characterizations of the relationship between the physical and the non-physical are consistent with a robust, anti-physicalist emergentism according to which certain non-physical properties are metaphysically necessitated by physical properties and the metaphysically necessary connections between the physical and the non-physical properties are fundamental and *sui generis* (Horgan, 1993, 2006; Kim, 2005; Wilson, 2005). Supervenience is incapable of properly distinguishing between physicalism and competing views. Consequently, it fails to come to terms with the type of metaphysical priority that physicalism assigns to the physical.

4. Reduction and Conceptual Analysis

Another attempt to show that the physical is more fundamental than the non-physical consists in providing "conceptual" analyses of all sentences that contain non-physical terms in terms of only physical and physically acceptable terms. The idea that we can *actually* provide such analyses of all non-physical statements is, we shall assume, a chimera. But the fact that such a project is in-practice untenable need not fetter one's ambitions. One can still offer a theoretical account of how such analyses *could* proceed and thereby make it plausible that the requisite redescriptions and definitions are, at least in principle, forthcoming. David Lewis advances precisely such an account (Lewis, 1970, 1972).

For Lewis, an important component of the meaning of referential expressions is provided by a set of conditions that permit a subject to specify their reference given certain hypothetical scenarios or descriptions. For instance, one has a grasp of the meaning of "water"—in one sense of "meaning"—if one is able to determine the reference of "water" when one is provided with certain descriptions of how things are or might have been. Such reference conditions are assumed to be a component of the possession of the concepts or expressions under question and, furthermore, they are taken to be common knowledge among component speakers of the relevant language. Often one can collect all such reference conditions associated with a set of terms in a theory. In the case of mental terms—"pain," "belief," "desire", etc.—let us say that *T* is the theory that collects such conditions.

Lewis held that the meanings of theoretical terms are definable functionally, that is, by reference to their causal roles. And in doing so, theoretical terms are eliminable: they can be replaced "by their definientia" (1972, p. 254). As such, we can rewrite psychological terms in a way that they wear their physical (or at least, causal/functional) nature on their sleeves. Let us articulate this idea in a bit more detail and explain how it can be used as an attempt to show how the physical is fundamental.

Let "T" stand for a psychological theory that is stated using two sorts of terms: T-terms ($t_1, t_2, \ldots t_n$) and O-terms. T-terms are theoretical terms that are introduced by the psychological theory. For simplicity's sake let us assume that T-terms are names.[13] O-terms are any terms other than T-terms and they get their meanings in some way outside the theory. In contrast, what we know about their meanings of T-terms is told in the theory: they are in other words implicitly defined by the theoretical context in which they occur. Following Ramsey, Lewis presents a way to define the T-terms *explicitly*. Here are the steps. First, produce the postulate of T by forming a single, long conjunction of all the sentences that make up theory T. The postulate which has the form "$T[t_1, t_2, \ldots, t_n]$" states of the entities *named* by the T-terms that they occupy certain relations to one another and to other entities named by O-terms. Second, replace uniformly all of the T-terms that the postulate contains with variables that do not already occur in theory T. This yields the realization formula of T which is of the form "$T[x_1, x_2, \ldots x_n]$." Any n-tuple of entities (that is, any ordered set of n entities) that satisfies the realization formula is a *realization* of theory T. Third, prefix existential quantifiers binding each of the n variables to the realization formula of T. The result is the Ramsey sentence:

$$\exists x_1 \exists x_2 \ldots \exists x_n\, T[x_1, x_2, \ldots x_n].$$

The formulated Ramsey formula states that there is some realization of the theory.[14] Lewis holds that unless T is uniquely realized, the T-terms are denotationless.[15] Thus, we can modify the Ramsey sentence in a way that asserts that there is a *unique* realization of T:

$$\exists_! x_1 \exists_! x_2 \ldots \exists_! x_n\, T[x_1, x_2, \ldots x_n].$$

Finally, each T-term can be defined as follows: $t_i =_{def}$ the ith member of the n-tuple of entities that uniquely realizes theory T.[16]

What one gets out of this analysis is the simultaneous functional definition of psychological terms via the use of a Ramsey sentence of the relevant psychological theory. Of course, one need not stop at psychological concepts; one can carry the Lewisian analysis to all non-physical statements and terms. That is, one can hold that all non-physical statements that are true about our world can be translated into statements containing functional-role concepts and then argue that the referents of such functional concepts are physical entities.

Lewis's account of how to define theoretical terms finds a natural home in the project of reductive physicalism. The project of reductive physicalism is often conceived as a two-step project. First, one defines the properties that are to be reduced functionally using Lewis's approach. Functional analysis of this sort is often an a priori process that aims to "[work] the concept of the property to be reduced 'into shape' for reduction by identifying the causal role for which we are seeking the underlying mechanisms" (Levine, 1993, p. 132). In other words, functional analyses turn non-physical vocabulary into "materialistically kosher" terms (Horgan, 1993, p. 556). Second, one finds the physical property that fulfills the functional role that was specified in the first step. Lewis explicitly uses this model in arguing for a certain type of psychophysical identifications (Lewis, 1972). According to Lewis, mental states are individuated by their causal-functional profiles. And, indeed, folk psychology implicitly defines mental terms by their causal-functional roles. That is, a mental state *M* can be analyzed a priori to be the state that occupies causal role *R*. Now, if it can be shown empirically that brain state *B* is the occupant of the causal role *R*, then we can conclude that *M* is identical to *B* (*ibid*., p. 249). This idea is not exclusive to mental terms and states. It can be applied to all non-physical states with the hopes of showing how such states can be reduced to physical states (Kim, 1998b, pp. 98–99; Jackson, 1994 articulate similar reductive accounts).

There are two assumptions underwriting the project of reductive physicalism that ought to be made transparent. First, the non-physical phenomena that call for explanation are such that the terms that are involved in their respective theories can be analyzed functionally (Chalmers, 1996, p. 44). Indeed, this assumption is crucial for the success of reductive physicalism. Without it, we have no reason to think that the phenomena that call for an explanation are amenable to a reductive explanation.

Second, the process of being able to identify the target non-physical phenomenon with a physical state or phenomenon that occupies the causal-functional role assigned to the non-physical phenomenon is thought to be enough to vindicate physicalism. We look at what our preferred theory of the world says—for example, current physics—and if something plays the causal-functional role associated with a non-physical phenomenon then the phenomenon in question has found a place in our worldview: the phenomenon is entailed (indeed, a priori entailed) by what our preferred physical theory says. In this way, reductive physicalism is capable of offering answers to all sorts of "location problems" (Jackson, 1998). It allows us to say when and how a putative feature of our world has a place in our physicalist universe.

Putting these two assumptions together, we can see that the project of reductive physicalism offers a natural suggestion as how to construe the metaphysical priority of the physical.

(3) The physical is more fundamental than the non-physical if there is a reductive explanation of all non-physical phenomena in terms of physical phenomena.

Despite claims to the contrary, we think that this sort of reductive explanation of the non-physical to the physical fails to capture the spirit of physicalism, *if physicalism is understood as a dimensioned metaphysical view*. This claim might sound surprising. Yet, we believe that it follows once we have understood the limitations of reductive explanation and its relationship to fundamentality (or primacy).

Why doesn't (3) work? Why is it the case that reductive explanation is not sufficient to establish the primacy of the physical? To a first approximation, the reason is this: the fact that some theoretical terms (what Lewis calls "T-terms") can be defined in terms of a preferred vocabulary does not mean that the entities named by such vocabulary are metaphysically prior to the entities named by T. It might be true that physical entities in this world meet the functional or causal roles associated with non-physical entities. But why should one conclude from this fact that the non-physical entities are nothing over and above the physical entities?

The point can be made most forcefully if we turn to psychological phenomena. Here, we are drawing on Ned Block's (2015) criticism of reductive explanation. Assuming that psychological phenomena are multiply realizable, then it is possible that they can be found in a number of agents that are physically different from us. In each case there will be a reductive analysis of the phenomenon in question. Pain in humans, let us continue with philosophical fiction, is C-fiber stimulation; in octopuses, pain is something else. But such a reductive analysis fails to shed any light on the question of ground. What is exactly that which stands as the common ground of the multiply realizable mental phenomenon?

One possible suggestion is to follow Lewis in holding that *having pain* (and not pain itself) is a higher-order property that is common in humans, octopuses, and in any other organism that experiences pain. But such an attempt to locate commonality between different organisms fails to articulate any kind of *physical* similarity between the different pains. At most, what we have located is a *functional* commonality.

What if one were to say that multiply realizable phenomena are grounded in a disjunction? Accordingly, the ground of mental phenomenon M is physical state P_1 *or* physical state P_2 *or* . . . physical state P_n.Such an attempt to find ground seems unacceptable, at least from the perspective of metaphysical physicalism. Again, there is no common physical ground, only the illusion of one. In virtue of precisely what does *M* exist? The answer cannot be that *M* holds in virtue of one of the physical states (e.g., P_1) that compose the disjunction, for *M* could have been present even if the system or organism were not in that physical state. Thus, *M is* something over and above P_1. In turn, the ground of *M* cannot be all of the disjuncts taken together: each disjunct suffices for *M*. So, the ground, it seems, can only be the disjunction. But what a disjunction tells us is a commonality or a general relationship that holds between the disjuncts. The ground that a disjunction reveals is functional not physical (Block, 2015; Stoljar, 2010).[17]

Should our search for ground be more fine-grained? Perhaps we should not be looking for that which gives rise to a mental state as a *type* but rather for the ground of *tokens* of mental states: "Don't ask what is the ground of pain, but rather what is the ground of this particular dull pain that I am having right now." Although dialectically available, such a move is incongruous with the mandates of reductive explanation as presented earlier (but see Braddon-Mitchell & Jackson, 2007, p. 103). Indeed, the fact that mental states (such as pain) admit of a functional explanation suggests that we can talk about pain as such (or at least, *human* pain as a type) but if there is such a thing as pain as such (or human pain), then physicalism owes us an account of its ground: i.e., what is that in virtue of which pain occurs and renders it nothing over and above the physical? Furthermore, even if we move away from types of mental states and concentrate on tokens, we still have not arrived at the requisite metaphysical dependence relationship that is supposed to hold between the physical and the mental. What exactly is the relationship between the mental and the physical, considered on the level of tokens? If it is one of identity, then both the token of pain and the specific physical state are rendered equally fundamental—they are one and the same after all. But if the relationship is not one of identity, then what is it? We are still owed an account of their relationship.

In sum, assuming reductive physicalism, what is shown is that given how things are, physical entities happen to occupy the roles associated with non-physical terms. And because they occupy those roles, the non-physical follows. What is absent from such an account is an explanation of how the physical nature of our world plays a *distinctive* role in grounding its non-physical nature. Reductive physicalism is more functionalism than physicalism.

We anticipate three objections.

Objection 1: We have misunderstood reductive physicalism. *Proper* reductionism denies that there is something in addition to the physical entities that are the occupants of the various roles that explicate the non-physical entities. There is no pain and no water, only the realizers of such entities. Thus, to ask what is the metaphysical relationship between pain and the physical occupant of the pain-role is to have misunderstood reductive physicalism.

We have two thoughts with respect to this charge. First, it is not clear that we are guilty of a misunderstanding of the project of reductive explanation. Consider, for example, Jackson's solution to the various location problems that arise for the physicalist (Jackson, 1998). Jackson explicitly denies an eliminativist solution to such problems (1998, pp. 2–3) and offers instead as a solution his "entry by entailment thesis" (1998, p. 6). That is, a putative fact has a place in the physicalists' world if it is entailed by the way things are physically. Hence, there are two things that *appear* to exist (the putative non-physical fact and the way things are physically), the latter does not include in an obvious sense the former, and thus it is meaningful to ask about the metaphysical relationship between them (see also Nolan, 2005, p. 8). Second, if contrary to our claims reductive physicalism has to be understood as an eliminativist position, then reductive physicalism now falls outside of the scope of this chapter. Regardless of its merits and demerits, such an eliminativist take on reductive physicalism is not a dimensioned view.

Objection 2: We have misunderstood Lewis's version of reductive physicalism. Although Lewis looks like a functionalist, he is a type identity theorist: he identifies mental properties with certain neurophysiological properties (Lewis, 1966, 1972, 1994).

Undeniably, there is something right with claiming that Lewis is an identity theorist, but that is not the whole story. Lewis might be an identity theorist but he is so by way of functionalism (Smart, 2007). Although Lewis accepts as true that pain is identical to C-fiber stimulation (let us assume), he maintains that such an identity claim is contingent and kind-relative (Lewis, 1994, pp. 59–60): pain is C-fiber stimulation only for humans and only at the actual world. "Pain" is a non-rigid definite description. Linguistically, it behaves similarly to "the state that plays the pain role" and as such it refers to different things in different contexts. It is this feature of Lewis's position that makes it hard to see how the mental is nothing over and above the physical. Whatever physical state we decide is the occupant of the causal or functional role of pain in humans, then that is pain. But the fact that in our world (or even in all possible worlds) C-fiber stimulation is, let us say, the occupant of the pain-role does not explain how pain holds in virtue of or *arises out* of the physical.[18]

Objection 3: Our objection to reductive physicalism cannot be right. It cannot be right because it is too strong. It is too strong because, if successful, it shows that the failure of reductive physicalism is not restricted to the relationship that holds between the mental and the

> physical. That is, if we are right, reductive physicalism comes short of accounting for the metaphysical relationship that holds between the physical and *any non-physical functional entities or properties*. But that is absurd. Isn't it? No one thinks that mundane phenomena and entities such as screwdrivers, cars, parties, etc. pose a threat to physicalism. No one thinks that one cannot explain or account for those phenomena and entities in a physicalistically acceptable manner.

We accept the description of the objection, but we deny the implication. Our claim is not that higher-level, functional entities and properties stand somehow as obstacles to physicalism insofar as they are ontologically inconsistent with the mandates of physicalism. The claim is a different one. It is this: if one is (a) *not* an eliminativist about the higher-level functional entities and properties and (b) committed to the idea that over-and-aboveness needs to be spelled out in metaphysical terms, then one ought to offer, we maintain, an account of the metaphysical relationship that holds between the physical and those higher-level entities and properties. Reductive physicalism offers a *functional* explanation of the relationship between the two. But such a functional explanation is not one that points out how the *physical* gives rise to the non-physical. It simply shows that given that the physical does such and so, the non-physical follows. The emphasis is not on the physical but on the role that the physical plays. The physical is in a sense superfluous, replaceable in principle by alien entities. As such, we contend, reductive explanation does not ground the non-physical in the physical (Block, 2015).

Of course, one can deny that physicalism *ought* to care for an asymmetric metaphysical relationship between the physical and the non-physical that renders the latter nothing over and above the former—we are, in fact, sympathetic to this idea and develop it in the following chapters. Or one can respond by arguing that functionalism is all that physicalism needs; to ask for something more is to place the bar at an unreachable height. Fair enough. We are not pretending that such responses are not available. Our claim is simply that such responses are not positive answers to the metaphysical question. They do not specify the metaphysical relationship that is assumed to exist between the physical and non-physical. They deny either that it exists or that is part of physicalism.

5. A Priori Entailment

In presenting reductive explanation and specifically in showing how it is thought to provide a solution to various location problems for physicalists (Jackson, 1998), we stated that if Φ is reductively explained in terms of P, then truths about Φ are a priori entailed by truths about P. But in criticizing reductive explanation as failing to specify a relationship of metaphysical dependence, we paid no particular attention to this relationship of a priori entailment. Suppose now that the relationship between reductive explanation and a priori entailment is made explicit: Φ is reductively explained in physical terms, if truths about physics are such that a priori entail truths about Φ. Does an articulation of reductive physicalism as a thesis about a priori entailment help matters? It does not.

There are important differences between entailment and the metaphysical relationship that is presumed to hold between the physical and the non-physical and which renders the first fundamental. A sentence *P* might entail a priori a sentence *Q* even if *P* and *Q* are both false. But *Q* cannot metaphysically depend on *P*: an in-virtue-of relation cannot hold between false statements (or between the facts expressed by false statements) (Bolzano, 1837/1972; Tatzel, 2002). Perhaps, the comparison then should be between entailment in cases in which both statements are true. But again this does not seem to yield the requisite relationship. First, every true sentence *P* is entailed by itself. But the common view on metaphysical priority is that nothing is metaphysically prior to itself (Raven, 2015). Second, and more to the point, there are examples in which *P* a priori entails *Q*, but the fact expressed by *Q* does not hold in virtue of the fact expressed by *P*. Consider the following example given by Bernard Bolzano (1837/1972) while presenting his account of ground. The sentence "well-functioning thermometers stand higher in summer than in winter" a priori entails that it "it is warmer in summer than in winter," yet the fact expressed by the latter does not hold in virtue of the fact expressed by the former. A priori entailment, therefore, does not seem by itself capable of providing us with the relationship of metaphysical dependence for which we are looking.

6. Realization

Reductive physicalism fails to come up with the requisite account of metaphysical dependence that ought to hold between the physical and the non-physical. Does realization physicalism fare any better? The answer depends on the *variety* of realization physicalism that one has in mind.

As it turns out, it is not easy to say clearly what realization is. There is a fair bit of disagreement as to how to understand the thesis of realization and how it can be applied to physicalism (Gillett, 2002, 2003; Melnyk, 2003, 2006; Poland, 1994; Polger, 2007; Polger & Shapiro, 2008; Shoemaker, 2007; Wilson, 1999). For present purposes, we shall focus on two influential accounts of realization that have been employed in the service of physicalism: Andrew Melnyk's realization physicalism (Melnyk, 2003, 2006) and Jessica Wilson and Sidney Shoemaker's causal subset account of realization (Wilson, 1999, 2011; Shoemaker, 2001, 2007, 2011; see also Watkins, 2002). Our aim is to examine whether such articulations of realization can provide an account of the metaphysical primacy of the physical over the non-physical.

6.1. Melnyk's Physical Realization

Before considering Melnyk's realization account, it is useful to distinguish clearly between two types of properties: *higher-order* and *first-order*. A higher-order property is a property that involves quantification over other properties. A first-order property is one that does not. A higher-order property then can be truly predicated about a subject if the subject has some other properties that meet certain conditions or play a certain role. A functional property *F* with associated role *R*, for example, is a higher-order property: its instantiation consists in the instantiation of a number of other properties in a manner that they play role *R*.

On one popular account of what realization is, realization is a relationship that holds between property instances or tokens (e.g., Melnyk, 2003). But this is not the only account. One could also hold that realization is a relationship between types. Given that we will be focusing on Melnyk's account of realization, we follow Melnyk in understanding realization as a relationship between tokens. In his 2003 book, Melnyk characterizes realization as follows:

> Token *x* *realizes* token *y* iff (i) *y* is a token of some functional type, F, such that, necessarily, F is tokened iff there is a token of some or other type that meets condition, C; (ii) *x* is a token of some type that in fact meets C; and (iii) the token of F whose existence is logically guaranteed by the holding of condition (ii) is numerically identical with *y*.
>
> (p. 21; see also Melnyk, 2006, p. 129)

Suppose that after thinking hard about mousetraps (or, if you prefer, after we develop a complete and ideal science of mousetraps) we come up with a certain condition *C* such that if something meets *C*, then that something is an instance of a mousetrap (and if something is an instance of a mousetrap then it meets *C*). Now, according to Melnyk's definition, a particular physical structure (e.g., the box that one bought from the hardware store today) realizes a mousetrap if and only if anything that meets condition *C* is such that is necessarily an instance of a mousetrap, the item bought from the hardware store meets condition *C*, and that instance of mousetrap that is logically guaranteed by the fact that the item from the hardware store meets condition *C* is identical to the mousetrap realized by the item from the hardware store.

Can this formulation of realization shed light on the purported metaphysical primacy of the physical? Consider the following claim:

(4) The physical is more fundamental than the non-physical if the latter is realized by the former.

As it stands, (4) does not work. First, Melnyk's characterization of realization leaves it open as to whether the realized token is *identical* with its realizer (2003, p. 21). However, in the present context the realizer better not turn out to be identical to the realized token. If *x* realizes *y*, and *x* and *y* are identical, then it follows that *y* also realizes *x*. The possibility of identity between the realizer and the realized renders realization *non-symmetric* (i.e., neither symmetric nor anti-symmetric). Metaphysical dependence of the sort that is capable of spelling out the primacy of the physical ought to be asymmetric (i.e., both anti-symmetric and irreflexive).

Second, and relatedly, the fact that the non-physical is realized by the physical does not preclude the possibility that the non-physical can also realize the physical. And this issue persists even if we preclude the identity of the realizer with the realized. As far as we can tell, this criticism was first presented in Francescotti (2010) (for a detailed response, see Melnyk, 2016a). Here is an example. Take the physical type *having a location* and let us assume that this is a functional type and, necessarily, it is tokened iff something meets condition C (condition C might be *being able to be placed in a system of coordinates*).[19] Now let us ask whether a token of this physical type, e.g., *being located at x*, can be realized by an instance of the non-physical type *birthday party*. Given that we already specified that *having a location* is a functional type of the requisite kind, then according to the account of realization offered previously, *Olivia's birthday party* (a token of the non-physical type *birthday party*) will realize *being located at x* if (a) *Olivia's birthday party* meets condition C and (b) the token of the functional type *having a location* that is necessitated by the fact that *Olivia's birthday party* meets C is numerically identical with *being located at x*. But both requirements can be satisfied. First, *Olivia's birthday party* meets condition C: after all, it does take place somewhere (let's say her house). Second, assuming that her house is located at *x*, then *Olivia's birthday party* necessitates the existence of the token *being located at x*. If this example is admitted, then realization is incapable of capturing the metaphysical priority that the physical enjoys over the non-physical.[20]

In order to remedy these problems, one needs to specify the manner in which a physical token meets the condition associated with the essence of the higher-order realized property instance. It is in this spirit that Melnyk offers his characterization of *physical realization*. He writes:

> A token *x* of a functional type, F, is *physically realized* iff (i) *x* is realized by a token of some physical type, T, *and* (ii) T meets the associated condition for F solely as a logical consequence of the distribution in the world of physical tokens and the holding of physical laws.
>
> (2003, p. 23)

Using the notion of physical realization, we can then revise (4) as follows:

(4*) The physical is more fundamental than the non-physical if the latter is *physically* realized by the former.

(4*) is a clear improvement over (4). First, if we insist that the non-physical has to be *physically* realized by the physical, then we are assigning a certain priority to the physical: it is in virtue of the physical facts (the distribution of physical tokens and the holding of physical laws) that the token of a non-physical functional type is realized. Second, even though it seems plausible to hold that the non-physical is physically realized, it is not plausible to maintain that the non-physical non-physically realizes the physical: the physical does not hold in virtue of various non-physical facts (see Melnyk, 2016a).

Should (4*) then be accepted? One might worry that (4*) shares one of the shortcomings of reductive explanation: insofar as physical realization gives us a ground of the non-physical, it is a functional ground. If a token, *x*, of a non-physical type, *F*, is physically realized by a token, *y*, of a physical type, *T*, then *x*'s existence is logically guaranteed by the fact that the tokening of *y* meets, necessarily given the laws of physics and physical circumstances, condition, *C*. So, the ground of the non-physical token is specified by condition *C* and consequently it is functional not physical. But this is not necessarily so. The realized token might be a token of a *functional* non-physical type, but according to Melnyk, "functional type" ought to be understood broadly (see note 19). Thus, depending on how *C* is spelled out—i.e., what type of properties figure in *C*—the ground of non-physical tokens might after all end up being physical.

Daniel Stoljar objects to Melnyk's realization physicalism on the grounds that there is no way to spell out *C* in a way that does not render realization either identity physicalism or supervenience/necessitation physicalism (Stoljar, 2010, pp. 123–124, 2015). According to Stoljar, the properties that are included in condition *C*—the condition that spells out the essence of the higher-order non-physical property that is assumed to be physically realized by the physical—are either physical or realized by physical properties. If the former, then realization physicalism "will stand revealed as holding a version of identity physicalism (one level up, as it were), and thus will face the multiple realization objection" (Stoljar, 2015). If the latter, an infinite regress looms, and the way to stop it, according to Stoljar, is to accept a supervenience thesis.

Let us put aside the second horn of Stoljar's dilemma—Melnyk (2016a) shows that even if the properties involved in *C* are realized by physical properties no infinite regress ensues—and focus instead on the claim that the properties involved in *C* are physical. Does that show that realization physicalism is a version of identity physicalism? It is instructive to consider what Melnyk writes in response to this objection:

> [L]et us first ask whether, if a higher-order property *P* has an essence into which only physical properties enter, it follows that *P* is one and the same as a physical property. It may indeed seem to follow, on the grounds that the property can be specified in purely physical terms. But

> we shouldn't count a property as physical just because it can be specified in purely physical terms. We are speaking here of a higher-order property; and an instance of a higher-order property owes its reality to the property instance that realizes it. But the *realizing* property doesn't have to be physical just because the *property that it realizes* can be specified in purely physical terms . . . Suppose, for the sake of a concrete example, that being a mousetrap has a higher-order essence that can be specified in purely physical terms. Plausibly, it is still metaphysically possible for a mousetrap to be realized by a well-organized team of immaterial spirits. But if it *is* possible, then a mousetrap could exist that had no physical parts at all, and it seems wrong to call the property of being a mousetrap physical if there could be a mousetrap that had no physical parts at all. It doesn't follow, then, that *P* is one and the same as a physical property just because it has a higher-order essence into which only physical properties enter, and so the realization physicalist doesn't "stand revealed as holding a version of identity physicalism."
>
> (2016a)

What shall we make of this passage? Melnyk's aim is to show that the fact that a higher-order property has an essence that can be specified solely in terms of physical properties does not suffice to render the higher-order property *physical*. And if it is not physical, then it cannot be identical to a physical property.

Melnyk's suggestion echoes a point made previously in the context of reductive explanation. The fact that a property can be given a functional account that has a purely physical explication does not entail that such a property is nothing over and above the physical. But if that is so, isn't Melnyk's account *also* incapable of accounting for how the non-physical is nothing over and above the physical? If the essences of non-physical functional types are specified in purely physical terms and yet such properties fail to be physical—because they can be realized by entities incompatible with physicalism, as the quoted passage states—then realization physicalism does nothing to fix the metaphysical priority of the physical over the non-physical.

This point can be put in another way. The phrase "*P* has an essence into which only physical properties enter" is at least ambiguous. It can mean that the only way to spell out *P*'s essence is by appealing to physical and only to physical properties. Or, it can mean that although it is possible to spell out *P*'s essence by appealing only to physical properties, it is also possible to spell it out by appealing to other kinds of properties (for instance, properties that are antithetical to physicalism). Melnyk's example of mousetrap supports the latter understanding. However, one could protest that if the essences of higher-order properties are such that could be spelled out by both physical and other types of properties, then those higher-order properties are, most fundamentally, functional properties. But insofar as they are functional, they are not nothing over and above the physical, even if in our world tokens of those properties are physically realized by tokens of physical types.

Melnyk's position appears to be faced with a dilemma: either higher-order properties are physical or not. If they are not, then realization physicalism is incapable of showing how non-physical properties are nothing over and above the physical. Indeed, realization physicalism offers no clear improvement over reductive physicalism. If, however, they are physical properties, then Stoljar's objection returns: realization physicalism appears to be a form of identity physicalism. And an identity thesis has the wrong features for establishing fundamentality. If the non-physical turns out to be identical to the physical, then not only is the former nothing over and above the latter, but also vice versa.

Stoljar's objection notwithstanding, realization physicalism carries the promise of giving rise to the sought-after relationship of metaphysical dependence. First, physical realization assigns a priority to the physical over the non-physical: the non-physical is physically realized (i.e., made *real*) by physical tokens. Second, physical realization is an internal relation insofar as the fact that *y* physically realizes *x* holds in virtue of facts about *y* and *x* (Melnyk, 2016a, 2016b). As such, the physicalist incurs no metaphysical costs by embracing physical realization. Finally, physical realization is hyperintensional insofar as it is more fine-grained than necessitation. If the physical physically realizes the non-physical, then the former necessitates the latter, but not everything that is metaphysically necessitated by the physical is physically realized by the physical. For all these reasons, realization physicalism and Stoljar's objection are worthy of the physicalists' time. Perhaps there is a sense in which the non-physical *is* physical without, however, being identical to the physical. In that case, physical realization owes us an explanation of how that is possible.

6.2. Subset Realization

According to the "traditional" account of realization, of which Melnyk's version is one possible articulation, the realized property (or instance of property) is a higher-order property that is defined in terms of a functional role and the realizers of this property are the first-order properties (or property instances) that perform this role. Both Jessica Wilson and Sydney Shoemaker have advanced and developed alternative articulations of realization. For the purposes of this chapter, we focus exclusively on Shoemaker's view.[21] We assess whether his version of realization, which holds that "all states and properties of things, of whatever kind, are physical or physically realized," is indeed, and according to his own words, "the most revealing characterization of physicalism itself (Shoemaker, 2007, p. 1).

For Shoemaker, properties are individuated in terms of their causal profiles.[22] Although Shoemaker is a famous proponent of the causal theory of properties, i.e., the theory according to which properties have their causal profiles *essentially* (see Shoemaker, 1980, 2007), he maintains—at least in his *Physical Realization*—that his account of realization physicalism does not presuppose such a strong view regarding property individuation. Instead, Shoemaker argues that all that is needed is the weaker view that each property "is individuated by a causal profile in the sense that it and it alone has the profile in the actual world and worlds nomologically like it" (2007, p. 142). As we point out below, and as Shoemaker ultimately concedes, this weak view does not secure physicalism. But, importantly, a substitution of this weak view with the stronger claim according to which properties have their causal profiles essentially is no solution either.

How does Shoemaker understand realization? One property realizes another just in case a certain membership relationship holds between the causal profile of the realizer and that of the realized (Shoemaker, 2007, p. 12, cf. 2001, p. 78). Specifically:

Realization$_{subset}$ Property *P* realizes property *Q* iff *Q*'s causal features constitute a subset of *P*'s causal features.

Does Shoemaker's version of realization account for the metaphysical priority of the physical over the non-physical? In other words, should (5) be accepted?

(5) The physical is more fundamental than the non-physical if the latter is realized$_{\text{subset}}$ by the former.

There are at least two reasons that speak against (5). First, as noted before, subset realization is insufficient by itself to guarantee the truth of physicalism (Kirk, 2009; McLaughlin, 2009; Stoljar, 2010). Although Shoemaker insists that the "occurrence of realized states is 'nothing over and above' the occurrence of their realizers" (2007, p. 2), such a constitutive relationship does not follow from the weak account of property individuation. Consider, for example, the relationship between a mental property, *M*, and a physical property, *P*. *P* will realize *M* just in case the causal features of *M* are a subset of those of *P*. Now if properties are contingently individuated in terms of their causal features (2007, p. 2, n. 2), then even though it might be the case that in the actual world the instantiation of *P* (the physical realizing property) gives rise to an instance of *M* (the realized mental property), it is not guaranteed that *M* will be instantiated in all possible worlds in which *P* is instantiated. And *pace* Shoemaker (2007), this difficulty does not disappear by expanding the realizer of *M* to include not only *P* but also the holding of the laws of nature that obtain in the actual world (see Kirk, 2009, p. 150; McLaughlin, 2009). Hence, it is a mistake to hold that the tokening of the mental property in question is *nothing over and above* the occurrence of its physical realizer. A subset account of realization fails to account for the metaphysical primacy of the physical over the non-physical.

In response to this difficulty, one could endorse Shoemaker's causal theory of properties and maintain that properties have their causal features essentially. Such a move is indeed one that Shoemaker himself makes in later works (see, e.g., Shoemaker, 2011) and although it avoids the problem raised above, it does require the acceptance of a controversial account of property individuation. Is this a fair price to pay? It is hard to tell. For present purposes, what matters is whether this stronger version of Shoemaker's account of realization can help us to specify the metaphysical dependence relationship between the physical and the non-physical that we are after.

Suppose that we follow Shoemaker in holding that according to physicalism, all non-physical properties are physically realized. What this means is that the causal features of each and every instantiated non-physical property is a subset of the causal features of some instantiated physical property. But doesn't such an understanding of the relationship between the physical and the non-physical render Shoemaker's account of realization a form of identity thesis? (See Kim, 2010; Pereboom, 2016; but also Wilson, 2011.) If non-physical properties are constituted by their causal features, and such causal features are, in virtue of the fact that non-physical properties are realized by physical properties, the features which constitute physical properties, then non-physical properties are physical properties after all.[23] The point here is not that non-physical properties should be identified with their realizers but rather that non-physical properties just *are* physical properties. Subset realization is revealed as a form of identity physicalism and as such, it is a flat view. Hence, even if we grant that properties possess their causal powers *essentially*, subset realization physicalism still does not deliver the sought-after metaphysical relationship between the physical and the non-physical that not only shows that the latter is nothing over and above the former but which also demonstrates that the former is in some sense prior or more fundamental than the former.[24]

7. Grounding

We have been looking for a relationship of metaphysical dependence that has the following features: (a) it holds between the physical and the non-physical; (b) it assigns metaphysical priority to the former; and (c) it renders the latter nothing over and above the former. Despite our best efforts, we came up short. Why is that?

One might suggest that the reason is simple. We could not find an account of the requisite metaphysical dependence by examining various existing formulations of physicalism because the relationship that we are after is *primitive*: it is Ground with a capital "G." Thus, proponents of physicalism who wish to capture the metaphysical nature of physicalism should offer a Grounding formulation of physicalism. In this section, we present this avenue for physicalists and raise a number of difficulties that need to be resolved (for more difficulties, see Wilson, 2016). Just like the previous avenues considered, this is not an easy road to take.

What is Grounding? It is common to take Grounding to be a primitive relation (Rosen, 2010, pp. 113–114; Schaffer, 2009, p. 364) either between facts (as per Rosen, 2010; Audi, 2012a) or entities (as per Jenkins, 2011; Schaffer, 2009) that expresses a kind of constitutive form of determination dependence ["something like metaphysical causation" (Schaffer, 2012, p. 122)].[25] Thus, to say that "*x* Grounds *y*" is to assert that *y* holds in virtue of *x: y is* what it is because of *x*. Proponents of Grounding maintain that such a notion helps one to structure reality (Schaffer, 2009) and to distinguish between what seems to exist (but perhaps does not) and what *really* exists (Fine, 2001; see, however, Audi, 2012b). If the mental is Grounded in the physical, then the physical is more fundamental than the mental. The mental depends in a strong metaphysical sense on the physical (it is constitutively determined by it) and as such it could be considered to be nothing over and above the physical.

Because of its primitive nature, Grounding is often introduced with the help of examples (Correia & Schnieder, 2012; Fine, 2012; Raven, 2015; Rosen, 2010; Schaffer, 2009). One cites plausible instances of Grounding and, on the basis of such instances, articulates the nature of Grounding by both relating it to and distinguishing it from other more familiar notions (e.g., explanation, supervenience, a priori entailment). One can also use Grounding in order to elucidate other notions (Schaffer, 2009). All of this is done with the aim of characterizing Grounding without, however, reductively defining it.

The primitiveness of Grounding is, as one would expect, a mixed bag. On the one hand, it invites skepticism both in regard to its meaning and its use. Some contend that Grounding is an esoteric or confused notion (e.g., Daly, 2012; Hofweber, 2009; Wilson, 2014). Others complain that as a primitive coarse-grained metaphysical relation, Grounding is bereft of any real metaphysical use (e.g., Koslicki, 2015; Wilson, 2014): it fails to resolve the questions that it is supposed to resolve. On the other hand, its primitiveness provides us with certain stipulative freedom, and we may be able to take advantage of that freedom in using Grounding in formulating physicalism. Accordingly, we make the following assumptions:

(a) Grounding is irreflexive: nothing Grounds itself.
(b) Grounding is asymmetric: if *x* Grounds *y*, then *y* does not Ground *x*.
(c) Grounding itself is not an explanatory relationship even though it underwrites explanations (see, e.g., Audi, 2012b; Schaffer, 2012)

Requirements (a)—(c) are placed in order to allow Grounding to capture the relationship of metaphysical dependence that is assumed to hold between the physical and the non-physical if physicalism is true.[26]

Consider thus (6):

(6) The physical is more fundamental than the non-physical if the non-physical is Grounded in the physical.

Now, if by definition "*x* Grounds *y*" means *x* is more fundamental than *y*, then Grounding captures a type of metaphysical priority. That much is clear. What is not clear is whether (6) captures the type of metaphysical priority that physicalism assigns to the physical. In what follows, we consider three complications in an attempt to offer a Grounding formulation of physicalism.

7.1. Grounding and Reduction

Not every proponent of Grounding accepts that Grounded facts are nothing over and above their Grounds. In fact, it is consistent with the notion of Grounding that if the physical Grounds the non-physical, then the latter could be something over and above the former. For example, Paul Audi writes: "The mere fact that some entity is grounded does not make it any more (or less) ontologically innocent. The grounded is every bit as real—and real in precisely the same sense—as that which grounds it" (Audi, 2012a, p. 102). Although permissible by the rules of Grounding, such an attitude is at odds with physicalism. The non-physical cannot be over and above the physical. So, if Grounding is to be of use to proponents of physicalism, Grounded facts or entities have to be nothing over and above what Grounds them.

Here we see an immediate issue with Grounding. It does not suffice to say that physicalism is the view according to which the non-physical is Grounded in the physical and leave it at that. One also needs to articulate how Grounding captures the relationship of nothing-over-and-aboveness.

So, what does it mean to say that *y* is nothing over and above *x*? In the present context, it cannot mean that *x* and *y* are identical (recall the features of Grounding). Following Trogdon (2013a), one could hold that *y* is nothing over and above *x* just in case the ontological commitments of the existence of *x* are the same as that of the existence of *y*. (Kelly Trogdon offers this as an account of reduction. Here we are utilizing it as an account of nothing-over-and-above-ness.) Such an account guarantees that the existence of *y* "weighs," ontologically speaking, no more than the existence of *x*. The benefit of such an understanding of the notion of nothing-over-and-aboveness is that it allows Audi's claim that the Grounded is real, perhaps even as real as that which Grounds it, but without having to admit that the Grounded is something over and above its Grounds.

Despite its merits, such an understanding of nothing-over-and-aboveness will not do for our purposes. Nothing-over-and-aboveness understood in terms of ontological commitments is a symmetric relationship (Trogdon, 2013a). As such, not only would the non-physical be nothing over and above the physical, but also vice versa.

A different understanding of nothing-over-and-aboveness can be found in Rosen's discussion of reduction (Rosen, 2010, Sect. X). Rosen argues for the following claim: if <p> (the proposition that p) is true and reduces to <q>, then [*p*] (the fact that p) is Grounded in [q]. What is it for one proposition to reduce to another? According to Rosen, <p> reduces to <q> if <q> is what we get when we offer a *real definition* (the definition of a thing/entity and not a verbal definition) (see Fine, 1994a) of p. Take for example the property *being a circle*. Its real definition is this: a circle is the set of all points in a plane that are equidistant from a given point (the center). The real definition tells us then that what it *is* to be a circle and it also tells us *how* to generate one. There is nothing more to being a circle than what its real definition offers us. Thus, following Rosen we can say that (i) <something is a circle> reduces to <something is the set of all points in a plane that are equidistant from a given point> and (ii) if <something is a circle> is true, then [something is circle] is Grounded in [something is the set all points in a plane that are equidistant from a given point].

How useful is this analysis to proponents of physicalism? As it stands, it is not very useful. Rosen's analysis offers a necessary condition for reduction. If we apply it to the case of the physical/non-physical, it tells us that *if* the non-physical reduces to the physical, then the physical Grounds the non-physical. The difficulty with this proposal is that now we need to figure out *how* to reduce (in Rosen's sense) the non-physical to the physical. And that means that we need to embark on a journey to figure out whether each non-physical existent has a *real definition* in terms of the physical such that the definition (i) does not render the non-physical identical to the physical and (ii) shows that reduction is both asymmetric (the non-physical reduces to the physical but not vice versa) and irreflexive (the physical does not reduce to itself, otherwise it would Ground itself). Perhaps such a task is achievable. But even if it is, the proponent of a Grounding formulation of physicalism has to show that the proposed reduction of the non-physical to the physical is different than the options considered previously (e.g., realization or reductive explanation). In effect, in order to motivate a Grounding formulation of physicalism, the proponent of such a definition would need to provide us with a story of how the non-physical is nothing over and above the physical. We are (more or less) back where we started.

7.2. Grounding and Necessitation

Suppose that the non-physical is Grounded by the physical. Does that mean that the physical necessitates the non-physical? Let "Γ" stand for the collection of all physical facts and let us assume that Γ Grounds a non-physical fact [q]. Does it follow that, necessarily, if all physical facts in Γ obtain, then [q] obtains? Many proponents of Grounding accept that Grounding carries such a modal commitment (e.g., Audi, 2012b; Dasgupta, 2014; deRosset, 2013; Rosen, 2010; Trogdon, 2013b). For example, Rosen (2010) writes that "[t]he facts that ground a given fact collectively ensure that it obtains as a matter of metaphysical necessity" (p. 118) and notes that such a necessary connection between Grounds and what is Grounded allows the proponent of Grounding physicalism to distinguish her position from dualism.

Although it seems promising to hold that Grounding entails necessitation, not everybody agrees. Indeed, in the literature one finds counterexamples to the claim that Grounding carries modal entailment (e.g., Leuenberger, 2014; Schnieder, 2006; Skiles, 2015).[27] Here, we are not interested in adjudicating this debate, which is internal to the Grounding literature. Still, the debate matters to proponents of Grounding formulations of physicalism. If there can be instances of Grounding without (metaphysical) necessitation, then the question of whether the Grounded is nothing over and above its Grounds returns. A necessitation relationship is a necessary condition for nothing-over-and-aboveness: If the physical Grounds obtain and a non-physical Grounded fact does not, then something in addition to the physical facts is needed in order to make it the case that the non-physical fact obtains (see also Witmer, 2001). Hence, an account of Grounding that does not entail that what is Grounded is necessitated by its Grounds would fail to capture the spirit of physicalism.[28,29]

7.3. Grounding and Grounding Facts

Lastly, according to our Grounding proposal, the physical Grounds the non-physical. But what exactly is the status of those facts about Grounding? Are they themselves Grounded in something or not? Questions about the status of Grounding facts have attracted the attention of both proponents and critics of Grounding (Bennett, 2011; Dasgupta, 2014; deRosset, 2013; Sider, 2011; Wilson, 2016). Indeed, some have thought that the status of those Grounding facts constitutes an obstacle to Grounding formulations of physicalism (e.g., Sider, 2011). Consider the following Grounding claim:

> [GC]: The fact that Greece is a parliamentary representative democratic republic is Grounded in facts concerning voting regulations and the activities of the various governmental branches.

Is [GC] Grounded? Suppose that it is not. [GC] is then arguably[30] fundamental. But [GC] involves in addition to facts about voting regulations and activities of governmental branches, mention of Greece and of parliamentary representative democracy. Such an involvement seems problematic. If physicalism is true, a fundamental description of the world better not include talk of Greece or types of democracies (Sider, 2011; see also Dasgupta, 2014; deRosset, 2013; Trogdon, 2013a). After all, they are supposed to be nothing over and above the physical. Physicalists would then seem to be committed to holding that [GC] is Grounded. But what fact would Ground [GC]? And if [GC] is Grounded in a fact, then that further fact would also need to be Grounded, and so on. A proliferation of Grounds and Grounding facts would ensue.

Karen Bennett (2011) and Louis deRosset (2013) both argue that [GC] is Grounded in a fact that it contains. More generally, if [p] Grounds [q], then [[p] Grounds [q]] is itself Grounded in [p]. Such a proposal also takes care of the worry of an infinite regress: not only is [[p] Grounds [q]] Grounded in [p], but also [[[p] Grounds [q]] is Grounded in [p]] is Grounded in [p]. Hence, assuming that [Greece is a parliamentary representative democratic republic] is Grounded in physical facts about voting regulations and the activities of the various governmental branches, then [GC] itself, a fact about Grounds, is also Grounded in physical facts about voting regulations and the activities of governmental branches.

A different solution to the question of what Grounds [GC] is found in Dasgupta (2014). Without going into the details of his position, Dasgupta holds that [GC] is Grounded in facts concerning the essences of entities involved in [GC] together with some other facts pertaining to [GC]. What is important for our purposes is that, according to Dasgupta, the facts concerning the essences of entities involved in Grounding facts are Ungrounded. Still, he denies that this feature renders them fundamental. Rather, what this shows according to Dasgupta is that such facts are "autonomous" insofar as they are not apt for having a Ground in the first place.

Both solutions have their merits. On the one hand, there is something right with Dasgupta's attitude that, at least within the context of physicalism, one need not Ground every single fact. Physicalism's scope is not unrestricted. It is not a theory about everything. Consequently, it is within physicalists' rights to exclude certain facts from the scope of their theory. On the other hand, Bennett and deRosset's suggestion is appealing to physicalists for the opposite reason. It shows that under the supposition that a non-physical fact is Grounded in a physical fact, then the fact that such Grounding fact obtains is also Grounded in a physical fact. Many things "follow" from the physical: not only the non-physical but also the very relationship between the physical and the non-physical that renders the latter less fundamental.

Still, one might have concerns about both proposals. In the case of Dasgupta's proposal, one might worry that physicalists have over-restricted the scope of their position. Essentialist facts are still facts and by not providing an account of how they are Grounded we leave out a description of how things are (deRosset, 2013). In the case of Bennett and deRosset's proposal, one might wonder whether their proposal offers a satisfactory *explanatory* connection between Grounding facts and their Grounds (Dasgupta, 2014). Figuring out the force that such concerns carry is important. We would like to know whether they pose serious obstacles to Grounding formulations of physicalism. But even without having to figure that out, we can still note that Grounding formulations of physicalism face difficulties that appear to be internal to the notion of Grounding (see also Melnyk, 2016a, 2016b; Wilson, 2016). Although this conclusion does not amount to an argument against Grounding formulations of physicalism, it raises questions about the use and value of the notion of Grounding in formulations of physicalism.

8. Lessons

It is time to take stock. The arguments provided in this chapter make clear, we believe, that there is no quick and easy way to provide a metaphysical formulation of physicalism. Although there is widespread agreement amongst physicalists that the non-physical is nothing over and above the physical, it is not clear how to capture this relationship of dependence via metaphysical notions. Despite such a setback, proponents of physicalism are not without options. We bring this chapter to an end by listing six possible ways moving forward and by indicating how we will proceed in the following chapters.

Option 1: One can reject the view that physicalism ought to care for a relationship of *metaphysical* dependence between the physical and the non-physical. In fact, if reductive physicalism does not have room for such a relationship, then so much the worse for our notion of metaphysical dependence. For example, Barbara Montero's understanding of physicalism is consistent with this approach. According to Montero (2013), supervenience of the mental on the physical is not even necessary for physicalism. If Montero is right, then physicalism can survive on a metaphysics-free diet. If we do not need supervenience, then we do not need a stronger relationship of metaphysical dependence.

Option 2: Physicalism lacks *physical* ground. What it can offer, however, is functional ground. And that is all that is needed. Functionalism is physicalism enough.

Option 3: One may try to repair one of the accounts of physicalism that were evaluated in this chapter. Realization physicalism seems to be the natural candidate since it fared better than the others. Or perhaps one should take to heart the idea that the relationship of metaphysical dependence in question is primitive and thus invest one's efforts in the notion of Grounding.

Option 4: One may look at other ways of formulating physicalism with the hopes of finding the requisite account of metaphysical dependence in them. Perhaps one should understand the relationship between the physical and the non-physical in terms of composition (e.g., Pereboom, 2011), part—whole relationship (e.g., Ehring, 2003; Elpidorou, manuscript), constitution (e.g., Baker, 1997), or the determinate-determinable relationship (e.g., Yablo, 1992; Wilson, 2009). None of these approaches is free of problems, but what else is new?

Option 5: At the onset of our discussion, we put aside identity physicalism and claimed that it does not have the right features to count as the relationship of metaphysical dependence that physicalism requires. In light of our conclusions, one may argue that our findings are a vindication for identity physicalism. In other words, the *right* lesson to draw from this chapter is that the only version of physicalism that is worth our time is that of identity physicalism (e.g., Hill, 1991, 2009a; Polger, 2004; Smart, 1959).

Option 6: One should not bother with formulating physicalism and its metaphysical commitments. This might mean that there is no question of physicalism (Crane & Mellor, 1990) or it might mean that we do not need a formulation of physicalism to address the important philosophical issues that surround physicalism (Stoljar, 2010).

In what follows, we take option 1, or something close to it. In other words, we undertake the task of explicating an account of physicalism that is not only free of most of its metaphysical commitments but also tied, inextricably so, to the empirical sciences of the mind and to the physical sciences. We take the findings of this chapter as a license to move beyond an understanding of physicalism that is necessarily given in metaphysical terms. In other words, even though our findings might not demonstrate that metaphysical formulations of physicalism are hopeless (this was never our intention after all), they still highlight a need to think hard about physicalism's character and its unquestioned ties to metaphysics. In the following chapters, we will offer an alternative characterization of physicalism that does not treat physicalism as a metaphysical thesis. In fact, according to our account, physicalism is neither necessarily linked to metaphysics nor a thesis. Instead, physicalism ought to be understood as an ongoing, empirically grounded, and interdisciplinary research project. Understood in this way, we shall show that physicalism is capable of rendering consistent the joint acceptance of AUSTERITY and PLURALITY and thereby vindicating the basic intuition behind physicalism. There is more to physicalism than metaphysics. Indeed, there is a better physicalism that is not metaphysics.

Notes

1. Contemporary usage of "physicalism" parts ways with the manner in which the term was originally used. For both Neurath (1931a, 1931b) and Carnap (1959) the term denoted, more or less, the methodological-cum-linguistic thesis that the *language* of physics is the language in which one should provide an account of the world (see Crane, 2000, p. 76; Stoljar, 2010, p. 10). "Physicalism," as it is currently used, expresses first and foremost a set of ontological commitments about what entities exist in our world.
2. It is often stated that physicalism is both a contingent thesis and one that has strong modal commitments (Lewis, 1983; Jackson, 1998; Stoljar, 2015). Its contingency is manifested in the claim that physicalism is a thesis about our world and even if it is true, it did not have to be so. Furthermore, the acceptance of physicalism entails a necessary determination thesis, one that articulates requirements for all possible worlds that stand in a similarity relationship to the actual one. The precise modal commitments of physicalism, however, depend ultimately on one's understanding of nothing-over-and-aboveness. In fact, the truth of physicalism in the actual world, which requires, we assume, that the

mental is, in some sense, nothing over and above the physical, might entail—depending on our understanding of nothing-over-and-aboveness—that there are no worlds in which the mental is basic. For an argument in support of such a conclusion, see Levine and Trogdon (2009). See also Crane (2000, p. 74) for a brief consideration of the contingency/necessity of "monism," a position that in certain respects is similar to physicalism.

3. Entities exist concretely insofar as they exist spatiotemporally. An entity can play a causal role in our world even if it is a *mere* effect and not necessarily a cause.
4. Most informal characterizations of physicalism assert the metaphysical primacy of the physical. For the claim that according to physicalism the non-physical is nothing over and above the physical see, among many others, Byrne (1999, p. 348), Chalmers (1996, p. 41), Dowell (2006, p. 1), Jackson (1998, p. 9), Leuenberger (2008a, p. 145), Lewis (1994, pp. 51–52), Loewer (2001, p. 39), Melnyk (2003, p. 2), Pettit (1995, p. 142), and Wilson (2005, p. 426).
5. Different attempts to define "physical" are summarized and evaluated in Chapter 3. See also Ney (2008) and Stoljar (2015).
6. The holding of this relationship implies that one of the relata is more fundamental than the other (Cameron, 2008; Schaffer, 2010; Rosen, 2010). Having said that, we do not mean this to be a claim about ontological (or metaphysical) dependence *as such*. There could be instances of ontological dependence that are symmetric. See, e.g., Barnes (forthcoming) but also consider Berker (manuscript). All that we require is that insofar as physicalism is concerned, the dependence relationship assumed to hold between the physical and the non-physical is asymmetric.
7. It is our view that physicalism is inconsistent with fundamental mentality. The existence of fundamental mentality would violate what we take to be a necessary condition of physicalism, namely, that the non-physical is nothing over and above the physical. So, if *b* is both fundamental and mental, then physicalism ought to be rejected. Although not everyone would agree with such an assessment, we defend our claim in Chapter 4 where we articulate our preferred version of physicalism.
8. What happens if the in-virtue-of relationship is not well founded? Does physicalism require that there must be a final fundamental level? (See, e.g., Lewis (1994, p. 52)). Or is physicalism consistent with the possibility of an infinite descent of dependence (*a* holds in virtue of *b*, *b* holds in virtue of *c*, *c* holds in virtue of *d*, . . . , *ad infinitum*)? Schaffer (2003, p. 507) argues that physicalism is an "irreparably fundamentalist doctrine." Physicalism, Schaffer holds, requires a fundamental level because in the absence of such a level one cannot draw a distinction between the primary (i.e., the physical) and the derivative. Montero (2006) and Levine and Trogdon (2009) respond to Schaffer.
9. We will not discuss a truthmaking approach to physicalism. For an examination of whether physicalism can be formulated in terms of truthmaking, we direct the reader to Morris (2016).
10. Alastair Wilson's (2017) discussion of Grounding complicates matters. He distinguishes between nomological causation and metaphysical causation (only the former is mediated by a law of nature) and argues that Grounding should be understood as metaphysical causation. If Wilson is right, then there is a systematic connection between Grounding and causation. Be that as it may, the claims made in this paragraph are about nomological causation which by itself fails to fix ontological dependence. See also Schaffer (2016, Sect. 4.5) for a discussion of the differences between causation and Grounding.
11. Making the notion of global supervenience precise is no child's play. For some attempts and discussions, see Bennett (2004), McLaughlin and Bennett (2014),

Leuenberger (2009), Paull and Sider (1992), Shagrir (1999), and Stalnaker (1996).

12. David Mark Kovacs (2016) argues that a pattern of both modal and set-theoretical facts is capable of giving rise to an explanation of metaphysical dependence. Kovacs's account can thus be read as a way of showing how necessitation (or supervenience) can be explanatory.
13. It is unlikely that all T-terms of a theory will be names. Theories will most likely contain in addition to names, predicates and functors. Still, the assumption that T-terms are names appears to be harmless for it is plausible to suppose that one could replace all T-term with names. For example, let "F" be a predicate included in a theory T. According to Lewis (1970), we can replace sentences of the form "Fx" with sentences of the form "x has the property F-hood" where "F-hood" is a name. A similar substitution could be performed in the case of functors. Finally, in order to transform predicates and functors into names, the O-language has to contain already the copulas needed for those transformations. Lewis assumes that these are to be found in the O-language (1970, p. 429).
14. Logically, T is stronger than the Ramsey sentence. T does not only specify that there is an entity (or an n-tuple) of entities that they have such-and-so causal roles. It also specifies what are the entities (pain, desire, belief, etc.) that have those roles. Still, given that "pain", "desire", "belief", etc. are implicitly defined by their roles, it cannot turn out that something other than pain occupies the pain-role. By definition, whatever occupies the pain-role is pain.
15. In cases where the theory is multiply realized, Lewis used to hold that the terms are denotationless. This seems to be Lewis's view at least in (1970) and (1972). His reasoning supporting this conclusion is that a theory that fails to be uniquely realized is in a sense a failed theory (1970, pp. 432–433). In later works, Lewis allows that terms of theories which are multiply realized are not denotationless but indeterminate insofar as they do not distinguish between the various realizers. For more on this issue, see Lewis (1997 and 2008), and Wolfgang Schwarz's (2015) outstanding presentation of Lewis's analytic functionalism.
16. There will be cases in which the theory T although not realized is *very nearly realized*. In such a case, Lewis holds that we can construct a weaker theory T* which is implied by T but does not imply it such that an n-tuple of entities is a realization of T* iff it is a near realization of T. We can then work with T* instead of T and it is the former that is "the real term-introducing theory" (1970, p. 432).
17. In a different context, Paul Teller raises the same concern. He writes: "Now what, I want to ask, makes it appropriate to call a property 'physical' when it is such a disparate and infinitely long disjunction of disjuncts each of which is probably already an uncountable conjunction of finite physical descriptions? Yes, it is a Boolean combination of physical properties, but I feel that to call it 'physical' threatens to be misleading. Which physical characteristics is it that all the things satisfying the individual disjuncts have in common?" (Teller, 1984, p. 59).
18. We take the following passage from Lewis to support our reading of his position: "When we describe mental state *M* as the occupant of the *M*-role . . . [i]t says nothing about what sort of state it is that occupies the role. It might be a non-physical or a physical state, and if it is physical it might be a state of neural activity in the brain, or a pattern of currents and charges on a silicon chip, or the jangling of an enormous assemblage of beer cans" (Lewis, 1994, p. 58).
19. Melnyk understands "functional type" liberally. It "refer[s] to any type whose tokening just is the tokening of some or other type that meets a specific associated condition, where this condition could be of *any* kind, and needn't be the playing of a causal role" (2006, p. 129).
20. One could protest that *having a location* is not a physical type and thus the provided example does not threaten (4). In response to this objection, we offer

the following considerations. First, claims about the location of entities figure prominently in physical theories and descriptions of the world. As such, we have a reason to count the type in question as physical. Second, it is possible to give additional examples of cases in which non-physical tokens realize tokens of physical types (see Francescotti, 2010, pp. 605–606). Importantly, these examples are ones that involve tokens of unambiguously physical types. Third, there are additional problems with enlisting (4) in the services of physicalism, ones that go beyond the issue of whether non-physical tokens can realize tokens of physical types. Consider, for example, token *a* of functional type, *A*, whose associated condition is some role, *R*. Token *a* could be realized by token *b*, which is the token of a physical type, and plays role *R*. Now, if it turns out that, while playing role *R*, *b* behaves in a manner that is contrary to the laws of physics, then token *a* is not rendered nothing over and above the physical, even though it is realized by a physical token (Melnyk, 2003, pp. 23–24).

21. (Andreas Elpidorou) In the version of this chapter that served as the editorial introduction to the special issue on physicalism (Elpidorou, 2017), I titled this section "Shoemaker's realization." I have now come to realize that this was an unfortunate mistake. Although it is the case that in the editorial introduction my focus was Shoemaker's version of subset realization and not Wilson's, the label "Shoemaker's subset realization" suggests that Shoemaker is the originator of this position. In print, however, the first articulation of subset realization is found in Wilson (1999) and Wilson has done much work in developing the position further (Wilson, 2005, 2009, 2010). Thus, at the very least, the position should be attributed to both Wilson and Shoemaker. For a discussion on the history of subset realization, see the following blog post by Wilson: http://philosopherscocoon.typepad.com/the_campaign_for_better_c/2015/03/jessica-wilson-toronto-on-the-pedigree-of-the-subset-view-of-realization.html.
22. According to Shoemaker (2007, p. 12) the causal profile of a property includes both "forward-looking causal features" (how the tokening of the property gives rise to various effects) and "backward-looking causal features" (what are the states of affairs that can give rise to the instantiation of the property). Shoemaker no longer insists that the backward-looking causal features are part of the causal profile of a property. See Shoemaker (2011). This move is a return to his previous position on properties (Shoemaker, 2001).
23. If it is possible for non-physical properties to be realized by properties which are incompatible with physicalism, then non-physical properties are not identical to (some or other) physical properties: the causal features which are constitutive of the non-physical properties are not physical. In this case, however, the fact that such non-physical properties are actually realized by physical properties does not render them nothing over and above their physical realizers.
24. For some other problems with subset realization that, for reasons of space, we cannot discuss, see Gibb (2014), Gillett (2010), Pereboom (2011), and Tiehen (2014).
25. We speak of Grounding as a relation. However, not everyone would agree with this presentation. For example, Fine (2012) and Correia (2010) take Grounding to be a non-truth-functional sentential operator that connects sentences stating the Grounds and sentences stating what is being Grounded. What is more, not everyone accepts that Grounding is primitive. See, for example, Bricker (2006).
26. Requirement (c) is negotiable. That is for two reasons. First, some proponents of Grounding maintain that Grounding is an explanatory relation (Dasgupta, 2014; Fine, 2001). Second, one might argue that physicalism is at heart an explanatory position and the primacy of the physical ought to be captured in terms of an explanatory relation: It is the physical that explains the non-physical and not vice versa. As it will become clear in the following chapters that is

precisely our view, although we do not use Grounding but (scientific) composition to articulate the character of explanation that is at the heart of physicalism.

27. For instance, Leuenberger (2014, II.i) argues that it is possible to have a world *w* in which the property *red* is Grounded in the physical facts, but because of the presence of a non-physical blocker that makes visual phenomenology disappear, *red* is not instantiated even though the physical facts obtain. (For a discussion of blockers within the context of physicalism, see Hawthorne, 2002).
28. In the previous paragraph, we stated that Γ, the collection of all physical facts, Grounds a non-physical fact [q] and then asked whether it is possible for all physical facts in Γ to obtain and for [q] to fail to obtain. One might accept that Γ fails to necessitate [q] but deny that this shows that Grounding does not entail necessitation. That is because what Grounds [q] is not just Γ but rather Γ plus a totality fact—i.e., a fact that expresses that nothing more than physical facts obtain. So, both Γ and a totality fact necessitate [q]. Although it is beyond the scope of this chapter to evaluate this response, it is plausible that, in this case, Γ does *not* Ground the totality fact: otherwise, Γ alone would be sufficient to Ground [q]. Consequently, proponents of physicalism would need to consider whether such a totality fact, which is not Grounded in the totality of physical facts, is consistent with physicalism. For a more detailed discussion of this issue, see Leuenberger (2014). Rosen (2010) also briefly discusses the nature of the totality fact within the context of Grounding.
29. Even if Grounding does not entail metaphysical necessitation, it has been argued that Grounding entails a supervenience thesis that involves Grounds and what is Grounded: Specifically, any two worlds that are indiscernible with respect to their Grounds are indiscernible with respect to what is Grounded (Leuenberger, 2014; cf.; Schaffer, 2016, n. 10). Such a result, however, offers little solace to proponents of physicalism who are interested in using Grounding as a way to spell out the relationship between the physical and the non-physical. Given the many problems with supervenience as an attempt to explicate metaphysical priority, the fact that what is Grounded (the non-physical) supervenes on its Grounds (the physical) does not show that the former is nothing over and above the latter.
30. Not everyone identifies the fundamental with that which is not Grounded. See, e.g., Sider (2011) and Wilson (2014).

References

Audi, P. (2012a). A clarification and defense of the notion of grounding. In F. Correia & B. Schnieder (eds.), *Metaphysical grounding: Understanding the structure of reality* (pp. 101–121). Cambridge: Cambridge University Press.

Audi, P. (2012b). Grounding: Toward a theory of the in-virtue-of relation. *Journal of Philosophy*, *109*, 685–711.

Baker, L. (1997). Why constitution is not identity. *The Journal of Philosophy*, *94*, 599–621.

Barnes, E. (forthcoming). Symmetric dependence. In R. Bliss & G. Priest (eds.), *Reality and its structure: Essays in fundamentality*. New York: Oxford University Press.

Bennett, K. (2004). Global supervenience and dependence. *Philosophy and Phenomenological Research*, *68*(3), 501–529.

Bennett, K. (2011). By our bootstraps. *Philosophical Perspectives*, *25*, 27–41.

Berker, S. (manuscript). The unity of grounding.

Block, N. (2015). The Canberra plan neglects ground. In T. Horgan, M. Sabatés, & D. Sosa (eds.), *Qualia and mental causation in a physical world: Themes from the philosophy of Jaegwon Kim* (pp. 105–133). Cambridge: Cambridge University Press.

Bolzano, B. (1837/1972). *The theory of science: Die Wissenschaftslehre oder Versuch einer Neuen Darstellung der Logik* (R. George, Trans. and ed.). Berkeley/Los Angeles, CA: University of California Press.

Braddon-Mitchell, D., & Jackson, F. (2007). *Philosophy of mind and cognition: An introduction* (2nd edition). Malden, MA: Blackwell Publishing.

Bricker, P. (2006). The relation between the general and the particular: Entailment vs. supervenience. In D. Zimmerman (ed.), *Oxford studies in metaphysics* (Vol. 2, pp. 251–287). Oxford: Oxford University Press.

Byrne, A. (1999). Cosmic hermeneutics. *Philosophical Perspectives*, *13*, 347–383.

Cameron, R. P. (2008). Turtles all the way down: Regress, priority and fundamentality. *The Philosophical Quarterly*, *58*(230), 1–14.

Carnap, R. (1959). Psychology in physical language. In A. J. Ayer (ed.), *Logical positivism* (pp. 165–198). New York: The Free Press.

Chalmers, D. J. (1996). *The conscious mind: In search of a fundamental theory*. New York: Oxford University Press.

Chomsky, N. (2000). *New horizons in the study of language and mind*. Cambridge, UK: Cambridge University Press.

Correia, F. (2010). Grounding and truth-functions. *Logique et Analyse*, *53*, 251–279.

Correia, F. (2013). Metaphysical grounds and essence. In M. Hoeltje, B. Schnieder, & A. Steinberg (eds.), *Varieties of dependence: Ontological dependence, grounding, supervenience, response-dependence* (pp. 271–296). München: Philosophia.

Correia, F., & Schnieder, B. (2012). Grounding: An opinionated introduction. In F. Correia & B. Schnieder (eds.), *Metaphysical grounding: Understanding the structure of reality* (pp. 1–36). Cambridge, UK: Cambridge University Press.

Crane, T. (2000). Dualism, monism, physicalism. *Mind & Society*, *1*(2), 73–85.

Crane, T., & Mellor, H. (1990). There is no question of physicalism. *Mind*, *90*, 185–206.

Daly, C. (2012). Skepticism about grounding. In F. Correia & B. Schnieder (eds.), *Metaphysical grounding: Understanding the structure of reality* (pp. 81–100). Cambridge, UK: Cambridge University Press.

Dasgupta, S. (2014). The possibility of physicalism. *The Journal of Philosophy*, *111*(9/10), 557–592.

Davidson, D. (1980). Mental events. In *Essays on actions and events* (pp. 207–225). Oxford: Clarendon Press.

deRosset, L. (2013). Grounding explanations. *Philosophers' Imprint*, *13*(7), 1–26.

Dowell, J. L. (2006). Formulating the thesis of physicalism: An introduction. *Philosophical Studies*, *131*(1), 1–23.

Ehring, D. (2003). Part-whole physicalism and mental causation. *Synthese*, *135*(3), 359–388.

Elpidorou, A. (2017). Introduction: The character of physicalism. *Topoi*. Published online. http://doi.org/10.1007/s11245-017-9488-2

Elpidorou, A. (manuscript). Part-whole physicalism: The neglected ontological significance of the third Logical Investigation.

Fine, K. (1994a). Essence and modality: The second philosophical perspectives lecture. *Philosophical Perspectives*, *8*, 1–16. doi: 10.2307/2214160

Fine, K. (1994b). Ontological dependence. *Proceedings of the Aristotelian Society*, *95*, 269–290.

Fine, K. (2001). The question of realism. *Philosophers' Imprint*, *1*, 1–30.
Fine, K. (2012). Guide to ground. In F. Correia & B. Schnieder (eds.), *Metaphysical grounding: Understanding the structure of reality* (pp. 37–80). Cambridge, UK: Cambridge University Press.
Francescotti, R. (2010). Realization and physicalism. *Philosophical Psychology*, *23*(5), 601–616.
Gibb, S. (2014). The entailment problem and the subset account of property realization. *Australasian Journal of Philosophy*, *92*(3), 551–566.
Gillett, C. (2002). The dimensions of realization: A critique of the standard view. *Analysis*, *62*, 316–323.
Gillett, C. (2003). The metaphysics of realization, multiple realizability, and the special sciences. *The Journal of Philosophy*, *100*, 591–603.
Gillett, C. (2010). Moving beyond the subset model of realization: The problem of qualitative distinctness in the metaphysics of science. *Synthese*, *177*, 165–192.
Hall, N. (2004). Two concepts of causation. In J. Collins, N. Hall, & L. A. Paul (eds.), *Causation and counterfactuals* (pp. 225–276). Cambridge, MA: MIT Press.
Hawthorne, J. P. (2002). Blocking definitions of materialism. *Philosophical Studies*, *110*(2), 103–113.
Hellman, G., & Thompson, F. W. (1977). Physicalist materialism. *Nous*, *11*(4), 309–345.
Hempel, C. (1969). Reduction: Ontological and linguistic facets. In S. Morgenbesser, P. Suppes, & M. White (eds.), *Philosophy, science and method: Essays in honor of Ernest Nagel* (pp. 179–199). New York: St. Martin's Press.
Hempel, C. (1980). Comments on Goodman's ways of worldmaking. *Synthese*, *45*, 139–199.
Hill, C. S. (1991). *Sensations: A defense of type materialism*. Cambridge, UK: Cambridge University Press.
Hill, C. S. (2009a). The identity theory. In T. Bayne, A. Cleeremans, & P. Wilken (eds.), *The Oxford companion to consciousness* (pp. 359–363). Oxford: Oxford University Press.
Hill, C. S. (2009b). *Consciousness*. Cambridge, UK: Cambridge University Press.
Hofweber, T. (2009). Ambitious, yet modest, metaphysics. In D. J. Chalmers, D. Manley, & R. Wasserman (eds.), *Metametaphysics* (pp. 260–289). Oxford, UK: Oxford University Press.
Horgan, T. (1993). From supervenience to superdupervenience: Meeting the demands of a material world. *Mind*, *102*, 555–586.
Horgan, T. (2006). Materialism: Matters of definition, defense, and deconstruction. *Philosophical Studies*, *131*(1), 157–183.
Jackson, F. (1994). Finding the mind in the natural world. In D. Chalmers (ed.), *Philosophy of mind: Classical and contemporary readings* (pp. 162–169). New York: Oxford University Press.
Jackson, F. (1998). *From metaphysics to ethics: A defence of conceptual analysis*. Oxford, UK: Oxford University Press.
Jenkins, C. S. (2011). Is metaphysical dependence irreflexive? *The Monist*, *94*(2), 267–276.
Kim, J. (1984). Concepts of supervenience. *Philosophy and Phenomenological Research*, *45*(2), 153–176.
Kim, J. (1993a). *Supervenience and mind: Selected philosophical essays*. Cambridge, UK: Cambridge University Press.

Kim, J. (1993b). Postscripts on supervenience. In *Supervenience and mind: Selected philosophical* (pp. 161–171). Cambridge, UK: Cambridge University Press.
Kim, J. (1998a). *Mind in a physical world: An essay on the mind-body problem and mental causation*. Cambridge, MA: MIT Press.
Kim, J. (1998b). The mind-body problem after fifty years. In A. O'Hear (ed.), *Current issues in philosophy of mind* (pp. 3–21). Cambridge, UK: Cambridge University Press.
Kim, J. (2005). *Physicalism, or something near enough*. Princeton, NJ: Princeton University Press.
Kim, J. (2010). Thoughts on Sydney Shoemaker's physical realization. *Philosophical Studies, 148*(1), 101–112.
Kirk, R. (2009). Physical realization. *Analysis, 69*(1), 148–156.
Koslicki, K. (2015). The coarse-grainedness of grounding. In K. Bennett & D. W. Zimmerman (eds.), *Oxford studies in metaphysics* (Vol. 9, pp. 306–344). Oxford, UK: Oxford University Press. doi: 10.1093/acprof:oso/9780198729242.001.0001
Kovacs, D. M. (2016). Grounding and the argument from explanatoriness. *Philosophical Studies*. doi: 10.1007/s11098-016-0818-9
Kripke, S. (1980). *Naming and necessity*. Cambridge, MA: Harvard University Press.
Leuenberger, S. (2008a). Ceteris absentibus physicalism. *Oxford Studies in Metaphysics, 4*, 145–170.
Leuenberger, S. (2008b). Supervenience in metaphysics. *Philosophy Compass, 3*(4), 749–762.
Leuenberger, S. (2009). What is global supervenience? *Synthese, 170*(1), 115–129.
Leuenberger, S. (2014). Grounding and necessity. *Inquiry, 57*, 151–174.
Levine, J. (1993). On leaving out what it's like. In M. Davies & G. Humphreys (eds.), *Consciousness: Psychological and philosophical essays* (pp. 121–136). Oxford, UK: Blackwell Publishing.
Levine, J., & Trogdon, K. (2009). The modal status of materialism. *Philosophical Studies, 145*, 351–362.
Lewis, D. (1966). An argument for the identity theory. *Journal of Philosophy, 63*, 17–25.
Lewis, D. (1970). How to define theoretical terms. *Journal of Philosophy, 67*, 427–446.
Lewis, D. (1972). Psychophysical and theoretical identifications. *Australasian Journal of Philosophy, 50*(3), 249–258.
Lewis, D. (1983). New work for a theory of universals. *Australasian Journal of Philosophy, 61*, 343–377.
Lewis, D. (1986). *On the plurality of worlds*. Oxford, UK: Blackwell Publishing.
Lewis, D. (1994). Reduction of mind. In S. Guttenplan (ed.), *A companion to the philosophy of mind* (pp. 51–63). Oxford, UK: Basil Blackwell.
Lewis, D. (1997). Naming the colors. *Australasian Journal of Philosophy, 75*, 325–342.
Lewis, D. (2008). Ramseyan Humility. In D. Braddon-Mitchell & R. Nola (eds.), *Conceptual analysis and philosophical naturalism* (pp. 203–222). Cambridge, MA: MIT Press.
Loewer, B. (2001). From physics to physicalism. In C. Gillet & B. Loewer (eds.), *Physicalism and its discontents* (pp. 37–56). Cambridge, UK: Cambridge University Press.
Lynch, M. P., & Glasgow, J. M. (2003). The impossibility of superdupervenience. *Philosophical Studies, 113*(3), 201–221.

McLaughlin, B. (2009). Review of Sydney Shoemaker's physical realization. *Notre Dame Philosophical Reviews*. Online journal.

McLaughlin, B., & Bennett, K. (2014). Supervenience. In E. N. Zalta (ed.), *The Stanford encyclopedia of philosophy*. http://plato.stanford.edu/archives/spr2014/entries/supervenience/

Melnyk, A. (1997). How to keep the "physical" in physicalism. *The Journal of Philosophy*, *94*(12), 622–637.

Melnyk, A. (2003). *A physicalist manifesto: Thoroughly modern materialism*. Cambridge, UK: Cambridge University Press.

Melnyk, A. (2006). Realization and the formulation of physicalism. *Philosophical Studies*, *131*(1), 127–155.

Melnyk, A. (2016a). In defense of a realization formulation of physicalism. *Topoi*. Published online. doi: 10.1007/s11245-016-9404-1

Melnyk, A. (2016b). Grounding and the formulation of physicalism. In K. Aizawa & C. Gillett (eds.), *Scientific composition and metaphysical ground* (pp. 249–270). London: Palgrave Macmillan.

Montero, B. G. (2006). Physicalism in an infinitely decomposable world. *Erkenntnis*, *64*(2), 177–191.

Montero, B. G. (2013). Must physicalism imply the supervenience of the mental on the physical? *The Journal of Philosophy*, *110*(2), 93–110.

Montero, B. G., & Brown, C. (2017). Making room for a this-wordly physicalism. *Topoi*. Published online. doi: 10.1007/s11245-017-9450-3

Morris, K. (2016). Physicalism, truthmaking, and levels of reality: Prospects and problems. *Topoi*. Published online. doi: 10.1007/s11245-016-9379-y

Neurath, O. (1931a/1983). Physicalism: The philosophy of the Vienna Circle. In R. S. Cohen & M. Neurath (eds.), *Philosophical papers 1913–1946* (pp. 48–51). Dordrecht: D. Reidel.

Neurath, O. (1931b/1983). Physicalism. In R. S. Cohen & M. Neurath (eds.), *Philosophical oapers 1913–1946* (pp. 52–57). Dordrecht: D. Reidel.

Ney, A. (2008). Defining physicalism. *Philosophy Compass*, *3*(5), 1033–1048.

Nolan, D. (2005). *David Lewis*. Chesham, UK: Acumen.

Paull, R. C., & Sider, T. R. (1992). In defense of global supervenience. *Philosophy and Phenomenological Research*, *52*(4), 833–854.

Pereboom, D. (2011). *Consciousness and the prospects of physicalism*. Oxford, UK: Oxford University Press.

Pereboom, D. (2016). Anti-reductionism, anti-rationalism, and the material constitution of the mental. In K. Aizawa & C. Gillett (eds.), *Scientific composition and metaphysical ground* (pp. 123–140). London: Palgrave Macmillan.

Pettit, P. (1995). Microphysicalism, dottism and reduction. *Analysis*, *55*(3), 141–146.

Poland, J. (1994). *Physicalism: The philosophical foundations*. Oxford: Clarendon.

Polger, T. (2004). *Natural minds*. Cambridge, MA: MIT Press.

Polger, T. (2007). Realization and the metaphysics of mind. *The Australasian Journal of Philosophy*, *85*, 233–259.

Polger, T. W., & Shapiro, L. A. (2008). Understanding the dimensions of realization. *The Journal of Philosophy*, *105*(4), 213–222.

Quine, W. V. (1948). On what there is. *Review of Metaphysics*, *2*(1), 21–38.

Raven, M. (2012). In defense of ground. *Australasian Journal of Philosophy*, *90*, 687–701.

Raven, M. (2015). Ground. *Philosophy Compass*, *10*(5), 322–333.

Rosen, G. (2010). Metaphysical dependence: Grounding and reduction. In R. Hale & A. Hoffman (eds.), *Modality: Metaphysics, logic, and epistemology* (pp. 109–136). New York, NY: Oxford University Press.
Schaffer, J. (2003). Is there a fundamental level? *Noûs*, *37*(3), 498–517.
Schaffer, J. (2009). On what grounds what. In D. J. Chalmers, D. Manley, & R. Wasserman (eds.), *Metametaphysics* (pp. 347–383). Oxford: Oxford University Press.
Schaffer, J. (2010). The internal relatedness of all things. *Mind*, *119*(474), 341–376.
Schaffer, J. (2012). Grounding, transitivity, and contrastivity. In F. Correia & B. Schnieder (eds.), *Metaphysical grounding: Understanding the structure of reality* (pp. 122–138). Cambridge, UK: Cambridge University Press.
Schaffer, J. (2016). Grounding in the image of causation. *Philosophical Studies*, *173*(1), 49–100.
Schiffer, S. (1987). *Remnants of meaning*. Cambridge, MA: MIT Press/Bradford.
Schnieder, B. (2006). Truth-making without truth-makers. *Synthese*, *152*, 21–46.
Schwarz, W. (2015). Analytic functionalism. In B. Loewer & J. Schaffer (eds.), *A companion to David Lewis* (pp. 504–518). Malden, MA: Wiley Blackwell Publishing.
Shagrir, O. (1999). More on global supervenience. *Philosophy and Phenomenological Research*, *59*(3), 691–701.
Shoemaker, S. (1980). Causality and properties. In P. Van Inwagen (ed.), *Time and cause* (pp. 109–135). Dordrecht: D. Reidel.
Shoemaker, S. (2001). Realization and mental causation. In C. Gillett & B. Loewer (eds.), *Physicalism and its discontents* (pp. 74–98). Cambridge, UK: Cambridge University Press.
Shoemaker, S. (2007). *Physical realization*. New York, NY: Oxford University Press.
Shoemaker, S. (2011). Realization, powers, and property identity. *The Monist*, *94*(1), 3–18.
Sider, T. (2011). *Writing the book of the world*. Oxford, UK: Oxford University Press.
Skiles, A. (2015). Against grounding necessitarianism. *Erkenntnis*, *80*(4), 717–751.
Smart, J. J. C. (1959). Sensations and brain processes. *The Philosophical Review*, *68*(2), 141–156.
Smart, J. J. C. (2007). The mind/brain identity theory. In E. N. Zalta (ed.), *The Stanford encyclopedia of philosophy*. https://plato.stanford.edu/archives/spr2017/entries/mind-identity/
Stalnaker, R. (1996). Varieties of supervenience. *Philosophical Perspectives*, *10*, 221–241.
Stoljar, D. (2010). *Physicalism*. New York, NY: Routledge.
Stoljar, D. (2015). Physicalism. In E. N. Zalta (ed.), *The Stanford encyclopedia of philosophy*. http://plato.stanford.edu/archives/spr2016/entries/physicalism
Tahko, T. E., & Lowe, E. J. (2015). Ontological dependence. In E. N. Zalta (ed.), *The Stanford encyclopedia of philosophy*. http://plato.stanford.edu/archives/spr2015/entries/dependence-ontological/
Tatzel, A. (2002). Bolzano's theory of ground and consequence. *Notre Dame Journal of Symbolic Logic*, *43*, 1–25.
Teller, P. (1984). Comments on Kim's paper. *The Southern Journal of Philosophy*, *22*(S1), 57–61.
Tiehen, J. (2014). Subset realization and the problem of property entailment. *Erkenntnis*, *79*(2), 471–480.
Trogdon, K. (2013a). An introduction to grounding. In M. Hoeltje, B. Schnieder, & A. Steinberg (eds.), *Varieties of dependence: Ontological dependence, grounding, supervenience, response-dependence* (pp. 97–122). München: Philosophia.

Trogdon, K. (2013b). Grounding: Necessary or contingent? *Pacific Philosophical Quarterly*, *94*, 465–485.

Watkins, M. (2002). *Rediscovering colors: A study in pollyanna realism* (Vol. 88). Berlin, Germany: Springer Science & Business Media.

Wilson, A. (2017). Metaphysical causation. *Noûs*. Published online. doi: 10.1111/nous.12190

Wilson, J. (1999). How superduper does a physicalist supervenience need to be? *Philosophical Quarterly*, *49*, 33–52.

Wilson, J. (2005). Supervenience-based characterizations of physicalism. *Noûs*, *39*, 426–459.

Wilson, J. (2009). Determination, realization, and mental causation. *Philosophical Studies*, *145*(1), 149–169.

Wilson, J. (2010). Non-reductive physicalism and degrees of freedom. *The British Journal for the Philosophy of Science*, *61*(2), 279–311.

Wilson, J. (2011). Non-reductive realization and the powers-based subset strategy. *The Monist*, *94*(1), 121–154.

Wilson, J. (2014). No work for a theory of grounding. *Inquiry*, *57*(5–6), 1–45.

Wilson, J. (2016). Grounding-based formulations of physicalism. *Topoi*. Published online. doi: 10.1007/s11245-016-9435-7

Witmer, G. (2001). Sufficiency claims and physicalism: A formulation. In C. Gillett & B. Loewer (eds.), *Physicalism and its discontents* (pp. 57–73). Cambridge, UK: Cambridge University Press.

Yablo, S. (1992). Mental causation. *The Philosophical Review*, *101*(2), 245–280.

3 Defining Physicalism

Philosophers generally treat physicalism as a thesis that is both metaphysical and empirically informed. They turn to science in order to determine what are the basic entities that exist in our world and use metaphysics to show that everything else follows from, and is nothing over and above, these entities. In the previous chapter, we surveyed the challenges facing attempts to characterize the metaphysical character of physicalism. Providing a metaphysical account of the nothing-over-and-above relationship has proven to be an extremely difficult philosophical task. As Daniel Stoljar (2010) suggests, it is hard to come up with a version of physicalism that is both true and worth having. Although it may seem like piling on, we are now going to concentrate on another well-known challenge facing physicalism: the problem of how to define the term "physical" as it figures in definitions and discussions of physicalism. To put this in a different way, we are now going to consider the particular difficulties associated with treating physicalism as an empirically informed position. Our purpose, though, is not to bury physicalism; instead, we want to transform it. Consideration of these issues will lead us to offer a reconstructive version of physicalism—one that sees physicalism as an empirical research program and thus retains a connection to scientific explanation that is missing from many, if not most, versions of physicalism. While this revisionist conception may not satisfy all of the desiderata traditionally assigned to physicalism by philosophers, we think that it is well motivated and, more importantly, will provide a means of outlining a minimal yet determinate version of physicalism that will enable us to clearly elaborate the challenge posed by consciousness.

In this chapter, we outline and defend our reconstructive approach to physicalism. Our argument unfolds in two steps. First, we contend that a well-known problem for physicalism, Hempel's Dilemma, is in fact more serious than it is typically taken to be and undermines any attempt to offer a version of the metaphysical thesis that defers to the physical sciences (an opinion that we admittedly share with others: e.g., Crane & Mellor, 1990; Hempel, 1980; Ney, 2008b). Second, we propose that there is a version of physicalism that better captures the views of researchers and philosophers who are actively engaged with the psychological and brain sciences. This version redefines physicalism as an interdisciplinary research program aimed at understanding how physical entities give rise to and thus explain natural phenomena. As a research program, physicalism has general commitments concerning what exists and what constitutes a good explanation but, ultimately, remains open to future theoretical and empirical developments (Lakatos, 1970, 1977; Laudan, 1977). We contend that the constrained flexibility of this approach enables it to overcome the challenge posed by Hempel's Dilemma. In the next chapter, we demonstrate that these commitments have enough teeth to them to establish conditions for the possible success or indeed failure of our brand of physicalism. In subsequent chapters, we will examine the challenge posed by consciousness against the background of these conditions.

1. Hempel's Dilemma

Physicalism is the historical successor of materialism. The general idea of either position is that we should explicitly defer to what physics (or perhaps microphysics) tells us about what the world contains. Although the historical transition from materialism to physicalism is somewhat complicated (Ney, 2008a; Papineau, 2001; Stoljar, 2015), the reason that contemporary philosophers tend to prefer the latter term to the former term is that it does not retain the ontological commitments associated with our folk intuitions about the nature of matter. This is a direct consequence of the fact that so much of contemporary physics fails to comport with our everyday understanding of objects (Montero, 1999, 2009). Deferring to physics to determine what there is creates a problem that has come to be known as "Hempel's Dilemma" (Hempel, 1980). This problem centers on a core question: To which physical theory should we defer when developing our inventory of what exists? Two options seem possible: either we choose current theory or some future theory. The dilemma arises because neither option seems promising. The problem with choosing current physical theory is that this would almost assuredly make physicalism false. Indeed, if we adopt an inclusive approach that encompasses the different fields of physics and the various theories they contain (Relativity Theory, Quantum Electrodynamics, etc.), the resulting physical theory is likely to be inconsistent (Wilson, 2006). Focusing on a particular subarea of physics may not help that much because the contemporary theory that it contains is still likely to be supplanted in the future. The problem with choosing a future theory—and usually the best option is taken to be a complete and ideal one—is that this threatens to rob physicalism of any metaphysical bite. Given that we do not know much about what this theory will look like (let alone whether or not it is attainable), who is to say that it will not posit irreducible mental entities. Our uncertainty about the structure of this theory also threatens to render physicalism too vague to resolve the relevant metaphysical questions.

By far the most popular response to this dilemma is to embrace the second horn (for reviews see Loewer, 2001; Ney, 2008a; Stoljar, 2015; although see Bokulich, 2011; Melnyk, 1997, 2003; Vicente, 2011 for attempts to embrace the first horn). A veritable cottage industry has emerged around this futurist strategy. Proponents tend to argue either (a) that we know enough about the rough outlines of a complete and ideal theory to know that it excludes irreducible mental entities or (b) that we can amend, enrich, or transform a complete and ideal physical theory in some way so that it does not face the problems associated with this horn of Hempel's Dilemma.

There are good reasons to think that neither of these forms of futurism will work. A central problem with the first is that, if the recent history of physics shows us anything, it is that the ontological commitments of future physical theories are very hard to predict. Philosophers switched from materialism to physicalism in the twentieth century because physical theories changed drastically over a relatively short period of time and dramatically contradicted what we thought we knew a priori about the substance of our world. While this history does not show that any particular hypothesis about the outlines of a complete and ideal physical theory is false, it does throw into question the very attempt to extrapolate anything meaningful about such a distant future theory from the details of current theory.

Supporters of this form of futurism propose that we can nevertheless draw some significant conclusions. To see how one might defend this claim, consider a prominent account offered by Janice Dowell (2006). She contends that a complete and ideal physical theory is going to, at the very least, exhibit the hallmarks of a unified scientific theory. According to her, these hallmarks should include the following (2006, pp. 38–39):

1. The inclusion of a set of explanatory hypotheses from which empirically testable implications can be derived.
2. Confirmation by the obtaining of a number and variety of test-implications of its explanatory hypotheses.
3. The provision of a unified explanation of a variety of empirical generalizations. The theory as a whole provides a unified explanation of the empirical generalizations that are among its testable implications.
4. Additional empirical support by its fit with that is antecedently known and independently observable.

Dowell proposes that we can derive a substantive account of the physical from the combination of these hallmarks with a commitment to fundamental physical entities. Together these two elements of a complete and ideal theory are supposed to provide a solution to the problem of indeterminacy. This account, though, has a significant weakness. In Dowell's words (2006, p. 27), "There's nothing in the very idea of a posit of our complete and ideal scientific theory that rules out that some mental properties are among those posits." Despite this, she argues that her futurist version of a posteriori physicalism has content (and thus avoids Hempel's Dilemma) because there are conditions under which it would be true and conditions under which it would be false. It would be false, for instance, if there were sui generis mental entities that were not part of a unified scientific theory. The problem is that it would still be true if the physics of the future posited fundamental mental entities within a theory that has the hallmarks of a scientific theory. Thus, while Dowell has shown that this form of futurist physicalism has some substance, she has not shown that it has enough substance to provide a full solution to the dilemma. The parameters that she outlines are too flexible to exclude meaningful forms of dualism and strong emergentism.

The perceived inability of this form of futurism to exclude fundamental mental entities is one of the primary reasons that some have adopted a second form of futurism that seeks to define physicalism through its opposition to sui generis mental properties. A couple of types are common. One adds a further constraint to our commitment to a future theory. Jessica Wilson (2006), for example, suggests that we should add a *No Fundamental Mentality Constraint* in order to preserve historical continuity with traditional forms of physicalism. By these lights, something can be a physical entity only if it is not a fundamental mental entity. Another seeks to equate the physical with the non-mental (Montero, 1999, 2009; Montero & Papineau, 2005; Spurrett & Papineau, 1999). A core justification for this alternative is the recognition that the central dispute between physicalists and dualists concerns whether or not the mental is ultimately non-mental.

This second form of futurism also faces significant challenges. First, it is difficult to shake the impression that it represents an ad hoc solution to a long-standing philosophical problem. Second, it is not clear that this approach represents a sufficient solution (Stoljar, 2010, 2015). Because there are other metaphysical theses such as vitalism and emergentism that are also incompatible with physicalism, non-mentalism could be true while physicalism is false (Judisch, 2007). Do we then need to posit a no fundamental élan vital constraint, no fundamental chemistry constraint, no fundamental morality constraint, no free will constraint, etc., or to equate physical with the conjunction of non-mental, non-vital, non-emergent, non-moral, etc.? Wilson (2006) anticipates this worry and offers a two-part response.[1] First, she contends that we can bracket off vitalism and emergentism because we have largely successful physical accounts of the relevant phenomena. Second, she argues that the remaining phenomena can be lumped together because they are likely to be constituted to some degree by mentality. This apparently systematic connection between these hypothetical counterexamples suggests that the no fundamental mentality constraint may be up to the task of excluding them. In other words, there is no need for additional constraints. We are not convinced. Wilson's primary argument seems to be that it is intuitively plausible that mentality underlies all of the interesting cases. But is this true? Does one's commitment to fundamental moralism require a commitment to fundamental mentalism? It seems prima facie possible to be a physicalist about the mental but an anti-physicalist about the moral. Beyond this, we question the reliance on a kind of philosophical traditionalism implicit in Wilson's response. After all, our understanding of the physical is not the only thing that is likely to change in the future; our understanding of mind, morality, and free will may also undergo significant changes. Given this, it seems reasonable to worry that the center will not hold and we will need separate constraints once again.

Thus far, we have treated indeterminacy as the primary difficulty associated with the appeal to a complete and ideal physical theory. Other difficulties may be waiting in the wings, though. Noam Chomsky (1994, 1995), for instance, argues that the appeal to such an all-powerful theory just makes the truth of physicalism trivially true. Another potential stumbling block is the undefended assumption that there is a single complete and ideal physical theory. As far as we know, no good argument excludes the possibility of more than one. Moreover, given that there are positive reasons to think that physical theory may be in principle underdetermined by the available evidence (Duhem, 1914/1954; Earman, 1993; van Fraassen, 1980), one might even argue that multiple complete and ideal theories are likely. If this is correct, then we are faced with the disturbing possibility that some complete and ideal physical theories may posit fundamental mental entities and some may not. Clearly, this would make the job of excluding mental entities that much more difficult. Finally, there is the very question of the possibility of a complete and ideal theory. Why think that such a thing exists? One might appeal to an inductive inference based on the historical success of physics, but surely this sort of inference is too weak to ensure the existence of such a theory.

In sum, Hempel's Dilemma exposes just how difficult it is to define physicalism in a way that defers to physics. This difficulty appears to arise from a fundamental feature of scientific investigation: its dynamic flexibility and continuous evolution (Poland, 2003).

2. The Perils and Promise of Reconstruction

Concerns such as these have led some to offer reconstructive approaches to physicalism that preserve a commitment to the ongoing nature of the physical sciences. This strikes us as the correct response to Hempel's Dilemma, and we are going to offer our own reconstructive approach here. First, though, we consider and critically appraise several extant proposals. Following that we will lay out a new reconstructive approach that builds on these but has advantages over each.

Melnyk (1997, 2003) adopts the rare strategy of embracing the first horn of Hempel's Dilemma. Roughly put, he suggests that we treat physicalism the way we would any established scientific theory: as something that we endorse, not because it is completely accurate, but because it is more probable than its rivals (dualism, neutral monism, idealism, etc.). For this reason, we should be realists about physicalism the way we are about other established theories. A clear virtue of this sort of currentist account is that it is neither devoid of content nor indeterminate. It is reconstructive because it does not require a belief in the truth of physicalism.

There has been a great deal of pushback against this move. One prominent complaint is that, because current physics in inconsistent, it is not possible to see it as more probable than the other theories (Wilson, 2006). Even if we choose to endorse a consistent subset of current physics, though, the likelihood that it will ultimately prove to be false would suggest that our endorsement is ultimately provisional. Worse, there seems to be good reason to suppose that the current theory will be replaced by a future theory that posits new entities and is more probable than the current one (Crook & Gillett, 2001). Ultimately, Melnyk's approach seems to struggle with the open-ended nature of scientific investigation.

A different reconstructive approach takes the open-ended nature of science as its starting point. This approach treats physicalism as the possession of a certain attitude rather than the object of a belief (Hempel, 1966; Ney, 2008b; van Fraassen, 2002). The motivation for this approach is made clear in a well-known passage from van Fraassen (2002, p. 58; note that he uses the older term "materialism"):

> How shall we identify what is really involved in materialism? Our great clue is the apparent ability of materialists to revise the content of their main thesis as science changes. If we took literally the claim of a materialist that his position is a simple belief, we would be faced with an insoluble mystery, for that belief would then consist in the claim that all is matter, as currently construed. If that were all there was to it, how would such a materialist know how to retrench when his favorite scientific hypotheses fail?

For van Fraassen, the answer to this puzzle is to see physicalism as a stance rather than a thesis. As he sees it, the physicalist vows to change her ontological commitments as physical theory progresses. Alyssa Ney (2008b, p. 9) suggests that physicalism amounts to a commitment to the following oath, "I hereby swear to go in my ontology everywhere and only where physics leads me." While this approach avoids Hempel's Dilemma (by denying that physicalism is something that can be true or false) and captures something important about the commitments of researchers who view themselves as physicalists, there are reasons to think that it is too flexible. After all, it clearly allows for future physical theories that contain fundamental mental entities.

Jeffrey Poland (1994, 2003) offers a third reconstructive approach (see also Hellman, 1985), which he refers to as "methodological physicalism." This approach is an attempt to flesh out "the spirit of physicalism" that van Fraassen identifies (Poland, 2003). On this construal, physicalism involves a commitment to an idealized, hierarchically structured theory inspired by contemporary physics and the presumed unification of the sciences. Where it diverges from standard futurist forms of physicalism is that the proposed physical principles are seen as regulative ideals rather than truth-evaluable claims. These principles prove their worth methodologically by helping us to frame hypotheses and evaluate competing theories. Although this approach provides a compelling picture of how physicalism might guide future research, it has two significant problems. First, it is not clear that the switch from metaphysical theses to regulative ideals actually solves the problem of indeterminacy associated with futurist versions of physicalism. Second, the methodological heft of these regulative ideals has been questioned. Carl Gillett (2001), for instance, disputes the claim that methodological physicalism has enjoyed a successful track record in the sciences and suggests that putative instances of its application can be blocked by "The Third Wheel Argument," which holds that the real methodological work is being done by an effort to expunge local intertheoretic incoherence (pp. 240–241). One advantage of trying to avoid local incompatibility with well-supported theories in other scientific domains is that, unlike methodological physicalism, it can explain instances of top-down and horizontal intertheoretic influences. This circumscribed approach would thus be both more modest with respect to its methodological principles and more general in its application.

3. A New Approach

We suggest that there is something right about each of these reconstructive efforts, but they tend to be either too rigid (and thus incompatible with the dynamic nature of science) or too vague. What is needed is a reconstructive account that can avail itself of the richness of contemporary physical theory while embracing the likelihood of significant theory change. We think that such an account is available and has been hiding in plain sight. When we look to the psychological and brain sciences we find an active commitment to a kind of physicalism that is both detailed and forward thinking. Physicalism, we propose, is an ongoing interdisciplinary research program. Philosophers and researchers of various stripes are actively exploring the question of how to explain the mental in terms of the physical. The goal is a unified, hierarchically structured scientific theory built on a foundation of physics. In other words, it seeks to explain natural phenomena by means of an integrated theory that posits fundamental physical entities.

The recent trend towards evermore multi-, inter-, and trans-disciplinary research in the psychological and brain sciences reflects a shared commitment to a kind of integrative pluralism. Many researchers justify this by means of a broad appeal to physicalism. For them, physicalism represents an effort to offer explanations of the mental that are tied to physical causes and often cashed out in terms of computational properties, neural mechanisms, bodily actions, environmental factors, etc. Unfortunately, this interdisciplinary form of physicalism has largely been ignored in the mainstream philosophical discussion of physicalism (as can be seen by its absence from recent encyclopedic reviews of the literature such as Ney, 2008a and Stoljar, 2010, 2015). Philosophers have instead viewed physicalism in general and consciousness in specific through the lens of the traditional mind-body problem inherited from analytic metaphysics.

We argue that we should redefine physicalism as an interdisciplinary research program that encompasses the physical sciences, the various sciences of the mind, and philosophy. The notion of a research program turns on distinguishing central commitments from peripheral ones (Kuhn, 1962; Lakatos, 1977; Longino, 1990; Quine, 1951). The core of a research program is made up of a matrix of elements that may include theoretical claims, positive exemplars, guiding metaphors, methodological principles, and some basic ontological commitments. The goal is to offer physically grounded explanations of higher-level phenomena such as cognition, emotion, and consciousness.

This project has two key components. The first is a view of the physical that is inspired by current physical theory. At a minimum, this presumes a universal physical theory (broadly similar in application and scope to current theory). The second is a conception of what would count as a physical explanation of the mental. Here past successes in providing physical explanations of biological and chemical phenomena may serve as positive exemplars. Research program physicalism seeks to offer a positive, empirically informed account of how the physical gives rise to or explains the mental. In other words, it seeks to defeat dualism, neutral monism, etc., in the same way that physicalism has historically defeated vitalism in biology and emergentism in chemistry: by offering the promise of an effective account of the relevant phenomena that does not advert to fundamental entities indigenous to the special science.

We need to say something about the scope of physicalism. Admittedly, we are using the term, *research program*, with a broader sense than is typical. Usually people have more circumscribed phenomena in mind. For instance, there has been a great deal of discussion recently concerning whether recent research inspired by Bayesian explanations for cognitive phenomena should be treated as part of an independent and viable research program or not. The relevant questions at play concern the theoretical cohesion of these accounts, the testability of their claims, and the degree to which they represent a break from standard cognitive science. Despite the traditional assumption that research programs are localized, we think that there is no reason in principle that the term cannot be applied at a larger level of grain. For one, there is no agreed upon magnitude for research programs. Indeed, recognized research programs come in many sizes. In addition, we think that physicalism contains the sort of core commitments that characterize a research program.

A real world example might help make our position clear. Recently, Siddhartha Mukherjee (2010) published a compelling panoramic history of cancer research. In it, he provides a riveting account of the various clinical and experimental successes and failures that characterize this history. Not surprisingly, he focuses most of his attention on developments in the twentieth and twenty-first centuries. His narrative is replete with dramatic successes, significant missteps, and regrettable examples of overreach. Mukherjee examines a number of specific research programs, including dramatic efforts to develop radical surgical interventions and chemotherapeutic treatments as well as independent explorations of the biological contributions of environmental influences, viruses, and genes. Although Mukherjee emphasizes the disjointed and often balkanized character of the last century of research, it is also the case that all participants recognize the eventual need for a multi-level integrated explanation of the behavior of cancer cells in petri dishes, animal models, and living human beings. Indeed, the book ends on a somewhat hopeful note because despite the great challenges posed by this complex, heterogeneous, and constantly evolving disease, we are beginning to get a richer understanding of its microbiological underpinnings and a better appreciation of how to leverage this understanding into effective treatments.

We suggest that, while it certainly makes sense to distinguish several independent research programs in this history, it also makes sense to view it as characterized by a larger, overarching research program with core commitments concerning what should and should not count as a successful explanation of the disease, its course, and how to treat it. In other words, we suggest that a kind of physicalism underlies and unites the last century of cancer research. One might object that, unlike consciousness, no one would argue that cancer is not a physical phenomenon. We agree. Certainly, no one today would argue this. But if we step back and include previous centuries, we find clear disagreement. Indeed, for much of its history, western medicine viewed disease and health in terms of a balance of humors. This was certainly true of cancer. The Roman physician, Galen, viewed cancer as trapped black bile (Mukherjee, 2010). Given the sui generis nature of the humors and their association with an implicit vitalism, there is little question that humoral medicine is incompatible with the physicalist approach that characterizes modern medicine. Our proposal is that it makes sense to claim that current research is part of a physicalist research program.

3.1. Advantages of the Research Program Approach

Treating physicalism as a research program builds on the strengths of the previous reconstructive accounts but avoids many of their weaknesses. Consider first Melnyk's version of currentism. He suggests that we treat physicalism realistically as we would an established theory or hypothesis. This has the advantage of making physicalism determinate (and thus avoiding the apparent emptiness or triviality of futurism), but it has the unfortunate consequence of making physicalism incoherent or false. Research programs, though, are by their very nature more flexible than established theories. Although they build on our current understanding of relevant phenomena, they are inherently oriented towards the future. Discovery is not only expected, it is the central goal (Lakatos, 1977). The whole point of a research program is theory development and innovation.

Consider next the attitude approach of Hempel, van Fraassen, and Ney. A selling point of this approach is that it captures the sense in which physicalists are committed to following where physics leads. Treating physicalism as an attitude removes the need to ascertain its truth-value, but it does so at the cost of a lack of substance. A familiar difficulty for this account is that it allows for the possibility that a future physics might include irreducible mental entities. Ney (2008b) suggests that we would still be able to criticize the physicalist attitude under this scenario—not because it gave the wrong answer, but because it involved a more circuitous route than the dualist attitude would have. In other words, given this scenario, we could legitimately view physicalism as pragmatically flawed in hindsight. The assumption that the route associated with the dualist attitude would necessarily be more direct because the thesis of dualism is closer to the truth strikes us as highly questionable. Perhaps a dualist attitude would have prevented us from finding the evidence demonstrating the implausibility of a unified physical account. This is not as outlandish as it might sound. Bill Wimsatt (2007) has persuasively argued that there are circumstances under which false theories can lead to better ones. Presumably Ney believes that, given our current evidence and available theories, physicalism is a more reasonable attitude than dualism would be. This normative assessment is not unequivocally negated by the eventual success of a physical theory that includes fundamental mental entities. The dualist, after all, might have just been lucky. While Ney may be correct that the physicalist attitude must have been deficient in some pragmatic way in the imagined scenario, the precise nature of this deficiency is not immediately apparent.

Research program physicalism, however, is straightforwardly incompatible with the presence of fundamental mental entities in our future theory because the presence of such entities would indicate that the research program has failed: It has not met its explanatory goal, namely, to make transparent how the non-physical arises out of the physical.

Finally, consider the methodological physicalism of Poland and Hellman. This approach treats a unified, hierarchically structured science built on the foundation of physical theory as the source of regulative ideals against which we can evaluate theories and research. This account suffers from two main drawbacks: (i) it does not appear to be determinate enough to exclude prominent forms of anti-physicalism, and (ii) there are questions concerning methodological justification of the proposed regulative ideals. As pointed out above, research program physicalism excludes the relevant forms of anti-physicalism. This takes care of the first drawback. With respect to the second drawback, methodological principles that are very similar to the regulative ideals posited by Polland and Hellman are built into the very fabric of the research program. A number of philosophers have pointed out that research programs have built-in methodological commitments (Kuhn, 1962; Lakatos, 1977; Longino, 1990). Our claim is simply that the regulative ideals central to methodological physicalism match up well with the central methodological commitments of research program physicalism. Currently, the best model of how to explain the mental in terms of the physical involves a unified, hierarchically structured science built on the foundation of physical theory. As a general rule, then, research and theories that fit with this model will be preferred to those that do not.

A consequence of this is that research program physicalism embodies elements of the prominent forms of futurism offered by Dowell and Wilson. It provides a general picture of future physics derived from current theory and actively excludes fundamental mental entities.

In sum, we have shown that the research program approach to physicalism preserves what is right about the existing reconstructive approaches while avoiding many of their primary drawbacks. This approach avoids the problems associated with futurism without incurring the brittleness of currentism. It also complements and enriches attitude approaches to physicalism. Physicalism on this construal is neither a metaphysical gambit nor an expression of fealty to physics but a positive and dynamic approach to explaining the natural world.

4. Understanding the Research Program

Research program physicalism is not a thesis that can be true or false. Rather, it is a collective enterprise that will prove to be either successful or unsuccessful. The conditions under which a research program is said to fail give rise to interesting philosophical issues. For example, the research program might fail for reasons that have nothing to do with explanation. In particular, there is the possibility of "failure" due to lack of imagination or ingenuity. While such a failure might not be due to specific features of the research program, it could be. We can conceive of overly complicated research programs that fail because they expose our cognitive limitations. Predicting just how cognitively baroque a research program needs to be in order to be out of reach is a somewhat tricky business, though. Nevertheless, we should acknowledge that mysterianism with respect to consciousness (McGinn, 1989) cannot be ruled out a priori. For now, it is enough to focus on the success conditions of physicalism and to offer a working conception of those conditions.

As a research program, physicalism is a multidisciplinary program that aims to offer a comprehensive explanation of the nature of the world. In order to elucidate the nature of research program physicalism two questions need to be answered:

(1) What are the relevant explananda? That is, what does physicalism aim to explain?
(2) What sort of explanation or explanations does physicalism aim to provide?

In this section, we focus on the first question. In the next chapter, we take up and answer the second question.

4.1. *The Reach of Explanation*

Understood as a metaphysical or ontological thesis, physicalism promises to offer a comprehensive account of the nature of our world: it tells us how everything is in our world. Understood as a research program, physicalism has similar comprehensive aspirations. Its objective is to explain (in a manner that is going to be articulated in Chapter 4) anything that is *capable* of having an explanation.

Research program physicalism thus distinguishes between those facts that are apt for explanation and those that are not. Something is not apt for explanation if it is not appropriate to ask physicalism to offer an explanation for it. Facts that are not apt for explanation fit in one of the following two categories: there are facts that must be taken for granted by physicalism and then there are facts that fall outside of physicalism's scope.

On the one hand, fundamental laws and principles, and certain states of affairs (e.g., the initial or near initial conditions of our universe) are not apt for explanation insofar as such facts are needed by physicalism in order to be in a position to offer explanations of all other facts. That is not to say, of course, that physicalism is not warranted to accept them as true. Physicalism as a research program can offer inductive support for such facts. What it cannot do however is to explain *why* they obtain.

On the other hand, facts about causally isolated entities, assuming that we have reasons to believe that such facts obtain, fall outside the purview of research program physicalism. The same could be said for the truths of logic and mathematics. The exclusion of logic and mathematics from the scope of physicalism is stipulative. Perhaps, there is an explanation of those realms that is forthcoming and physicalistically acceptable. However, our articulation of physicalism does not demand it. Research program physicalism can be successful even if those realms have not yet been explained in a physicalistically acceptable manner.

If such facts are not apt for explanation, then what is? The short answer is: everything else. Facts about microphysical and macrophysical goings-on call for an explanation. And so does the totality of chemical, biological, psychological, economical, geological, meteorological, etc., facts. Laws, generalizations, and principles connecting the various fields to the physical also have to be explained. In essence, everything but a rather small class of facts should be explained and the aim of physicalism is to do just that.

The requirement for explaining everything that is apt for explanation is an integral part of physicalism as it is usually understood. Traditionally, having this requirement in place is thought to preclude the possibility that in our world there are "loose ends": that is, phenomena that should have an explanation but have none. But the aim to explain all facts that are apt for explanation must be understood as an *ideal*: It is the aim toward which the research program strives without assuming that it will ever be reached. Indeed, as we discussed above, the very notion of an ideal and complete theory creates its own set of problems and its existence should not be demanded for the success of the research program.

Research program physicalism thus accepts a qualified version of the loose ends requirement—one that it allows the possibility that some explanations carry on forever or are altogether missing. For example, it is not yet known why there is an imbalance in baryonic matter over antibaryonic matter in the observed universe. Although there are competing hypotheses that purport to explain the observed imbalance (e.g., Farrar & Shaposhnikov, 1993; Sakharov, 1991), it is not clear whether one of them will eventually be confirmed or not. In fact, it is conceivable that we might never be able to explain baryonic asymmetry (Canetti, Drewes, & Shaposhnikov, 2012) or some other currently unexplained physical phenomenon. Such a failure should not necessarily count against physicalism. Research program physicalism may have comprehensive aspirations, but not all absences of explanation carry the same weight. If baryonic asymmetry is an unexplained phenomenon, then research program physicalism can decide to count it either as a phenomenon that is not apt for explanation after all (since it has to be taken for granted) or one that its explanation is not essential to the success of the research program.

This last point, namely, the realization that not all explanations carry the same weight allows us to articulate more clearly the core commitments of the research program. What is essential for the success of the research program is to be capable of explaining all phenomena that are central to the scientific understanding of our place in the world: among others, such phenomena include the numerous and diverse processes and mechanisms that constitute our bodies and minds and that make our worldly and social interactions possible.[2] If a proper subset of such phenomena cannot be explained, then physicalism is in trouble. The existence of such loose ends would give us reason to be skeptical of the viability of research program physicalism, in a way that some unexplained quantum mechanical or astrophysical phenomena would not. In the context of physicalism—at least as physicalism has figured in contemporary philosophical debates—the litmus test for the research program is whether it will succeed in explaining consciousness. If it could be shown that the research program has provided an explanation of consciousness, then the research program would appear to be successful: No aspect of human existence remains mysterious and is beyond our explanatory reach.

Although the no loose ends requirement is an important part of the research program, it is not sufficient to render the research program physicalistic in nature. Naturalism is consistent with the no loose ends requirement—it can offer a worldview according to which no phenomenon that is apt for explanation lacks an explanation. Similarly, a variety of dualism that takes consciousness to be a fundamental feature of the world alongside mass or spin and postulates psychophysical laws that are fundamental (and thus not apt for explanation; Chalmers, 1996) would also respect the no loose ends requirement. Thus, in order to render the research program a form of physicalism, one needs to assign primacy to the physical. But that is not hard to do. Physicalism as a research program demands not only that everything that is apt for explanation and central to our understanding of our place in the world is explained. Importantly, it also demands that facts about such phenomena are ultimately explained by the physical. As a research program, physicalism aims to explain the world. But it does so with a particular aim in mind: It aims to explain how everything is a part of, or fits within, a physical world.

4.2. *Vitalism as an Exemplar*

To put it in a manner that passes over many of the complexities that will be addressed later on, research program physicalism ultimately holds that the philosophical controversy concerning the metaphysical status of consciousness will go the way of an earlier controversy over the nature of living things (although see Chapter 7 for a discussion of the ways in which consciousness may remain special). Just as the concept of life in the biological sciences was eventually explained without the need of postulating a property that was antithetical to physicalism (e.g., élan vital, entelechies, or what have you), consciousness will be explained in a similar fashion.

We are not the first to note the apparent similarity between the current debate concerning the metaphysical status of consciousness and earlier debates concerning that of life. Indeed, drawing on this analogy often plays an important role in defenses of physicalism (e.g. Churchland, 1986, 2002; Dennett, 1996, 2005, 2013). The historical failure of vitalism and related ideas is often cited as a reason to think that a similar fate awaits anti-physicalist views of consciousness.

Let us begin with the analogy itself. Both life and consciousness present what are often referred to as placement problems (Jackson, 1998): That is, the central metaphysical question seems to be how to place life or consciousness into what appears to be a fundamentally physical world. These placement problems arise from an apparent disconnect between concepts associated with everyday features of human experience and those of the physical sciences. Certainly, the intuition that life represents a unique and special phenomenon is common. After all, the notion that living things are imbued with special characteristics that distinguish them from non-living things is shared by many cultures; a fundamental distinction between animate and inanimate objects is grammaticalized in many languages; and evidence suggests that our visual system is particularly sensitive to what has come to be called "biological motion" (Borst & Egelhaaf, 1989; Johansson, 1973; Neri, Morrone, & Burr, 1998).

An important component of the dispute between physicalists and anti-physicalists concerns the epistemic status of our ordinary concepts pertaining to our experiences. At the heart of many forms of anti-physicalism is the idea that any position that fails to explain persistent and purportedly ubiquitous intuitions[3] derived from our phenomenal experiences should be viewed with skepticism. Physicalists, on the contrary, tend to emphasize the transformative and, frankly, counterintuitive nature of scientific theories. Consider the case of *heat*. The historical shift from a caloric theory of heat, in which heat was thought of as a fluid that flowed between physical bodies, to one tied to the kinetic properties of molecules demonstrates the way in which physical explanation can amend and shape our everyday concepts (Chang, 2004; Fox, 1971; Psillos, 1999).

Physicalists tend to see the somewhat fraught relationship between our scientific and folk concepts as a common, if not virtuous, feature of an empirical approach to understanding our world (Churchland, 1986, 2002). Indeed, such a relationship seems to be an inherent feature of a basic, no-frills inductive argument for physicalism: Given that a wide and ever-growing variety of natural phenomena can be explained in physical terms, it seems reasonable to inductively infer that all natural phenomena can be similarly explained. Anti-physicalists, unsurprisingly, maintain that there is something special about our phenomenal concepts and their contents. In other words, they think that consciousness is special.

This is where the analogy to vitalism comes into play. As we pointed out above, the idea that life is special has a long history. We can certainly trace it back to the Epicureans and Aristotle (Mayr, 1982). However, the time period most relevant to the debate between physicalists and anti-physicalists begins in the seventeenth century. During this time period, a commitment to what has come to be known as mechanical philosophy (Garber, 2002) was shared by many key figures in the development of the physical sciences, including Borelli, Boyle, Galileo, Harvey, Hobbes, Huygens, and Newton (Crowe, 2007; Dijksterhuis, 1986). At the heart of this approach is the idea that all physical phenomena could be explained in terms of the size, shape, and motion of smaller entities or, more accurately, corpuscles.[4] Descartes is often considered the father of modern neuroscience because he was the first to systematically apply these ideas to neurophysiology and psychology. A succinct statement of his approach to explaining the nervous system's role in carrying out the biological functions associated with bodily movement, perception, and basic cognitive activities can be found in the famous last sentences of *The Treatise of Man* (Descartes, 1662/1998, p. 169):

> I desire, I say, that you should consider that these functions follow in this machine simply from the disposition of the organs as wholly naturally as the movements from a clock or other automaton follow from the disposition of its counterweights and wheels. To explain these functions, then, it is not necessary to conceive of vegetative or sensitive soul, or any other principle of movement or life, other than its blood and spirits which are agitated by the heat of the fire that burns continuously

in its heart, and which is of the same nature as those fires that occur in inanimate bodies.

Two things are clear in this passage: The first is a full-throated statement that these biological functions should be *explained* in mechanical terms and the second is the claim that this renders vitalist explanations unnecessary.

Descartes's famous remarks were the first shot in a hard fought war that lasted several centuries. While it would take too much time to cover this entire history, some examples seem instructive. Mechanical physiology received a big boost from a series of iconic experiments on frog legs by Jan Swammerdam in the seventeenth century (Finger, 1994; Wickens, 2015). In one of these, Swammerdam demonstrated that it was possible to elicit a muscle twitch in a detached frog leg by stimulating the exposed motor nerves with a scalpel. In another, he placed a frog leg muscle and the attached nerve in a sealed tube filled with water and found that the water volume did not change when he stimulated the nerve (Wickens, 2015). This result seemed incompatible with an account of nerve action that depended on a flow of animal spirits. Although this experiment has come to be seen as something of an *experimentum crucis*, it is important to recognize that vitalism did not go quietly into the night. Responding to such experiments and the theories that emerged from them, Robert Whytt (1751; cited by Wickens, 2015, p. 107) claimed that the idea that mechanical physiological processes could produce the biological functions associated with life was "a notion . . . too low and absurd to be embraced by any but the most minute philosophers." Whytt appealed to his own experimental work on frogs. He found that destroying a frog's brain initially caused its body to go flaccid but soon after the body would return a sitting position. While we would now explain this in terms of a spinal reflex, Whytt claimed that it was the result of a vital force that he called the "sentient principle" that resided in the spinal cord.

Clearly, the disagreement between vitalists and mechanists was seen by both sides as something that should be addressed through empirical investigation. Indeed, a great deal of research went into defeating the notion that vital forces were responsible for nervous system activity. The discovery of so-called animal electricity by Luigi Galvani and Alexander von Humboldt (Finger, 1994) in the late eighteenth century as well as the synthesis of urea from ammonium cyanate by Friedrich Wöhler in 1828 (Mukherjee, 2010) helped turn the tide in favor of mechanism because they seemed to break down the fundamental distinction between living and non-living processes (Wickens, 2015). Although some biologists held on to vitalism until well into the twentieth century (Mayr, 1982), vitalism ultimately fell out of favor for at least three reasons: (i) an inability to settle on a precise characterization of vital forces; (ii) our ability to offer physical explanations of phenomena that were thought to require a vitalistic explanation; and (iii) an emerging case for the causal closure of the physical (Papineau, 2001).

The historical failure of vitalism creates at least a prima facie challenge for anti-physicalists because it was a research program derived from a persistent placement problem that withered in the face of an opposing, inherently physicalist research program. Anti-physicalists often dismiss this as a weak argument from analogy (e.g., Chalmers, 2003). Analogies, though, have their place in science. Certainly, Charles Darwin drew heavily on an analogy between artificial and natural selection (Thagard, 1992). Some even argue that analogies are important components of scientific theorizing (Campbell, 1957; Hesse, 1966). Hence, a stronger argument for the anti-physicalist is not that arguments from analogy are weak but rather the claim that the two placement problems are in fact not analogous. Consciousness is special in a way that life is not.

Physicalists have the means to respond to this counterargument. For example, following Melnyk (2003), physicalists can respond with the suggestion that, while an enumerative induction based on the overall success of physicalism and the gradual demise of human-centered exceptions (in astronomy, biology, chemistry, etc.) may not be conclusive, it nevertheless raises the probability of physicalism.

Historical examples such as vitalism play a different, more central role in research program physicalism than they do in other forms of physicalism. Rather than serve as premises in defeasible arguments, they guide future research namely by providing rough guidelines for theorizing and empirically investigating heretofore unexplained phenomena. What the history of vitalism demonstrates is that vitalism (as a research program) faded away not because vital forces were shown to be inconceivable, logically contradictory, or somehow conceptually unsustainable. Vitalism's failure was primarily a practical and explanatory one: Simply put, vitalism had less to offer to researchers than mechanism did. Our contention is that the same will occur with consciousness.

Notes

1. Another response is available. Some philosophers deny that physics is univocal (Papineau, 2001; Spurrett & Papineau, 1999). If this is right, then we may be able to distinguish different types of physicalism that are associated with different constraints. Wilson (2006, p. 75) rightfully points out, "this strategy seems to invite, not avoid, the charge of unsystematicity."
2. Gene Witmer (2016) suggests that metaphysical naturalism can be understood in part as the idea that "Human Interest Phenomena" or HIP are not fundamentally different than other non-HIP phenomena. Physicalism is then a specific type of metaphysical naturalism. One way to make the no loose ends requirement more tractable would be to limit it to HIP. Adopting a "no HIP loose ends" requirement would at the least make the domain of quantification more circumscribed.
3. There is rarely any discussion of, let alone investigation of, the cross-cultural manifestation of these intuitions. Indeed, there is very little examination of the diachronic shifts in our understanding of subjective experience that have occurred within Anglophone analytic philosophy.
4. Corpuscles, like atoms, are used to explain macro-level phenomena. Unlike atoms, though, they are thought to be infinitely divisible. The fact that many contemporary

metaphysicians define physicalism in terms of a fundamental level means that they are unable to characterize this version of mechanism as physicalist. This seems to be an unfortunate consequence of imposing metaphysical intuitions on physics, and we see it as a problem for the definition on offer. This is not simply a historical worry, since a number of philosophers of physics have questioned whether current physics itself is compatible with this conception of physicalism (Healey, 2013; Ladyman, Ross, Spurrett, & Collier, 2007).

References

Bokulich, P. (2011). Hempel's dilemma and the domains of physics. *Analysis, 71*(4), 646–651.

Borst, A., & Egelhaaf, M. (1989). Principles of visual motion detection. *Trends in Neurosciences, 12*(8), 297–306.

Campbell, N. R. (1957). *Foundations of science: The philosophy of theory and experiment*. New York, NY: Dover.

Canetti, L., Drewes, M., & Shaposhnikov, M. (2012). Matter and antimatter in the universe. *New Journal of Physics, 14*(9).

Chalmers, D. J. (1996). *The conscious mind: In search of a fundamental theory*. New York: Oxford University Press.

Chalmers, D. J. (2003). Consciousness and its place in nature. In S. P. Stich & T. A. Warfield (eds.), *The Blackwell guide to philosophy of mind* (pp. 102–142). Malden, MA: Blackwell Publishing.

Chang, H. (2004). *Inventing temperature: Measurement and scientific progress*. New York, NY: Oxford University Press.

Chomsky, N. (1994). Naturalism and dualism in the study of language and mind. *International Journal of Philosophical Studies, 2*(2), 181–209.

Chomsky, N. (1995). Language and nature. *Mind, 104*(413), 1–61.

Churchland, P. S. (1986). *Neurophilosophy: Toward a unified science of the mind-brain*. Cambridge, MA: MIT Press.

Churchland, P. S. (2002). *Brainwise: Studies in neurophilosophy*. Cambridge, MA: MIT Press.

Crane, T., & Mellor, H. (1990). There is no question of physicalism. *Mind, 90*, 185–206.

Crook, S., & Gillett, C. (2001). Why physics alone cannot define the "physical": Metaphysics and the formulation of physicalism. *Canadian Journal of Philosophy, 31*(3), 333–360.

Crowe, M. J. (2007). *Mechanics from Aristotle to Einstein*. Santa Fe, NM: Green Lion Press.

Dennett, D. C. (1996). Facing backwards on the problem of consciousness. *Journal of Consciousness Studies, 3*(1), 4–6.

Dennett, D. C. (2005). *Sweet dreams: Philosophical obstacles to a science of consciousness*. Cambridge, MA: MIT Press.

Dennett, D. C. (2013). *Intuition pumps and other tools for thinking*. New York, NY: W. W. Norton & Company Ltd.

Descartes, R. (1662/1998). *The world and other writings* (S. Gaukroger, Trans.). Cambridge, UK: Cambridge University Press.

Dijksterhuis, E. J. (1986). *The mechanization of the world picture* (C. Dikshoorn, Trans.). Princeton, NJ: Princeton University Press.

Dowell, J. L. (2006). The physical: Empirical not metaphysical. *Philosophical Studies, 131*, 1–23.

Duhem, P. (1914/1954). *The aim and structure of physical theory* (P. W. Wiener, Trans.). Princeton, NJ: Princeton University Press.

Earman, J. (1993). Underdetermination, realism, and reason. *Midwest Studies in Philosophy, 18*, 19 38.

Farrar, G. R., & Shaposhnikov, M. E. (1993). Baryon asymmetry of the universe in the minimal Standard Model. *Physical Review Letters, 70*(19), 2833.

Finger, S. (1994). *Origins of neuroscience: A history of explorations into brain function*. Oxford, UK: Oxford University Press.

Fox, R. (1971). *The caloric theory of gases: From Lavoisier to Regnault*. Oxford, UK: Clarendon Press.

Garber, D. (2002). Descartes, mechanics, and the mechanical philosophy. *Midwest Studies in Philosophy, 26*, 185–204.

Gillett, C. (2001). The methodological role of physicalism. In C. Gillett & B. Loewer (eds.), *Physicalism and its discontents* (pp. 225–250). Cambridge, UK: Cambridge University Press.

Healey, R. (2013). Physical composition. *Studies in History and Philosophy of Science Part B: Studies in History and Philosophy of Modern Physics, 44*(1), 48–62.

Hellman, G. (1985). Determination and logical truth. *Journal of Philosophy, 82*(11), 607–616.

Hempel, C. (1966). *Philosophy of natural science*. New Jersey, NJ: Prentice Hall.

Hempel, C. (1980). Comments on Goodman's ways of worldmaking. *Synthese, 45*, 139–199.

Hesse, M. (1966). *Models and analogies in science*. Notre Dame, IN: Notre Dame University Press.

Jackson, F. (1998). *From metaphysics to ethics: A defence of conceptual analysis*. Oxford, UK: Oxford University Press.

Johansson, G. (1973). Visual perception of biological motion and a model for its analysis. *Perception & Psychophysics, 14*(2), 201–211.

Judisch, N. (2007). Why "non-mental" won't work: On Hempel's dilemma and the characterization of the "physical." *Philosophical Studies, 140*(3), 299–318.

Kuhn, S. (1962). *The structure of scientific revolutions*. Chicago, IL: University of Chicago Press.

Ladyman, J., Ross, D., Spurrett, D., & Collier, J. G. (2007). *Every thing must go: Metaphysics naturalized*. Oxford, UK: Oxford University Press.

Lakatos, I. (1970). Falsification and the methodology of scientific research programs. In I. Lakatos & A. Musgrave (eds.), *Criticism and the growth of knowledge* (pp. 91–196). Cambridge, UK: Cambridge University Press.

Lakatos, I. (1977). Introduction: Science and pseudoscience. In J. Worrell & G. Currie (eds.), *The methodology of scientific research programmes: Philosophical papers* (Vol. 1, pp. 1–7). Cambridge, UK: Cambridge University Press.

Laudan, L. (1977). *Progress and its problems: Towards a theory of scientific growth*. Berkeley, CA: University of California Press.

Loewer, B. (2001). From physics to physicalism. In C. Gillett & B. Loewer (eds.), *Physicalism and its discontents* (pp. 37–56). Cambridge, UK: Cambridge University Press.

Longino, H. (1990). *Science as social knowledge: Values and objectivity in scientific inquiry*. Princeton, NJ: Princeton University Press.

Mayr, E. (1982). *The growth of biological thought*. Cambridge, MA: Harvard University Press.
McGinn, C. (1989). Can we solve the mind-body problem? *Mind*, *98*(391), 349–366.
Melnyk, A. (1997). How to keep the "physical" in physicalism. *Journal of Philosophy*, *94*(12), 622–637.
Melnyk, A. (2003). *A physicalist manifesto: Thoroughly modern materialism*. Cambridge, UK: Cambridge University Press.
Montero, B. (1999). The body problem. *Nous*, *33*(2), 183–200.
Montero, B. (2009). What is the physical? In B. McLaughlin, A. Beckermann, & S. Walter (eds.), *Oxford handbook in the philosophy of mind* (pp. 173–188). Oxford, UK: Oxford University Press.
Montero, B., & Papineau, D. (2005). A defense of the via negativa argument for physicalism. *Analysis*, *65*(3), 233–237.
Mukherjee, S. (2010). *The emperor of all maladies: A biography of cancer*. New York, NY: Simon and Schuster.
Neri, P., Morrone, M. C., & Burr, D. C. (1998). Seeing biological motion. *Nature*, *395*(6705), 894–896.
Ney, A. (2008a). Defining physicalism. *Philosophy Compass*, *3*(5), 1033–1048.
Ney, A. (2008b). Physicalism as an attitude. *Philosophical Studies*, *138*, 1–15.
Papineau, D. (2001). The rise of physicalism. In C. Gillett & B. Loewer (eds.), *Physicalism and its discontents* (pp. 3–36). Cambridge, UK: Cambridge University Press.
Poland, J. (1994). *Physicalism: The philosophical foundations*. Oxford, UK: Oxford University Press.
Poland, J. (2003). Chomsky's challenge to physicalism. In L. M. Antony & N. Hornstein (eds.), *Chomsky and his critics* (pp. 29–48). Oxford, UK: Basil Blackwell.
Psillos, S. (1999). *Scientific realism: How science tracks the truth*. New York, NY: Routledge.
Quine, W. V. O. (1951). Two dogmas of empiricism. *The Philosophical Review*, *60*, 20–43.
Sakharov, A. D. (1991). Violation of CP invariance, C asymmetry, and baryon asymmetry of the universe. *Soviet Physics Uspekhi*, *34*(5), 392–393.
Spurrett, D., & Papineau, D. (1999). A note on the completeness of "physics." *Analysis*, *59*(261), 25–29.
Stoljar, D. (2010). *Physicalism*. New York, NY: Routledge.
Stoljar, D. (2015). Physicalism. In E. N. Zalta (ed.), *The Stanford encyclopedia of philosophy*. http://plato.stanford.edu/archives/spr2016/entries/physicalism
Thagard, P. (1992). *Conceptual revolutions*. Princeton, NJ: Princeton University Press.
van Fraassen, B. (1980). *The scientific image*. Oxford, UK: Oxford University Press.
van Fraassen, B. (2002). *The empirical stance*. New Haven, CT: Yale University Press.
Vicente, A. (2011). Current physics and "the physical." *British Journal for the Philosophy of Science*, *62*(2), 393–416.
Wickens, A. P. (2015). *A history of the brain: From stone age surgery to modern neuroscience*. New York, NY: Psychology Press.
Wilson, J. (2006). On characterizing the physical. *Philosophical Studies*, *131*(1), 61–99.
Wimsatt, W. C. (2007). *Re-engineering philosophy for limited beings: Piecewise approximations to reality*. Cambridge, MA: Harvard University Press.
Witmer, D. G. (2016). Physicality for physicalists. *Topoi*, 1–16. Advanced online publication. http://doi.org/10.1007/s11245-016-9415-y

4 A Physicalism With Bite

Last chapter, we argued that Hempel's Dilemma threatens to undermine any attempt to offer a substantial version of physicalism that treats it as a truth-evaluable thesis. We then took up revisionist approaches that have been developed in response to this challenge. In the end, we offered our own revisionist approach, research program physicalism, which we believe combines the best of the other revisionist approaches and avoids some of their pitfalls. Suppose that we are right, and research program physicalism is really the best available form of revisionism. An important question remains: Does this form of physicalism have enough bite to do the philosophical work that we traditionally associate with physicalism?

In this chapter, we argue that our moderate, empirically oriented variety of physicalism is up to the job. In particular, we contend that it provides an effective means of solving the core conundrum of physicalism: how to acknowledge the apparent plurality of entities in the world exposed by the special sciences while at the same time remain true to an austere ontology.

1. Explanation and Physicalism

An emphasis on explanation is not foreign to physicalism as it currently practiced and understood. Epistemic arguments against physicalism are premised on precisely a presumed lack of explanation of the relationship of consciousness to physical entitles and processes. Opponents of physicalism cite our inability to provide a satisfactory explanation of consciousness as support for the claim that physicalism is false (Chalmers, 1996, 2003/2010, 2006; Strawson, 2008). Explanation is intimately related to understanding. To explain a phenomenon is to render it intelligible. And, conversely, to be incapable of explaining it is to lack a firm understanding of its nature. Without a physical explanation of consciousness, physicalists cannot show how consciousness fits in a physicalist world.

The relationship between explanation and understanding is evident in traditional discussions of explanation in both philosophy of science and in physicalism. For example, Carl Hempel (1965, p. 337) describes the motivation behind the deductive-nomological model (DN) as follows:

> a DN explanation answers the question "Why did the explanandum-phenomenon occur?" by showing that the phenomenon resulted from certain particular circumstances, specified in C1, C2, . . . , Ck, in accordance with the laws L1, L2, . . . , Lr. By pointing this out, the argument shows that, given the particular circumstances and the laws in question, the occurrence of the phenomenon was to be expected; and it is in this sense that the explanation enables us to understand why the phenomenon occurred.

Similarly, David Chalmers insists that in order for physicalists to vindicate their position they need to offer an "explanation that makes transparent why some high-level truth obtains, given that certain low-level truths obtain" (2010, p. 313). For Chalmers (and Frank Jackson) the only type of explanation that is capable of rendering such a relationship transparent is that of reductive explanation (Chalmers & Jackson, 2001). Elsewhere, Chalmers provides a more detailed description of the nature of reductive explanation by describing it in terms of logical supervenience:

> A natural phenomenon is reductively explainable in terms of some lower-level properties if the property of instantiating that phenomenon is globally logically supervenient on the low-level properties in question. . . . If the property of exemplifying a phenomenon fails to supervene logically on some lower-level properties, then given any lower-level account of those properties, there will always be a further unanswered question: Why is this lower-level process accompanied by the phenomenon?
>
> (Chalmers, 1996, p. 48; cf. Chalmers & Jackson, 2001)

The point that both of these discussions of explanation underscore is that explanation is an appropriate focus for physicalists. The reason why we are after an explanation of a phenomenon is because only through explaining it can we render it intelligible and place it in our world. If the physicalist's goal is to render consistent PLURALITY with AUSTERITY, then explanation seems well suited to accomplish such a goal.

We mention Chalmers and Jackson's approach of reductive explanation as an example of how to connect explanation to physicalism, but we do not recommend it. Although both the research program and Chalmers and Jackson's version of physicalism are related insofar as they aim to explain all phenomena in terms of the physical, the two differ in crucial ways.

First, a priori entailment physicalism assumes both a static picture of mental phenomena and a complete physical theory. In other words, it assumes that we have a sufficient understanding of consciousness that is forever fixed and that we can safely postulate a complete (at least in principle) physical theory. Our approach, on the contrary, rejects both assumptions. It is a premise of our approach that physicalism is an ongoing research program. As such, both the character of physics and our understanding of consciousness are likely to change. In regard to the latter possibility, our sciences of the mind are incomplete and our philosophy of the mind is still in flux. While many claim that we have special epistemic access to our phenomenal experience, there remains significant disagreement about fundamental features of core concepts such as qualia (Crane, 2001). In this sense, the situation does not seem to be that different from other folk theories prior to arrival of successful empirically grounded theories.

Second, unlike a priori physicalism, research program physicalism is an explicitly *scientific* undertaking. What is sought is a scientific explanation of consciousness. While it is true that some philosophers continue to appeal to the type of explanations presupposed by a priori physicalism, the DN model in specific and hypothetico-deductive accounts of explanation in general have largely fallen out of favor in the philosophy of science. On a hypothetico-deductive approach, explanations involve predictions derived from general laws and initial conditions. Philosophers of science have become disenchanted with this approach for a number of reasons. As Hempel himself recognized, this approach struggles to account for explanations involving statistical laws (1965). Given the centrality of statistical laws to many contemporary explanations in various sciences, this is no small problem. Even if it is possible to address this lacuna, there is the larger problem that deductions seem neither necessary nor sufficient for explanation. They do not seem necessary because many explanations offered in biology and psychology appeal to generalizations that fall well short of the sort of strict lawfulness required for deduction (Bechtel, 2008; Woodward, 2014). They do not appear to be sufficient because there are a number of well-known counterexamples. First, there are so-called explanatory asymmetries that cannot be captured on deductive approaches. One can often take an explanation from a set of laws and specific initial conditions and create a parallel derivation from the previous explanandum and the set of laws to the initial conditions. These so-called backward derivations (Woodward, 2014) do not seem to be explanatory. Perhaps the most famous example involves the shadow of a flagpole (Bromberger, 1966). We can derive the height of the flagpole from laws concerning the propagation of light, trigonometry, and the length of the shadow but, under normal circumstances, the height of the flagpole explains the length of the shadow and not the reverse. Another class of counterexamples involves explanatory irrelevancies. A famous one comes from Wesley Salmon (1971): We are asked to consider the inference from the generalization that men who take birth control pills regularly do not get pregnant and the fact that a particular man takes birth control pills regularly to the prediction that he will not get pregnant. Clearly, this inference does not adequately explain his failure to get pregnant. Something has gone wrong.

One might respond to these objections by taking a strong stance on the necessity requirement. In other words, one might defend the necessity of the relevant deductions while abandoning the claim that they are sufficient. This move faces several challenges. First, it is not clear how this requirement fits with the fundamental purpose of the hypothetico-deductive approach, which is to provide a rational reconstruction of the activity of scientists. Second, given that there are both scientific theories that do not meet the necessity requirement and a number of accounts of scientific explanation that do not have it, we are still owed independent reasons for it. Finally, any defense of this requirement needs to show that it is not being imposed to satisfy one's prior metaphysical commitments but is instead the result of an attempt to make sense of the practice of science.

Philosophers of science have generally abandoned the hypothetico-deductive approach for these reasons. Indeed, this is not a new development. Unfortunately, the discussion surrounding the role of explanation in physicalism has yet to catch up with this fact. Of course, a defender of the orthodoxy could maintain that physicalism, as it is traditionally construed, requires deductive explanation, perhaps as a consequence of some variant of the nothing-over-and-above thesis. Still, even if this sort of traditionalism has any merit (and we have already offered reasons to question this move), it does not apply to research program physicalism because it is reconstructive and explicitly committed to viewing physicalism as a scientific enterprise.

A number of approaches to understanding scientific explanation do not require deductive structure. Indeed, the hypothetico-deductive skeptic seems to face an embarrassment of riches. Some philosophers suggest that explanation should be understood in statistical terms. For instance, Salmon (1971) proposes that explanations elaborate what factors are statistically relevant to the occurrence of the explanandum. Others argue that explanations involve fitting disparate phenomena within the purview of a unified theory (Friedman, 1974; Kitcher, 1981). One way of thinking about such accounts is that they treat explanation as the application of schema to a wide range of phenomena (Thagard, 1992). In keeping with this, several attempts have been made by cognitive scientists to offer explicit versions of this thesis that incorporate experimental work on concepts (Abelson & Lalljee, 1988; Churchland, P. M., 1989, 2012; Schank, 1986). Yet another approach treats explanation as an act of communication. To give an example, Bas van Fraassen (1980) views explanations as answers to why-questions. An important feature of such answers is that they often involve contrasting the role of certain factors with that of other possible factors. In a similar vein, Peter Achinstein (1983) views explanation as an illocutionary act intended to elicit understanding.

Perhaps the most prevalent approach holds that scientific explanations are inherently causal (e.g., Cartwright, 1989; Miller, 1987; Salmon, 1984; Woodward, 1989). The general idea is that what matters for scientific explanation are the causal relationships between different entities and not the deductive relationships between theories. Providing a description of a relevant mechanism is often seen as an important part of this enterprise because such a description involves identifying the relevant entities that produce, underlie, or maintain the phenomenon in question (Craver & Tabery, 2017; Glennan, 1992, 1996). While there are a number of definitions of mechanisms on offer (e.g., Bechtel & Abrahamsen, 2005; Glennan, 2002; Machamer, Darden, & Craver, 2000), the literature has generally moved towards ecumenicalism (Illari & Williamson, 2012).

Some theorists attempt to preserve the connection of explanation to reduction while removing the deductive component. For example, Theurer (2013) argues that the problem is not reductionism per se but, rather, the assumption that it requires accepting the deductive-nomological model. She contends that new mechanistic approaches provide a manner of understanding reduction in a way that fits with the older, less restrictive account of John Kemeny and Paul Oppenheim (1956).

While there is a general acknowledgement that causal mechanisms play an important role in many scientific explanations, one might wonder whether or not some types of non-mechanistic explanations are also important. Within neuroscience, for instance, it is not hard to find what on their face seem to be exemplars of non-mechanistic explanations involving general network properties, dynamical laws, or computational processes (although for the view that such explanations are in fact compatible with mechanism see Kaplan, 2015; Kaplan & Craver, 2011; Levy & Bechtel, 2013). This has led some to suggest that we should adopt some form of explanatory pluralism (Marom, 2010; Stepp, Chemero, & Turvey, 2011; Weiskopf, 2011; Woodward, 2013).

Clearly, the topic of scientific explanation is a fecund area of philosophical research. In retrospect, the demise of the hypothetico-deductive approach seems to be more of a beginning than an ending, and philosophers of science have developed a number of robust non-deductive accounts of explanation. Despite the apparent heterogeneity, it remains possible that these accounts could be unified by some underlying principle (e.g., Thagard, 1992). Even if the different approaches cannot be unified, we only need to establish the existentially quantified claim that it is possible to explain consciousness physically to block anti-physicalism. After all, the onus is on the anti-physicalist to show that *no* physical explanation is possible.

2. Compositional Explanation

The central idea of naturalism is that we should look to the sciences for answers to our metaphysical questions. However, naturalism leaves room for what we have referred to as PLURALITY without AUSTERITY. It is often accompanied by a realism with respect to the ontological posits of the special sciences, but it does not require any sort of particular connection between these and those of physics. In this section, we address an important question that we have left unanswered: How exactly is research program physicalism a type of *physicalism*?

In response to this question, we propose that research program physicalism imposes additional requirements on explanations that result in a kind of ontological austerity. Specifically, we develop the notion of compositional explanation and use it to distinguish between naturalistic explanations that are compatible with the research program as a form of physicalism and those that are not. Our contention is not that compositional explanation is the only scientifically acceptable form of explanation. Rather, our claim is that understood as a form of *physicalism*, the research program strives to offer compositional explanations of all phenomena that are apt for explanation and which are central to our understanding of our place in nature (consciousness, life, etc.).

2.1. *A Case Study*

Recall that according to our proposal, physicalism is understood to be an explanatory interdisciplinary project. Its aim is to explain the phenomena in a way that renders them physical and as such, it succeeds or fails on the basis of how adequately it explains the natural world.

But what type of explanation does physicalism strive to offer? Given that we understand physicalism to be an interdisciplinary research project, the explanation should be one that figures prominently in our sciences. Even a cursory glance at our sciences shows that successful explanations often take the shape of *compositional* explanations: a target phenomenon Φ (the "whole") is compositionally explained if it is explained in terms of the workings of its components ("parts").[1] Compositional explanations set out to capture the compositional relations that are assumed to exist in nature. By studying how entities (individuals, properties, or processes) are composed, one discovers compositional relations. Such relations are *vertical* insofar as they relate the individuals, properties, or processes of one level to the individuals, properties, or processes of another level. Furthermore, compositional relations are determinative and hold between relata that are synchronous. Accordingly, a demonstration of how the various components of the target phenomenon work together is sufficient to explain the existence of the phenomenon. In other words, in the case of a successful compositional explanation, the presence of the components and their interconnections suffice to realize ("to make real") the phenomenon in question. A compositional explanation of consciousness would be a clear demonstration of how consciousness arises out of its (physical) components. Hence, the research program, as conceived here, is successful if, and when, consciousness is compositionally explained.

It is best to introduce compositional explanations with the use of an example. For ease of explication, we shall discuss a well-known example from physical chemistry. The different properties of allotropes of carbon are explained in virtue of the bonding behavior between carbon atoms. A carbon atom contains six electrons and in the ground state the electron configuration is $1s^2 2s^2 2p_x^{\ 1} 2p_y^{\ 1}$. In such a state, carbon is divalent, for only the unpaired electrons in p_x and p_y are available for bonding. However, carbon normally bonds with four other atoms (i.e., it is tetravalent). Such tetravalent bonding cannot be accounted for by the simple sharing of the two unpaired p electrons. Instead, the bonding is the result of *orbital hybridization*. In carbon allotropes (and compounds), several different orbits mix their characteristics (*hybridize*) in order to yield the most energetically stable structure. In the case of carbon, there are three types of hybrid orbitals: sp^3, sp^2, and sp (Atkins & De Paula, 2015; Carter & Norton, 2013).

The small energy difference between 2s-and 2p-orbital makes it possible to promote one of the s electrons from the 2s-orbital to the previously empty $2p_z$-orbital. Such excitation results in a new electron configuration, $1s^2 2s^1 2p_x{}^1 2p_y{}^1 2p_z{}^1$ and hybridization occurs between the single 2s orbital and the three 2p orbitals ($2p_x$, $2p_y$ and $2p_z$). The result of such hybridization is four identically shaped hybrid orbitals called "sp^3" with different spatial orientations, each oriented around the carbon nucleus at 109.5° from all the other sp^3-orbitals and pointing towards the corners of an imaginary regular tetrahedron. In this hybrid state, the carbon atom has four $2sp^3$ orbitals instead of two 2s and two 2p. Its valence state is four instead of two, and as such, the hybridized atom is ready to form covalent bonds with other carbon atoms.[2]

In the case of diamond, each sp^3-hybridized carbon atom is bonded to four other carbon atoms located $1.544 \times 10{-}^{10}$ meters away from it. The four sp^3-orbitals of each hybridized carbon atom bond to the orbitals of four other carbon atoms forming a strong covalent sigma (σ) bond pointing in a tetrahedral direction (Figure 4.1). The overall result of such bonding is a strongly held together three-dimensional, covalent lattice structure (Figure 4.2).

As mentioned above, a carbon atom can assume different hybridized forms. Indeed, in addition to the sp^3 hybrid orbital, two other orbitals are possible. Whereas the structure of diamond is accounted by sp^3 hybridization, graphite structures are explained by a different type of hybridization, namely, sp^2 hybridization. Such a hybrid state arises also from the promotion of a 2s electron to a 2p orbital but, unlike sp^3 hybridization, only two of the three 2p orbitals hybridize with the single 2s orbital. This results in three sp^2 hybrids and in one unhybridized free 2p orbital. The three identical sp^2 hybrids are in the same plane and their orientation of maximum probability forms a 120° angle between each orbital. The unhybridized 2p orbital lies perpendicular to the plane of the sp^2 hybrid orbital and it is available to form a pi (π) bond with other atoms. In the case of graphite, each sp^2-hybridized carbon atom bonds to three other sp^2-hybridized carbon atoms forming sheets of flat interconnected hexagonal rings (Figure 4.3). The bond between the sp^2-hybridized atoms is a strong covalent bond: The lopsided configuration of the sp^2 orbital permits a substantial overlap between the other sp^2 orbitals. Similarly to the sp^3 orbital, the sp^2 orbital is directional and it forms a sigma (σ) bond. But in addition to the σ bond, a π bond is also present in graphite. The free delocalized electron, which is perpendicular to the plane, forms a bond by pairing with another delocalized electron of the

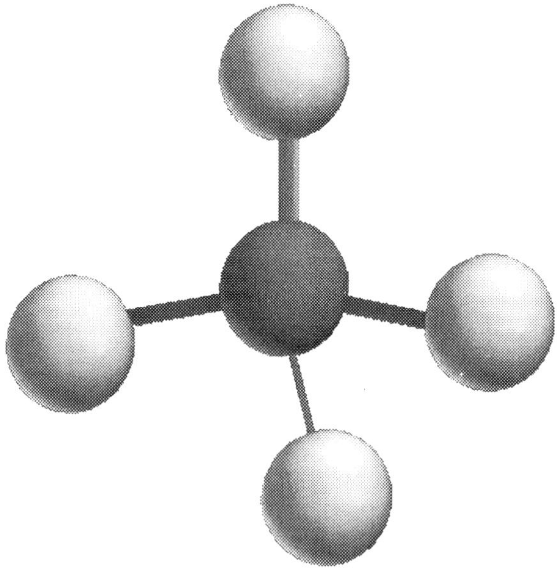

Figure 4.1 Bonding of sp3-Hybridized Carbon Atom to Four Other Carbon Atoms

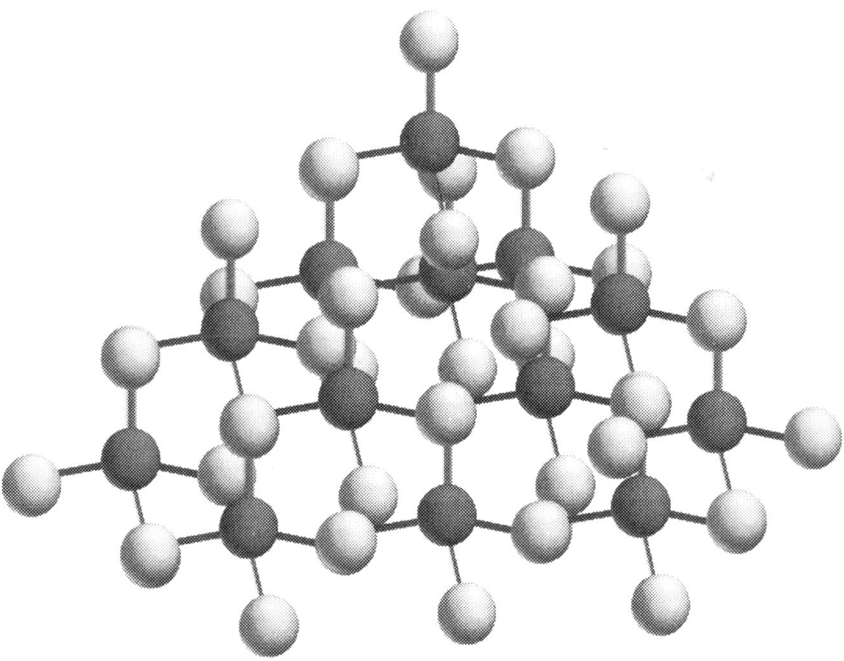

Figure 4.2 Atomic Structure of Diamond

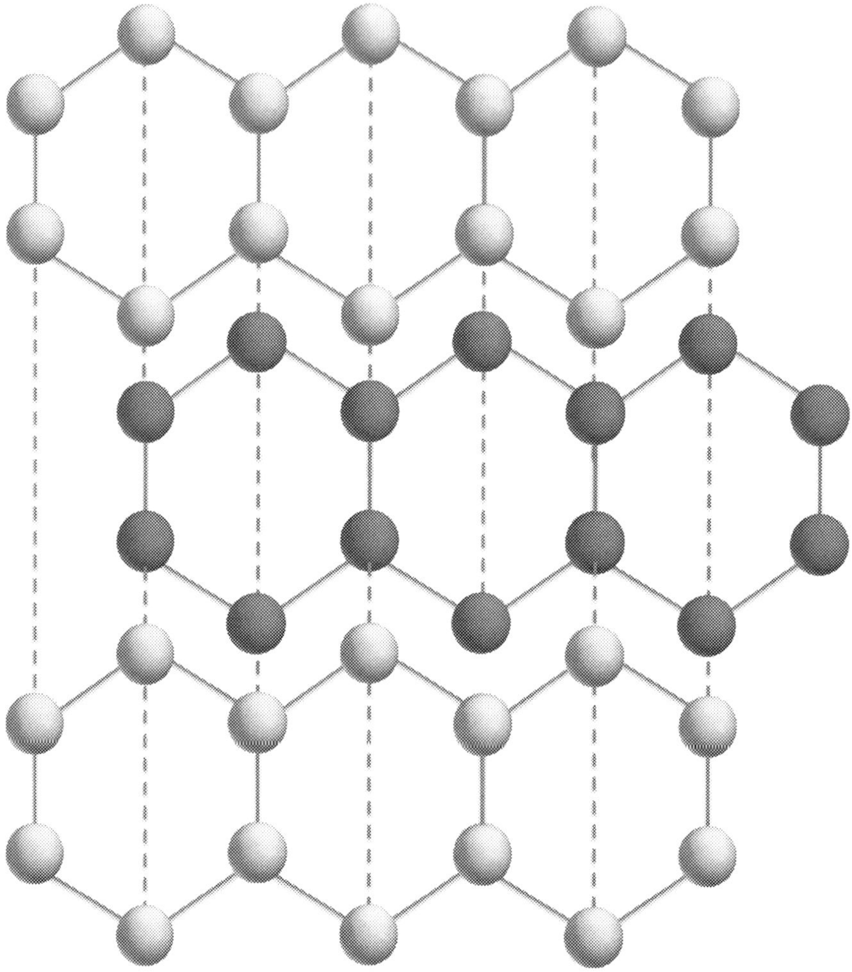

Figure 4.3 Atomic Structure of Graphite. Solid lines indicate covalent bonds between sp^2-hybridized carbon atoms. Dotted lines indicate van der Waals interactions between delocalized electrons from adjacent planes.

adjacent plane. As such, graphite is composed of a series of stacked parallel planes. The sheets that compose graphite are held to each other via van der Waals interaction, which is much weaker than the covalent bonds of the in-plane carbon atoms.

The respective atomic structures of diamond and graphite explain their physical/mechanical, electrical, thermal, and optical properties. On the one hand, the extreme hardness of diamond is explained by the presence of the network of strong covalent bonds that permeates the structure. Its great resistance to compression is explained by its tetrahedral structure. Its thermal conductivity (which is the highest of any solid in room temperature) is explained by lattice vibration and its ability to permit the flow of phonons (Berman, 1992; Evan, 1992; Pierson, 1993; Singer, 1990). Its high electrical resistivity is explained by the strength of the electron bonds that renders the excitation of electrons unlikely. And lastly, its brightness is explained by the fact that, given the high strength of the bonds, virtually all of visible light is either reflected or refracted. On the other hand, graphite is characterized by anisotropy: its properties may vary (and considerably so) depending on which direction of the solid we are considering. For example, graphite conducts electricity well within its sheets but not between them. Electrical conductivity within the plane is explained by the fact that the planar structure of graphite permits the movement of electrons. Electrical resistivity perpendicular to planes is explained by the fact that the spacing between the sheets is relatively large and by the absence of a mechanism for the movement of electrons from one plane to the other. The fact that graphite can be used as a lubricant or in pencils is explained by the fact that the bonds between the planes (or sheets of hexagonal rings) are held together by weaker forces and as such, they can be easily separated. Many other properties of graphite (and diamond) are explained in a similar fashion, i.e., by appeal to their atomic structure. The cases of diamond and graphite are clear and remarkable illustrations of the power of compositional explanations. A number of differing and diverse phenomena on the so-called "macro-level" (electrical conductivity, brightness, anisotropy, strength, etc.) are fully explained in terms of the workings of lower-level entities.

Compositional explanations abound in the sciences: phase transition, elasticity, friction, electrical conductivity, oxidation-reduction, biological decomposition, adaptive immunity, economic inflation, and countless other phenomena are all explained in terms of their components. Even if compositional explanation is not the be all and end all of scientific explanations, it is both ubiquitous in the sciences and exemplary of how one phenomenon is explained in virtue of another (its components) *without remainder*. Successful compositional explanations leave no questions answered. This is not because one can deduce (*a priori*) the target phenomenon using statements involving its components (and perhaps certain bridging principles); scientists are not in the business of semantic or *a priori* reductions of the sort that have dominated philosophical discussions. Rather, compositional explanations explain because by laying bare the compositional nature of a target phenomenon we have rendered it intelligible; we have explained how nature is ordered and how everything fits together. Such a scientific attitude is reflected in Steven Weinberg's remarks about explanation and deduction:

> We may even say that something is explained even when where we have no assurance that we will ever be able to deduce it. Right now we do not know how to use our standard model of elementary particles to calculate the detailed properties of atomic nuclei, and we are not

> certain that we will ever know how to do these calculations, even with unlimited computer power at our disposal. (This is because the forces in nuclei are too strong to allow the sort of calculation techniques that work for atoms or molecules.) Nevertheless, we have no doubt that the properties of atomic nuclei are what they are because of the known principles of the standard model. *This "because" does not have to do with our ability to actually deduce anything but reflects our view of the order of nature*
>
> (Weinberg, 1994, p. 28; emphasis added).

Physicalists often describe their project as one of finding a place for a non-physical phenomenon (social, biological, economic, mental, etc.) in the physical world (Jackson, 1998). Physicalism succeeds when all putatively existing non-physical phenomena are fitted in the physical world. Compositional explanations have the power of doing precisely that: By showing how non-physical phenomena are composed of physical entities, we have placed them in the natural order. We have done so not by eliminating them from the world—diamonds and graphite structures are still here. Rather, we have placed them in the natural world by showing that they hold in virtue of the workings of their physical components.

We would like to head off a potential misinterpretation of our appeal to composition, however. There is an unfortunate tendency among physicalists to presuppose that the notion of composition is a settled one, or at least one that is properly in the domain of metaphysics, and not within the purview of physics or other sciences. By these lights, the job of physics is simply to furnish the fundamental entities or to characterize the fundamental level (Kim, 1993; Oppenheim & Putnam, 1958). This is often viewed in the context of an appeal to a final and complete physical theory. At a minimum, this presupposition faces two significant challenges. First, as a number of philosophers have noted (Healey, 2013; Ladyman, Ross, Spurrett, & Collier, 2007; Schaffer, 2003), there are compelling reasons to think that physics will not provide the sort of fundamental entities that most metaphysical conceptions of compositions require. Second, and perhaps more importantly, the very notion of composition employed by physical theories has changed over time. Richard Healey (2013) drives this home through an example: the different ways in which historical theories have decomposed light into parts. Newton took light to be composed of heterogeneous corpuscles, classical wave theory took it to be the superposition of waves with different wavelengths and polarizations, and quantum theory takes it to be a collection of photons or quantized electromagnetic fields depending on context. Each of these theories employs a different mathematically derived conception of how light is composed of parts, most of which are incompatible with our intuitive conception of composition. We suggest that this flexibility should be a characteristic feature of a scientifically engaged commitment to compositional explanation.

2.2. Features of Compositional Explanation

With the example of the allotropes of carbon in mind, we can now highlight a number of key features of compositional explanations. Here we draw upon Carl Gillett's thorough discussion of compositional explanations (Gillett, 2016a, Chapter 2; 2016b). We focus primarily on those features that can be utilized in the service of offering an explanatory characterization of physicalism.

(a) Asymmetry

Compositional explanations involve relations that are asymmetric. The target phenomenon (the "whole") is explained in terms of its components (the "parts") and not vice versa. For instance, the electric conductivity of graphite is explained in terms of its components (i.e., carbon atoms and their bonds) insofar as such components give rise to or non-productively determine electrical conductivity. But the carbon atoms of graphite and their configuration do not hold in virtue of nor are non-productively determined by electrical conductivity. As the Weinberg quotes makes evident, in positing compositional explanations, scientists posit an order in nature. And compositional explanations posit a "downward" order: the whole is explained by its parts.

(b) Irreflexivity

Relatedly, compositional relations are irreflexive: within the scientific practice of compositional explanations, one does not find instances in which a phenomenon is explained in terms of itself. Graphite is not a component of itself nor is its anisotropy explained in terms of anisotropy.

COMMENT

Features (a)—(b) allow us to see how compositional relations and explanations are applicable to the case of physicalism. If a phenomenon (e.g., a biological phenomenon) is compositionally explained and its components are physical, then the phenomenon itself is *physically* explained. At the same time, such an explanation establishes an order of priority: the biological phenomenon is explained in terms of its ultimately physical components and not vice versa.

(c) Transitivity

It is plausible that the relations that compositional explanations posit are transitive. For example, aspects of the adaptive immune system are explained in terms of the workings of T lymphocytes, which are taken to be components of adaptive immunity, and the various properties of T lymphocytes (e.g., the fact T lymphocytes produce cytokines) are explained in terms of the lower-level entities and processes that compose lymphocytes and their workings. Having said that, we do not insist that compositional relations are necessarily transitive. Whether transitivity holds between different levels is an empirical matter.

(d) Relata as "Entities"

What is the status of the relata of compositional explanations? We describe the relata of compositional relations as "entities" in order to signify our permissiveness as to what type of things (individuals, properties, or processes) can enter into compositional explanations (see also Gillett, 2016a). For instance, in the case of graphite, graphite itself is taken to be an individual that is composed of other individuals (carbon atoms) and their properties. The electrical conductivity of graphite (a property) is compositionally explained either in terms of individuals (carbon atoms) and their properties or in terms of a process (flow of phonons). The process of leaving marks on a paper while writing with a pencil is explained by the processes that take place when force is applied on graphite and which result in the separation of the sheets of hexagonal rings that compose it.

(e) Relata as "Working" Entities

Following Gillett (2016a), we shall describe the relata of compositional explanations not only as entities but as "working" entities. Such qualification is crucial for it indicates what types of entities are used in compositional explanations and consequently it informs us of the scope of compositional explanations. The relata are *working* entities insofar as they are entities that are individuated at least partly in terms of what they *do* (their powers or causal profiles). Scientists target only causally potent or powerful phenomena and explain such phenomena in terms of other causally potent or powerful phenomena. Such a feature of compositional explanation and scientific practice should not be taken to mean that no non-causal properties or relationships may figure either in compositional explanations or in the specification of individuals, properties, or processes implicated in such. For instance, a complete compositional explanation of the hardness of the diamond may require an account of the geometric or spatial properties of carbon atoms.

Still, the target phenomenon of a compositional explanation *is* a causally potent or powerful phenomenon and its explanation must include a specification of its working—i.e., powerful—components and their mostly powerful properties. Thus, compositional explanations only target causal goings-on and are not applicable in cases of abstract phenomena or entities that figure, for instance, in logic, set theory, mathematics, or ethics.

(f) Synchronicity and Verticality

Compositional relations hold between entities that are synchronous to each other. This feature clearly demarcates compositional relations from causal and other productive relationships. Furthermore, the relata are not *distinct*, as they typically are in cases of causal relationships. For instance, when we are offering a compositional explanation of graphite, the carbon atoms that figure as the components of graphite are, in some sense, the graphite itself. In other words, compositional relationships are "vertical" (Aizawa & Gillett, 2016; Gillett, 2016a): They hold between higher-level entities and lower-level entities and the former are explained in virtue of the latter. As mentioned above, this feature of compositional explanations permits us to establish an explanatory and consequently, an ontological priority.

(g) Determination and Necessitation

Successful compositional explanations demonstrate how one phenomenon is *determined* by the workings of its components. There are different ways of expressing this feature of compositional explanations, but the essence is simple. When we have offered a compositional explanation of a phenomenon, the phenomenon follows; we have grounded it or made it real. As Gillett puts it:

> When we have successfully identified certain components under the relevant conditions, then we have identified lower-level entities in the explanans that non-productively suffice for, and hence explain the existence of, the higher-level entity, under those circumstances, which is the explanadum.
>
> (2016b, p. 226)

The existence of the higher-level entity that has been explained in terms of lower-level entities is necessitated by those lower-level entities and their interactions. Such necessitation is that of natural or nomological necessitation. Stated otherwise, given the laws of nature and certain conditions, the presence of lower-level entities suffices for the target phenomenon.

COMMENT

To some, an appeal to nomological necessity might appear to be woefully insufficient to capture the character of physicalism. They might protest that the fact that a higher-level entity follows as a matter of nomological necessary from the instantiation of various lower-level entities (its components) does not show that such an entity is nothing over and above the components. They might ask, "Couldn't there a possible world (or scenario) in which the components exist precisely as they exist in this world but where the higher-level phenomenon is either absent or different?" "Certainly!" they would respond. But if so, something more is needed in addition to nomological necessity—some extra metaphysical or logical/conceptual "glue" that would bind the higher-level entity to its components across all (metaphysically or logically) possible worlds.

Although understandable, such a reaction is, from our perspective, unacceptable. If one begins with the assumption that physicalism is at heart either a metaphysical or conceptual position, then, of course, one ought to describe physicalism in terms that will guarantee its presumed force. Consequently, talk of "determination," "sufficiency," or "nothing over and above" would need to be explicated in terms that would guarantee the *impossibility* (logical or metaphysical) of a situation in which the components are present but the composed entity is not. As we have discussed in detail in Chapter 2, there are problems with traditional metaphysical approaches to physicalism, ones that do not appear to be so easily surmountable. Furthermore, our understanding of physicalism is no longer one that follows the tradition in demanding that according to physicalism the non-physical is conceptually or metaphysically nothing over and above the non-physical. By focusing on explanation and by understanding physicalism as an explanatory position, we have loosened the metaphysical and conceptual holds on physicalism. For us, physicalism holds that all non-physical phenomena are physically explained. And that means that most of them (if not all of them) will be compositionally explained by their physical components. Physicalism is understood to be an interdisciplinary research project that aims to explain the world. From the perspective of physicalism as a research program, consciousness is a problem not because of any metaphysical issues that arise on account of conceivability arguments, e.g., but rather because we lack a compositional explanation of consciousness that makes consciousness *intelligible* in the same way, e.g., that properties of allotropes of carbon are made intelligible by appealing to their atomic structure. Qua research program, research program physicalism is thus not concerned with metaphysical or conceptual necessities. One could argue that such necessities follow from a successful compositional explanation. But if one chooses to do so, then one would be doing metaphysics and not pursing the research program. Our version of physicalism is revisionist. Its fate does not depend on the presence of conceptual or metaphysical necessities.

Compositional explanations are common in the neurosciences. Indeed, this is true at various levels of granularity. Consider, for instance, explanations of how the propagation of action potentials arises from the dynamic interaction between membrane structures and elements of the extra-and intra-cellular milieu; explanations of how the organization of neural pathways and circuits shapes the activity of individual cells in primary sensory cortex as they respond to relevant stimuli within their receptive fields; explanations of how specific ganglia (i.e., populations of neurons) within the hippocampus and surrounding cortical areas support the encoding of certain aspects of memory; or explanations of the role that morphological changes play in neurological disorders such as Alzheimer's or Multiple Sclerosis. Echoing this, the preface to the most widely used and well-respected comprehensive textbook in the neurosciences (Kandel, Schwartz, Jessell, Siegelbaum, & Hudspeth, 2013) begins with the following sentence:

> The ultimate goal of neuroscience is to understand how the flow of electrical signals through neural circuits give rise to mind—to how we perceive, act, think, learn, and remember.
>
> (p. xli)

We suggest that compositional explanation is the glue that holds this project together. The vision of neuroscience on offer is, not as something that renders the explanations of other special sciences irrelevant or moot, but rather as something that supports and enriches them. This conception fits with the explicit attempt by the editors of the textbook to merge ideas from a wide range of disciplines, from developmental biology and population genetics to cognitive science and psychiatry. Indeed, the preface itself finishes with the claim that "the study of mind and consciousness defines the frontier of biology" (p. xlii).

It should be emphasized that research program physicalism expands the commitment to compositional explanation beyond the confines of the neurosciences. In keeping with this expansion, research program physicalism is compatible with embedded, embodied, and enactive accounts of mind. Indeed, it is compatible with dynamical explanations of psychological phenomena that depend on the active coupling of agents with elements of their environment (e.g., Chemero, 2009; Chemero & Silberstein, 2008; Kelso, 1995; Van Gelder, 1995).

In sum, explanation requires intelligibility but intelligibility demands neither a priori entailment nor metaphysical connections that hold across all possible worlds. It may turn out to be the case that a compositional explanation of consciousness is beyond our reach. We may never understand consciousness in terms of the workings of some physical entities. That is all well and good and it would result in the failure of the research program and the rejection of (our version of) physicalism. But such a failure would be a direct consequence of what our sciences tell us about consciousness and not what metaphysics or logic dictates.

(h) Non-Identity

Compositional explanations hold between entities that are not identical to each other. The adaptive immune system is not identical to any of its components (e.g., T lymphocytes) nor is it identical to the set of all of its components. The same holds for graphite and for other entities that are compositionally explained. There are at least two reasons that speak against positing an identity relationship between the relata of compositional explanations.

First, a philosophical or conceptual reason: compositional relations are often one-many insofar as a whole set of interconnected entities is shown to compose another entity (Gillett, 2016a). However, identity is traditionally understood to be a one-to-one relationship. Hence, the claim that compositional relations express identity relations would need to be supplemented by the non-trivial task of defending that a plurality of entities is identical to a singular entity (see Cotnoir & Baxter, 2014; Wallace, 2011).

Second, and more importantly for our purposes, a presumed identity relationship between the relata of compositional explanations stands, at least prima facie, in opposition to the scientific practice of compositional explanations. On the one hand, if compositional relations are relations of identity, then compositional explanations are symmetric and reflexive. But as it was mentioned above, compositional explanations are often employed in establishing a type of explanatory and ultimately ontological priority: Compositional explanations are advanced in the hope of carving out certain "vertical" relationships in nature that hold between the more and the less fundamental entities. If compositional explanations were to be understood as expressions of identity relations, then such pronouncements would be empty.

On the other hand, in many cases the target phenomenon that has been compositionally explained cannot be identified with *any* particular set of components. Consider again the case of graphite. Graphite has been compositionally explained in terms of its atomic structure but we find *no* particular structure of carbon atoms that is identical with graphite. Different assemblages of carbon atoms may compose graphite and slight alterations to the atomic structure of a sample of graphite do not render that sample a distinct substance. Thus, claims of identity between the target phenomenon and its components appear to be incongruous to compositional explanations, at least as they are practiced in the sciences.

(i) Multiple Realizability

Compositional explanations are compatible with the presumed multiple realizability of certain higher-level entities. In other words, a phenomenon Φ can be compositionally explained by its components and still be multiply realized. In fact, compositional explanations provide a model for when and how such multiple realizability occurs. Suppose that a higher-level property P is multiply realized insofar as instances of P are realized by the instantiation of $Q_1, Q_2, \ldots,$ and Q_n. According to compositional explanation, each instance of $Q_1, Q_2, \ldots Q_n$ realizes an instance of P because each instance of P is compositionally explained by $Q_1, Q_2, \ldots Q_n$. Solidity, for example, is realized not only by an assemblage of sp^3-hybridized carbon atoms each of which is bonded to four other similarly hybridized carbon atoms (diamond) but also in a wide arrange of atomic configurations. In the case of compositional explanations, multiple realizability will occur when heterogeneous sets of working components give rise to a higher-level homogeneity (i.e., an entity of the same type) (Gillett, 2016a, p. 77).

(j) Novelty

Compositional explanations are consistent with the existence of novelty, both as an ontological phenomenon and as an epistemic phenomenon. On the one hand, compositional explanations permit ontological novelty in the sense that the entity that has been compositional explained often has properties and powers that are qualitative different than the properties and powers of its components. There is nothing mysterious with this phenomenon as our discussion of carbon allotropes makes manifest. Although no carbon atom is hard, we can understand how an assemblage of such atoms may be. On the other hand, compositional explanations may yield unexpected or novel results. In case of connectionist networks, for example, unexpected behavior may arise from simple interactions between simple units. Still, connectionist networks can be compositionally explained.

COMMENT

Is it possible to have a different kind of novelty or emergence in the case of compositional explanation? And if so, is that kind of novelty or emergence consistent with physicalism as understood here? In order to address these questions, we need to disambiguate between different kinds of emergence.

Consider first what might be called "epistemic emergence": a type of epistemic novelty that involves a violation of expectations. Such a notion of epistemic novelty is obviously subject-dependent, and thus one may insist that epistemic novelty is an inappropriate guide to understanding the structure of nature and specifically, the relationship between the higher-level entity and its components. A better alternative, one may suggest, is a notion of emergence that is tied to the notions of deducibility or a priori entailment. Thus, one may ask whether compositional explanation requires that true statements about the phenomenon that is compositionally explained can be deduced from true statements about the instantiation and workings of the lower-level entities that compose the higher-level phenomenon. Different answers are possible to such a question. First, one may accept that compositional explanations require deducibility from lower-level statements to higher-level statements. Second, one could argue that compositional explanations do not require such deducibility or a priori entailment, but they do require the presence of a metaphysical connection between the components and the higher-level entity. Third, one may reject that compositional explanations require deducibility or a priori entailment but refuse to offer an alternative connection (metaphysical or anything stronger than nomological) between the components and the higher-level composed entity. As it should be clear from what came before, we take the third alternative. No logical or metaphysical connections are cited as part of compositional explanations when scientists provide such explanations. No physical chemistry textbook explains the anisotropy of graphite by illustrating how one may (even in principle) use true statements about carbon atoms and their properties to deduce the fact that carbon has the type of anisotropy that it has. Nor does an explanation of anisotropy involve discussion of metaphysically possible scenarios. Our attitude should be clear by now. We do not accept the fundamental assumption that physicalism should be understood as a position that involves metaphysical or conceptual connections between the non-physical and the physical. Physicalism, as we understand it, is first and foremost an explanatory project and, as the history of science demonstrates, we can have perfectly adequate explanations in the absence of metaphysical or logical connections.

Research program physicalism, we stated, is compatible with the idea that composed entities can have properties and powers that are qualitatively different from the properties and powers of their components. Still, it is incompatible with a different type, a stronger or more demanding kind, of ontological emergence ("Robust ontological emergence"), which holds that consciousness (or some other biological or psychological entity) is *not* composed of physical entities. Such a failure of compositional explanation would be established if the scientific study of consciousness were to yield no physical parts or components of consciousness. It would also be established if a "top-down" constitutive relationship were to be found in the case of consciousness—i.e., consciousness, as a whole, has a constitutive or determinative effect on its components. In either case, consciousness would not be compositionally explained and the research program would fail. Robust ontological emergence is a live possibility and cannot be ruled out a priori.

(k) Ontological Unity, or Reduction

Finally, compositional explanations establish that the composed entity is *nothing* more than its components and their interconnections. The composed higher-level entity requires no addition in being once all of its components are instantiated. Furthermore, and as was mentioned above, the instantiation of its components suffices for the instantiation of the composed, higher-level entity. Such claims have to be understood in light of nomological necessity—it is only given the laws of nature and certain conditions that such determination or sufficiency applies. Consequently, compositional explanations ought to obey a certain type of neutrality or conservation principle between the components and the composed entity. Gillett (2016a), for example, suggests that in the case of successful compositional explanations there must be a "mass-energy neutrality" requirement: the combined mass-energy of the components should equal the mass-energy of the composed entity. (Gillett [2016b, p. 206] relaxes the requirement a bit by requiring either mass-energy neutrality or force neutrality between the components and the composed entity.) Although Gillett's proposal sounds reasonable, we do not wish to preclude additional or different conservation principles. What is important for our purposes is that there exists a scientific measure that permits us to conclude that the composed entity is, nomologically speaking, nothing more and nothing less than its components.

2.3. Summary

What renders the research program a form of physicalism is its commitment to the claim that consciousness can be compositionally explained in terms of its physical parts. The research program's success is thus predicated on the eventual compositional explanation of consciousness. If successful, the research program will find a place for consciousness in the natural world order. It will show how consciousness is the natural (and not the metaphysical or logical) consequence of the workings of its parts. In other words, consciousness will be shown to be nothing over and above its physical parts for it would be asymmetrically and non-causally determined by its parts.

We can imagine variations of our research program. That is, research programs that demand that consciousness (or some other currently unexplained psychological or biological phenomenon) is explained, not compositionally, but in some other manner. Given the many different accounts of explanations that philosophers of science have articulated in the recent years, it would be foolish to rule out such related research programs a priori. However, given that we offer research program physicalism as a form of physicalism, we must take a stance that is strong enough to capture the core tenets of physicalism. To this end, we believe that a commitment to compositional explanation is strong enough to have rendered the non-physical target phenomenon (consciousness, memory, life, reproduction, inflation, etc.) *physical*: the former is both non-causally determined and composed by the physical. Still, our proposal is weaker than both metaphysical and conceptual approaches to physicalism. What drives the research program and its ontological commitments is explanation. Consciousness, as it occurs in our world and only in our world, is physical if it can be compositionally explained. Research program physicalism is both thoroughly scientific and physicalistic.

3. Theoretical Precursors

We are not the first to suggest that physicalism should be viewed in terms of its empirical promise with respect to understanding the mind. We conclude this chapter by highlighting what research program physicalism shares—and does not share—with previous empirically oriented approaches to explanation in the psychological and brain sciences. As was the case earlier with reconstructive approaches to physicalism, we maintain that our position preserves what is best about these precursors and inoculates against their weaknesses. More broadly, we hope to demonstrate the real promise of an approach to physicalism that focuses on scientific (and specifically, compositional) explanation.

In many ways, the contemporary discussion of the challenge posed by consciousness to physicalism (as opposed to the older notion of materialism) began in the middle of the twentieth century when a number of philosophers (e.g., Feigl, 1958; Lewis, 1966; Place, 1956; Smart, 1959) proposed that mental state types could be identified with brain state types. Identity theory was generally motivated by a deep commitment to science. J.J.C. Smart, for example, offers the following observation as an explanation of the impetus behind his proposal that sensations are brain processes (1959, p. 143): "It seems to me that science is increasingly giving us a viewpoint whereby organisms are able to be seen as physico-chemical mechanisms." Others went further and explicitly proposed that identity theory was a scientific hypothesis (Feigl, 1958; Place, 1956). Despite the ontological clarity of identity theory and its conceptual simplicity, it ultimately fell out of favor because it appeared to be incompatible with the presumed multiple realizability of mental states (Putnam, 1967/1975). While there has been some recent pushback against these arguments (e.g., Polger & Shapiro, 2016), we take it to be a significant benefit of our approach that it allows for, and even predicts, multiply realized properties and entities.

Over time the philosophical discussion of physicalism has moved away from the empirical investigation of mind and come to be viewed primarily in metaphysical terms. In the ensuing decades philosophers interested in the psychological and brain sciences have generally avoided direct consideration of the metaphysical puzzles that have occupied so much of the analytic literature and pursued their interests against the background of an assumed, if not explicit, physicalism. We think that it is time for physicalism to be returned to the foreground and reunited with empirically oriented philosophy of mind. In keeping with this, it is important to recognize that research program physicalism shares much with previous attempts to characterize the mind in physicalist terms. Three prominent approaches are particularly relevant: neurophilosophy, neo-mechanism, and dynamical systems theory. Below we examine the ways in which our approach fits with these precursors.

Neurophilosophy (Churchland, P. S., 1989, 1994, 2005) embodies the idea that neuroscience provides important input for addressing significant philosophical questions such as the nature of consciousness. It enjoys something of an equivocal status in philosophy. On the one hand, few would deny the breadth of its influence on empirically oriented philosophy of mind. Indeed, any list of the philosophers of psychology and neuroscience who owe an intellectual debt to neurophilosophy would be quite long. On the other hand, it has not received a lot of attention in the discussion of the metaphysics of consciousness. In an address entitled, "Can Neurobiology

Teach Us Anything About Consciousness?", Patricia Churchland pushes back against this marginalization and lays her cards out on the table:

> I am convinced that the right strategy for understanding psychological capacities is essentially reductionist, by which I mean, broadly, that understanding the neurobiological mechanisms is not a frill but a necessity. Whether science will finally succeed in reducing psychological phenomena to neurobiological phenomena is, needless to say, yet another empirical question. Adopting the reductionist strategy means trying to explain the macro levels (psychological properties) in terms of micro levels (neural network properties).
>
> (1994, p. 23)

What is striking about this defense is how little it directly addresses the metaphysical issues thought to be central to the topic of consciousness. Granted, much of the address attempts to defang the traditional thought experiments. Nevertheless, it is clear that Churchland thinks the real strengths of a reductionist approach are more pragmatic in character. First, she refers to reductionism as an empirical research strategy that may or may not pan out. In other words, she views reductionism not merely as an a posteriori thesis but also as a promising methodological ploy (see also Bechtel, 2008; Bechtel & Richardson, 1993; Wimsatt, 2007). Second, she focuses on the importance of explaining macro-level phenomena in terms of micro-level phenomena. Both of these non-standard elements fit well with our conception of an empirically supported research program, but neither directly addresses the placement problems at the heart of traditional conceptions of physicalism.

Although there are clear parallels between neurophilosophy and our approach, there are also substantial differences. First, they differ with respect to scope. Neurophilosophy specifically defends the importance of neuroscience to the empirical and philosophical investigation of mind. By contrast, we are offering a reconstructive version of physicalism. While neuroscience will undoubtedly play a fundamental role in future theory, this status is not a core claim of our position. In fact, there has been a recent trend towards including embodied and ecological factors in explanations of psychological phenomena (a trend that Churchland, 2005 herself acknowledges). This trend, which emerged after neurophilosophy was first formulated, informs the research program but does not fit well with the brain-centric focus of neurophilosophy (Clark, 2008). There is nothing in our characterization of compositional explanation that precludes the body or the environment from being components of psychological phenomena. Second, there are important differences between reductive explanations (as they are traditionally understood) and compositional ones. Reduction is thought to involve inter-level identities, which are inherently symmetric, while composition does not. Finally, the two approaches differ with respect to their epistemic commitments. Reduction, at least in its Nagelian form, requires a semantic transparency in which macro-level generalizations are derivable or predictable from micro-level ones. Composition makes no such demands.

Many philosophers who have been inspired by neurophilosophy have moved away from the classical, Nagel-style reductionism at its heart. This shift has occurred largely because of the perception that this approach is not descriptively adequate. The recognition that in practice many, if not most, explanations in the psychological and brain sciences fail to involve reductive identities has led many philosophers to look for new conceptual frameworks to understand how explanations in these fields actually work. At this time, the most influential of these focuses on the importance of mechanistic explanations. This neo-mechanism (to distinguish it from the earlier corpuscular version held by Descartes) has been explicitly developed to capture contemporary explanations in the biological sciences. One of the most cited philosophy of science papers in recent memory begins with the straightforward, seemingly quotidian observation, "In many fields of science what is taken to be a satisfactory explanation requires providing a description of a mechanism" (Machamer et al., 2000). Neo-mechanism as a philosophical enterprise seeks to understand the role that such an appeal to mechanism plays in practice and in principle with respect to special science explanations. Although several distinct definitions of mechanism have been offered (e.g., Bechtel & Abrahamsen, 2005; Glennan, 2002; Machamer et al., 2000), an ecumenical consensus has emerged which views mechanistic explanation in terms of the identification the relevant entities that produce, underlie, or maintain the phenomenon in question (Craver & Tabery, 2017; Illari & Williamson, 2012).

Even though there is a great deal of affinity between this neo-mechanism and our approach, the two accounts ought to be clearly distinguished. First, an appeal to compositional explanation is in at least one sense broader than an appeal to mechanistic explanation. Our account does not require that consciousness (or some other psychological phenomenon) must be given a mechanistic explanation. All that it requires is that such phenomenon is explained compositionally.

In addition, when enlisted in the services of the research program, compositional explanations are ontologically speaking more demanding than mechanistic explanations. Both neo-mechanism and the research program aim to explain. However, only the latter demands that the provided explanation is one that shows that the explained phenomenon is physical. Stated otherwise, in the context of the research program, compositional explanations aim to show not only that a target phenomenon (the "whole") is produced out of its physical components ("parts") but also, and importantly, that the target phenomenon is nothing over and above those physical parts. It is unclear, however, whether neo-mechanistic accounts are capable of capturing the relationship between the whole and the parts that physicalism requires. Such a conclusion is corroborated by the following two facts.

First, many proponents of neo-mechanism do not require that mechanistic explanations bottom out at a physical level. The target phenomenon can be mechanistically explained without being explained in terms of the activities of its *physical* components. On the contrary, in order for the research program to be a type of physicalism, it must show that consciousness and other psychological phenomena are compositionally explained in terms of their physical parts. As mentioned before, research program physicalism does not demand that there is a fundamental physical level at which all compositional explanations bottom out—in theory, compositional explanations could carry on forever. Nor does it require that all compositional explanations utilize the same "level" physical parts—some may utilize the posits of condensed-matter physics, others may invoke quantum mechanical phenomena. Still, the components or parts of the explained phenomenon have to be physical.

Second, compositional explanations not only explain a phenomenon in terms of its physical components, they also aim to show how the target phenomenon is constituted by its components. After all, successful compositional explanations show that the whole is composed by (i.e., it is *just*) its parts. There is nothing more to a diamond, for example, than its carbon atoms and their interconnections. Now, although neo-mechanists offer accounts of mechanistic constitution (i.e., the relationship that successful mechanistic explanations posit between the explained phenomenon and the mechanisms underlying it), it is not immediately obvious that mechanistic constitution is sufficiently strong to capture the ontological unity that the research program physicalism demands and that compositional explanation delivers.

Consider, for instance, one of the most popular articulations of mechanistic explanations, that of Carl Craver (2007). Craver develops a model of mechanistic explanations that are, according to him, *constitutive*: When we have mechanistic explanations, Craver holds, the explained phenomenon is shown to be constituted by the activities of its components (its underlying mechanism) (p. 129). Simplifying matters a bit, a component, x, is a constitutive part of a system, S, if (a) x is a part of S; (b) manipulating x's behavior can change S's behavior; and (c) manipulating S's behavior can change x's behavior. The three conditions, however, do not jointly guarantee that the mechanistically constituted phenomenon is nothing over and above its composing parts. The fact that a change in the behavior of the parts of a whole can bring about a change in the behavior of the whole, and vice versa, shows neither that the whole is its parts nor that the whole is composed by its parts. Gillett (2016b) presents a vitalist scenario according to which a biological process (say, digestion) is not composed by any cellular and molecular entities yet is nomologically connected to such entities by brute laws. Assuming that digestion is a property of biological individuals and that the cellular and molecular entities that are nomologically connected with the uncomposed biological process are spatially contained within (and thus parts of) the biological individuals, then all three conditions of Craver's constitution are satisfied. Yet, the vitalist scenario is a clear case of a phenomenon that is "mechanistically constituted" by some entities without being *composed* by those components. Indeed, the target phenomenon—in this case, vitalist digestion—appears to be ontologically distinct from the various cellular and molecular entities with which it is nomologically connected.

It is beyond the scope of this chapter to examine whether Craver's account has the means of responding to this issue. Nor is it important to provide a comprehensive review of other neo-mechanistic accounts of constitution (e.g., Couch, 2011; Harbecke, 2010) and to examine whether they are capable of giving rise to the requisite ontological unity. The point that we wish to make is that unlike mechanistic explanations, compositional explanations clearly do the trick: They render the explained phenomenon both physical and nothing over and above its parts. Neo-mechanistic accounts are not "enemies" of the research program—obviously, there is nothing anti-physicalist about them. Still, scientifically minded physicalists are better served by compositional explanations than by mechanistic explanations.

One of the primary criticisms of neo-mechanism is that there appear to be other legitimate explanatory practices that do not involve an appeal to mechanisms. While few would flatly deny the importance of mechanistic explanations to the biological sciences, it is not difficult to find apparently non-mechanistic explanations that appeal to general network properties or dynamical laws. Voicing their opposition to a mechanism-only approach, for instance, Michael Silberstein and Tony Chemero (2013, p. 960) claim, "that systems biology and systems neuroscience contain robust dynamical and mathematical explanations of some phenomena in which the essential explanatory work is not being done by localization and decomposition." Dynamical systems theory represents an attempt to capture and defend certain system-level explanations. On its face, because of the commitment to the failure of functional decomposition, it seems that dynamical systems theory excludes compositional explanation outright. We suggest that this is mistaken and argue that our approach is in fact compatible with many dynamical explanations.

To make this clear, we consider a well-known example that is often used to highlight the basic elements of a dynamical explanation (our discussion follows that of Shapiro, 2013). This example involves the relationship between changes in the number of predators and prey in a closed territory. To keep it simple, we will only consider the case where there is one species of each and all other environmental factors are kept constant. The key insight behind the relevant dynamical explanation is that the fates of predators and prey are intimately linked. More prey means more food for the predators and more predation means less prey. In the 1920s, Vito Volterra and Alfred Lotka independently developed a pair of differential equations that describe how the two populations change in relation to each other. Letting the variable x stand for the prey, y stand for the population of predators, and t for time, we can express these equations as follows:

$$dx/dt = \alpha x - \beta y$$

$$dy/dt = \gamma xy - \delta y$$

The Greek letters represent the fixed parameters of the system: α is the growth rate of the prey in the absence of predators; β is the predation rate; γ is the growth rate of the predators given a specific number of prey; and δ is the death rate of predators in the absence of prey. The differential equations thus describe how changes in one population are connected to changes in the other: The first equation describes how the population of prey changes over time as a function of its growth rate minus the predation rate and the second equation describes how the population of predators changes over time as a function of the number of prey minus the natural loss of predators.

These equations serve as a model of the relationship between predators and prey in a fixed environment. As is the case with any model, this one depends on a number of idealizations. Perhaps the most alarming of these is the assumption that there is a continuous rate of change between the two populations. Clearly, this is unrealistic since populations of organisms change discretely. Although we could have chosen a different phenomenon that involves continuous change (see Beer, 1995, 1999; Kelso, 1995 for other examples), we are going to stick with this example because the way in which the populations are coupled is intuitively clear. What is important about the model is that it makes clear predictions: Given initial population sizes and the relevant parameters, the equations map out a trajectory in a two-dimensional state space defined relative to the possible combinations of numbers of a predators and prey. Importantly, this model identifies a point at which the two populations will achieve equilibrium. In other words, it predicts that, given a set of initial conditions, a certain predator-prey population pair will act as an attractor and, over time, the system will tend to settle into this fixed state.

Suppose we apply this model to a population of foxes and rabbits. Imagine that we have good evidence for the environmental parameters. The model predicts that the two populations will fall into a specific equilibrium. When we measure the population sizes, we find that they match the predicted equilibrium. Suppose further that we are able to manipulate the system—say by increasing the amount of food and shelter available to the rabbits. Given that this should change the parameters of the system (including perhaps the both the rabbit growth rate and the predation rate), the model predicts that the two populations will change over time and settle into a new equilibrium. If the model were to be successful again, we would have greater confidence in its accuracy and then seem to have some justification for treating the model as part of an explanation of how the populations of the change in a systematic way.

A strategy of functional decomposition will not work for this system, because the relevant variables depend on each other. You cannot know what will happen to the rabbit population without knowing what will happen to the fox population and you cannot know what will happen to the fox population without knowing what will happen to the rabbit population. Any attempt to examine the population shifts of either species independently will miss the relevant generalizations. Thus, the dynamical equations capture a systems level relationship that cannot be understood in terms of the properties of the parts of the system.

As the quote from Silberstein and Chemero earlier indicates, supporters of the view that dynamical systems theory represents a dramatic break from the commitment to mechanism that has characterized recent philosophy of biology see this sort of failure of decomposition as a central point of contention between these approaches. Whether or not this is the case (and some mechanists have argued that it is not; e.g., Bechtel & Richardson, 1993), our point is that this failure is completely compatible with what we are calling a compositional explanation. Indeed, this sort of failure is an important design feature of our approach. Recall our discussion of the hardness of diamonds. This property is explained, not by the hardness of the carbon atoms, but by the presence of the network of strong covalent bonds that permeates the structure. Simply put, hardness is a system-level property. The ability to capture such properties is directly built into compositional explanation because it explicitly disavows identity and symmetry. Compositional explanation requires that wholes are understood in terms of the collective workings of the parts and nothing else; it does not exclude the possibility that such workings are fundamentally interactive and occur at a systems or network level. To put the point more directly, we suggest that neither diamonds nor predator-prey relationships provide a serious challenge to physicalism. The fact that compositional explanation can handle both speaks in its favor.

We want to be clear though. We are not saying that all dynamical explanations are compatible with our approach. Compositional explanation requires that wholes are realized by and comprised of their parts. It does not leave room for *sui generis* entities, downward constitutive influence of wholes on their parts, or other forms of radical ontological emergence. Our fox-rabbit scenario passes muster because, although the relevant variables of the model cannot be disentangled, the system consists of interacting physical entities. We readily acknowledge that dynamical explanations that are incompatible with compositional explanation are logically possible, but we maintain that these should in fact be considered to be violations of physicalism.

To be sure, we have only briefly surveyed a small portion of the relevant theoretical topography. A great many questions remain to be answered. For instance, there have been attempts to reconsider the nature of reduction (Theurer, 2013) and the promise of identity theory (Polger, 2004; Polger & Shapiro, 2016; Shapiro, 2004). There have been defenses of radical forms of eliminitivism (Bickle, 1998, 2003). There is also an ongoing debate considering the degree to which the conception of mechanism should be linked to causal explanation (Glennan, 1996, 2002; Craver & Tabery, 2017; Illari & Williamson, 2012). Although many have worried that mechanistic explanation may be too limited in scope, others have sought to extend mechanistic explanations to include dynamical and other systems level explanations (Bechtel, 2008; Bechtel & Abrahamsen, 2005). Questions persist concerning the completeness or adequacy of dynamical explanations. We do not pretend to have the answers to these questions. Instead, we see their resolution as part of the interdisciplinary project to understand the mind and its place in nature—a project that includes philosophy as an actively engaged participant. What we hope to have shown is that compositional explanation is both constrained enough to give research program physicalism real theoretical bite and yet flexible enough to allow for a degree of explanatory pluralism. We think physicalism should make the challenge posed by consciousness clear (in our case: that it may not be possible to provide an empirically supported compositional explanation of relevant conscious phenomena). At the same time, it should leave some substantial explanatory questions open and unresolved (such as the relative importance of mechanistic vs. dynamical explanations in the sciences of the mind) and relax its excessively strong epistemic and metaphysical commitments.

Notes

1. Our understanding of compositional explanation owes a great deal to Carl Gillett's work on scientific reduction and explanation as this is developed primarily in Gillett (2016a and 2016b).
2. It is worth emphasizing that these hybrid orbitals occur only in the bonding process with other atoms.

References

Abelson, R. P., & Lalljee, M. (1988). Knowledge structures and causal explanation. In D. J. Hilton (ed.), *Contemporary science and natural explanation: Commonsense conceptions of causality* (pp. 175–203). New York, NY: New York University Press.

Achinstein, P. (1983). *The nature of explanation*. Oxford, UK: Oxford University Press.

Aizawa, K., & Gillett, C. (2016). Introduction: Vertical relations in science, philosophy and the world: Understanding the new debates over verticality. In K. Aizawa & C. Gillett (eds.), *Scientific composition and metaphysical ground* (pp. 1–38). London, UK: Palgrave Macmillan.

Atkins, P., & De Paula, J. (2015). *Elements of physical chemistry* (5th edition). New York, NY: W. H. Freeman and Company.

Bechtel, W. (2008). *Mental mechanisms: Philosophical perspectives on cognitive neuroscience*. London, UK: Routledge.

Bechtel, W., & Abrahamsen, A. (2005). Explanation: A mechanist alternative. *Studies in History and Philosophy of Science Part C: Studies in History and Philosophy of Biological and Biomedical Sciences*, 36(2), 421–441.

Bechtel, W., & Richardson, R. C. (1993). *Discovering complexity: Decomposition and localization as strategies in scientific research*. Princeton, NJ: Princeton University Press.

Beer, R. (1995). Computational and dynamical languages for autonomous agents. In R. F. Port & T. van Gelder (eds.), *Mind as motion* (pp. 121–147). Cambridge, MA: MIT Press.

Beer, R. (1999). Dynamical approaches to cognitive science. *Trends in Cognitive Sciences*, *4*, 91–99.

Berman, R. (1992). Thermal conductivity of vapour deposited and isotopically enriched diamonds. In J. E. Field (ed.), *Properties of natural and synthetic diamond* (pp. 291–300). London, UK: Academic Press Ltd.

Bickle, J. (1998). *Psychoneural reduction: The new wave*. Cambridge, MA: MIT Press.

Bickle, J. (2003). *Philosophy and neuroscience: A ruthlessly reductive account*. Dordrecht: Kluwer Academic Publishers.

Bromberger, S. (1966). Why questions. In R. G. Colodny (ed.), *Mind and cosmos* (pp. 86–111). Pittsburgh, PA: University of Pittsburgh Press.

Carter, C. B., & Norton, M. G. (2013). *Ceramic materials: Science and engineering*. New York, NY: Springer Science & Business Media.

Cartwright, N. D. (1989). *Nature's capacities and their measurement*. Oxford, UK: Oxford University Press.

Chalmers, D. J. (1996). *The conscious mind: In search of a fundamental theory*. New York: Oxford University Press.

Chalmers, D. J. (2003). Consciousness and its place in nature. In S. P. Stich & T. A. Warfield (eds.), *The Blackwell guide to philosophy of mind* (pp. 102–142). Malden, MA: Blackwell Publishing. Revised version in Chalmers, 2010, pp. 103–140.

Chalmers, D. J. (2006). Phenomenal concepts and the explanatory gap. In T. Alter & S. Walter (eds.), *Phenomenal concepts and phenomenal knowledge: New essays on consciousness and physicalism* (pp. 167–194). Oxford, UK: Oxford University Press.

Chalmers, D. J. (2010). *The character of consciousness*. New York: Oxford University Press.

Chalmers, D. J., & Jackson, F. (2001). Conceptual analysis and reductive explanation. *Philosophical Review*, *110*, 315–361.

Chemero, A. (2009). *Radical embodied cognitive science*. Cambridge, MA: MIT Press.

Chemero, A., & Silberstein, M. (2008). Defending extended cognition. In V. Sloutsky, B. Love, & K. McRae (eds.), *Proceedings of the 30th annual conference of the cognitive science society* (pp. 129–134). New York, NY: Psychology Press.

Churchland, P. M. (1989). *A neurocomputational perspective: The nature of mind and the structure of science*. Cambridge, MA: MIT Press.

Churchland, P. M. (2012). *Plato's camera: How the physical brain captures a landscape of abstract universals*. Cambridge, MA: MIT Press.

Churchland, P. S. (1989). *Neurophilosophy: Toward a unified science of the mind-brain*. Cambridge, MA: MIT Press.

Churchland, P. S. (1994). Can neurobiology teach us anything about consciousness? In *Proceedings and addresses of the American Philosophical Association* (Vol. 67, No. 4, pp. 23–40). American Philosophical Association.

Churchland, P. S. (2005). A neurophilosophical slant on consciousness research. In V. A. Casagrande, R. W. Guillery, & S. M. Sherman (eds.), *Progress in brain research* (Vol. 149, pp. 285–294). Amsterdam, Netherlands: Elsevier.

Clark, A. (2008). *Supersizing the mind: Embodiment, action, and cognitive extension*. New York, NY: Oxford University Press.

Cotnoir, A. J., & Baxter, D. L. (eds.). (2014). *Composition as identity*. New York, NY: Oxford University Press.

Couch, M. B. (2011). Mechanisms and constitutive relevance. *Synthese*, *183*(3), 375–388.

Crane, T. (2001). The origins of qualia. In T. Crane & S. Patterson (eds.), *History of the mind-body problem* (pp. 164–194). London: Routledge.

Craver, C. F. (2007). *Explaining the brain: Mechanisms and the mosaic unity of neuroscience*. Oxford, UK: Clarendon Press.

Craver, C. F., & Tabery, J. (2017). Mechanisms in science. In N. Zalta (ed.), *The Stanford encyclopedia of philosophy*. https://plato.stanford.edu/archives/spr2017/entries/science-mechanisms

Evan, S. (1992). Surface properties of diamond. In J. E. Field (ed.), *Properties of natural and synthetic diamond* (pp. 181–214). London, UK: Academic Press Ltd.

Feigl, H. (1958). The "mental" and the "physical." In H. Feigl, M. Scriven, & G. Maxwell (eds.), *Concepts, theories and the mind-body problem: Minnesota studies in the philosophy of science* (Vol. 2, pp. 370–497). Minneapolis, MN: University of Minneapolis Press.

Friedman, M. (1974). Explanation and scientific understanding. *The Journal of Philosophy*, *71*(1), 5–19.

Gillett, C. (2016a). *Reduction and emergence in science and philosophy*. Cambridge, UK: Cambridge University Press.

Gillett, C. (2016b). The metaphysics of nature, science, and the rules of engagement. In K. Aizawa & C. Gillett (eds.), *Scientific composition and metaphysical ground* (pp. 205–248). London, UK: Palgrave Macmillan.

Glennan, S. (1992). Mechanisms, models, and causation. PhD dissertation. Chicago, IL: University of Chicago.

Glennan, S. (1996). Mechanisms and the nature of causation. *Erkenntnis*, *44*, 49–71.

Glennan, S. (2002). Rethinking mechanistic explanation. *Philosophy of Science*, *69*(Suppl.), S342–S353.

Harbecke, J. (2010). Mechanistic constitution in neurobiological explanations. *International Studies in the Philosophy of Science*, *24*, 267–285.

Healey, R. (2013). Physical composition. *Studies in History and Philosophy of Science Part B: Studies in History and Philosophy of Modern Physics*, *44*(1), 48–62.

Hempel, C. (1965). *Aspects of scientific explanation and other essays in the philosophy of science*. New York, NY: Free Press.

Illari, P. M., & Williamson, J. (2012). What is a mechanism? Thinking about mechanisms across the sciences. *European Journal for Philosophy of Science*, *2*(1), 119–135.

Jackson, F. (1998). *From metaphysics to ethics: A defence of conceptual analysis*. Oxford, UK: Oxford University Press.

Kandel, E. R., Schwartz, J. H., Jessell, T. M., Siegelbaum, S. A., & Hudspeth, A. J. (2013). *Principles of neuroscience* (5th edition). New York, NY: McGraw Hill.

Kaplan, D. M. (2015). Moving parts: The natural alliance between dynamical and mechanistic modeling approaches. *Biology and Philosophy*, *30*(6), 757–786.

Kaplan, D. M., & Craver, C. F. (2011). The explanatory force of dynamical models. *Philosophy of Science*, *78*, 601–627.

Kelso, S. (1995). *Dynamic patterns: The self-organization of brain and behavior*. Cambridge, MA: MIT Press.

Kemeny, J. G., & Oppenheim, P. (1956). On reduction. *Philosophical Studies*, *7*(1), 6–19.

Kim, J. (1993). *Supervenience and mind: Selected philosophical essays*. Cambridge, UK: Cambridge University Press.

Kitcher, P. (1981). Explanatory unification. *Philosophy of Science*, *48*(4), 507–531.

Ladyman, J., Ross, D., Spurrett, D., & Collier, J. G. (2007). *Every thing must go: Metaphysics naturalized*. Oxford, UK: Oxford University Press.

Levy, A., & Bechtel, W. (2013). Abstraction and the organization of mechanisms. *Philosophy of Science*, *80*(2), 241–261.

Lewis, D. (1966). An argument for the identity theory. *The Journal of Philosophy*, *63*(1), 17–25.

Machamer, P., Darden, L., & Craver, C. F. (2000). Thinking about mechanisms. *Philosophy of Science*, *67*(1), 1–25.

Marom, S. (2010). Neural timescales or lack thereof. *Progress in Neurobiology*, *90*(1), 16–28.

Miller, R. (1987). *Fact and method: Explanation, confirmation and reality in the natural and social sciences*. Princeton, NJ: Princeton University Press.

Oppenheim, P., & Putnam, H. (1958). Unity of science as a working hypothesis. In H. Feigl, M. Scriven, & G. Maxwell (eds.), *Concepts, theories and the mind-body problem: Minnesota studies in the philosophy of science* (Vol. 2, pp. 3–36). Minneapolis, MN: University of Minnesota Press.

Pierson, H. O. (1993). *Handbook of carbon, graphite, diamond, and fullerenes: Properties, processing and applications*. Park Ridge, NJ: Noyes Publications.

Place, U. T. (1956). Is consciousness a brain process? *British Journal of Psychology*, *47*(1), 44–50.

Polger, T. (2004). *Natural minds*. Cambridge, MA: MIT Press.

Polger, T., & Shapiro, L. (2016). *The multiple realization book*. Oxford, UK: Oxford University Press.

Putnam, H. (1967/1975). The nature of mental states. In H. Putnam (ed.), *Mind, language and reality: Philosophical papers* (Vol. 2, pp. 429–440). Cambridge, UK: Cambridge University Press.

Salmon, W. C. (1971). Statistical explanation. In W. Salmon (ed.), *Statistical explanation and statistical relevance*. Pittsburgh, PA: University of Pittsburgh Press.

Salmon, W. C. (1984). *Scientific explanation and the causal structure of the world*. Princeton, NJ: Princeton University Press.

Schaffer, J. (2003). Is there a fundamental level? *Noûs*, *37*(3), 498–517.

Schank, R. C. (1986). *Explanation pattern: Understanding mechanically and creatively*. Hillsdale, NJ: Erlbaum.

Shapiro, L. (2004). *The mind incarnate*. Cambridge, MA: MIT Press.

Shapiro, L. (2013). Dynamics and cognition. *Minds & Machines*, *23*, 353–375.

Silberstein, M., & Chemero, A. (2013). Constraints on localization and decomposition as explanatory strategies in the biological sciences. *Philosophy of Science*, *80*(5), 958–970.

Singer, S. (1990). Diamond: A high-power optical material. *SPIE Proceedings*, *1275*, 2–9.

Smart, J. J. (1959). Sensations and brain processes. *The Philosophical Review*, *68*(2), 141–156.

Stepp, N., Chemero, A., & Turvey, M. T. (2011). Philosophy for the rest of cognitive science. *Topics in Cognitive Science*, *3*(2), 425–437.

Strawson, G. (2008). Real materialism. In *Real materialism and other essays*. Oxford, UK: Oxford University Press.

Thagard, P. (1992). *Conceptual revolutions*. Princeton, NJ: Princeton University Press.

Theurer, K. L. (2013). Seventeenth-century mechanism: An alternative framework for reductionism. *Philosophy of Science*, *80*(5), 907–918.

van Fraassen, B. (1980). *The scientific image*. Oxford, UK: Oxford University Press.

van Gelder, T. (1995). What might cognition be, if not computation? *Journal of Philosophy*, *91*, 345–381.

Wallace, M. (2011). Composition as identity: Part 1. *Philosophy Compass*, *6*(11), 804–816.

Weinberg, S. (1994). *Dreams of a final theory*. New York, NY: Random House.

Weiskopf, D. A. (2011). Models and mechanisms in psychological explanation. *Synthese*, *183*(3), 313–338.

Wimsatt, W. C. (2007). *Piecewise approximations to reality: Engineering a philosophy of science for limited beings*. Cambridge, MA: Harvard University Press.

Woodward, J. (1989). The causal/mechanical model of explanation. In P. Kitcher & W. C. Salmon (eds.), *Scientific explanation (Minnesota studies in the philosophy of science)* (pp. 357–383). Minneapolis, MN: University of Minnesota Press.

Woodward, J. (2013). II—Mechanistic explanation: Its scope and limits. In *Aristotelian society supplementary volume* (Vol. 87, No. 1, pp. 39–65). London, UK: Blackwell Publishing.

Woodward, J. (2014). Scientific explanation. In E. N. Zalta (ed.), *The Stanford encyclopedia of philosophy* (Fall 2017 edition). https://plato.stanford.edu/archives/fall2017/entries/scientific-explanation/

5 The Explanatory Gap and Consciousness

Following the influential work of Joseph Levine (1983), it is often said that with regards to consciousness we are faced with an *explanatory gap*. If the locution "explanatory gap" is meant to denote the fact that we do not *yet* have a complete physical theory of consciousness, then postulating the existence of an explanatory gap is an uncontroversial claim. But that is not how the explanatory gap often figures in philosophical discussions pertaining to consciousness and physicalism. Indeed, the claim that there is an explanatory gap quickly becomes *the* crucial premise in a variety of arguments that seek to establish either conclusions about our epistemic abilities or conclusions about the ontological nature of consciousness. Thus, even though the explanatory gap is first presented as an uncontentious claim—one that we are all enjoined to accept—in reality, it is a loaded philosophical claim. Two features of the explanatory gap as it is used in philosophical discourse make this evident. First, the gap is often assumed to be permanent and not temporary. Second, the gap is typically seen as bridgeable *only* if one can show that truths about consciousness are a priori deduced from (or somehow conceptually connected to) truths about its physical (biological, neuronal) nature. These two features often run together. If the explanatory gap can be bridged only if truths about consciousness are shown to be logically or conceptually connected to truths about its physical nature, then the absence of such connections is evidence for the claim that the gap cannot, even in principle, be bridged.

It should be clear that, in order for the existence of the gap to be a cause of concern for physicalists, it must be a permanent feature of all physicalistically acceptable theoretical attempts to understand consciousness. This, we believe, is an important point that often, however, recedes in the background of discussions about the viability of physicalism. Stated otherwise, the explanatory gap is an issue for physicalism only if either physicalism can never overcome it or any solution to the gap is such that requires a major revision of physicalism's ontological commitments. In philosophical discussions of consciousness, at least in those aimed to expose difficulties with physicalism, the explanatory gap is then seen as a limitation of our cognitive abilities and explanatory practices that is necessarily associated with the adoption of a physicalist outlook.

1. The Explanatory Gap in Action

1.1. A Brief Look at the Literature

The belief that the explanatory gap is permanent is widespread in the literature on physicalism and specifically, in writings that purport either to object to physicalism or to showcase its limitations. To begin with, consider how Thomas Nagel describes the difficulty that physicalism faces when it comes to explaining the phenomenal character of consciousness. He writes:

> If physicalism is to be defended, the phenomenological features must themselves be given a physical account. But when we examine their subjective character it seems that such a result is impossible. The reason is that every subjective phenomenon is essentially connected with a single point of view, and it seems inevitable that an objective, physical theory will abandon that point of view.
>
> (1974, p. 437)

Nagel asserts that a defense of physicalism requires that physicalism will eventually bridge the explanatory gap. However, given physicalism's unwavering commitment to offering descriptions of the workings of the mind from a third-person (objective) perspective, he concludes that the qualitative nature of mentality lies beyond the reach of physicalism (see, however, pp. 449–450). Truths about consciousness are subjective and as such, an understanding of them requires the adoption of a specific point of view. On the contrary, truths of science can be understood from different points of view and, indeed, such truths are objective precisely because their understanding does not depend on the adoption of a *particular* point of view. Consciousness' subjective character thus turns out to be incongruous with attempts to render consciousness physical. To understand consciousness we need subjectivity, but physicalism only gives us objectivity. The explanatory gap that physicalism faces is not contingent upon our current epistemic situation, but rather a product of physicalism's character and specifically, its commitment to objective descriptions.

Frank Jackson's (1982, 1986) "knowledge argument" is even more explicit in making the claim that, as long as we remain committed to a physicalistic ontology, the explanatory gap will not dissipate. Jackson asks us to imagine a brilliant scientist, Mary, who from birth has been kept confined in a black-and-white room and never had any colored experience (not even colored dreams, afterimages, or hallucinations). Mary is unique not only in terms of her experiential history, but also in her incredible capacity for knowledge. In fact, Jackson postulates that Mary has been able to learn all that there is to know about the physical nature of the world. He writes:

> She knows all the physical facts about us and our environment, in a wide sense of "physical" which includes everything in *completed* physics,

> chemistry, and neurophysiology, and all there is to know about the causal and relational facts consequent upon all this, including of course functional roles.
>
> (Jackson, 1986, p. 291; emphasis in original)

In the hands of Jackson, Mary's hypothetical existence is quickly turned into an argument against physicalism. According to Jackson, the truth of physicalism entails that a subject such as Mary, i.e., a subject who is an ideal reasoner and knows all physical facts, ought to know *all* facts. "For to suppose otherwise," Jackson writes, "is to suppose that there is more to know than every physical fact, and that is just what physicalism denies" (ibid.). But Mary, Jackson insists, does not know all that there is to know. Some facts escape her. Which ones? Those which pertain to the subjective character of colored experiences. Mary has never seen a red object, for instance, in her room and, according to Jackson, if Mary is shown a red tomato she will learn something new. She will come to learn what it is like to have a red experience. But if so, then physical facts do not exhaust all facts and consequently, physicalism is false. Whatever one makes of Jackson's argument, it is clear that the argument requires the permanence of the explanatory gap. Mary, we are told, knows "*everything* there is to know about the physical nature of the world" and yet she still does not know everything about consciousness (ibid.; emphasis added). What Mary's case illustrates is that there is more to consciousness that what a complete physical story of the world can ever give us. This supposition about the limits of our scientific understanding of the world both lies at the heart of the knowledge argument and is an expression of the permanence of the explanatory gap. Indeed, if the knowledge argument did not require the permanence of the explanatory gap then either Mary would have complete phenomenal knowledge in her black-and-white room or she would still lack such knowledge but only because of some fact specific to her situation. In the former case, the knowledge argument would be of no concern to physicalists. In the latter case, the knowledge argument would fail to show that Mary's epistemic situation is indicative of our inability to scientifically explain consciousness.

The conceivability argument against physicalism operates on a similar assumption. A popular version of the argument is premised on the observation that it is conceivable that there could be a world that is in every physical (or microphysical) respect identical to ours, but which differs in some phenomenal (or conscious-related) respect. If such a world is conceivable, then, the argument goes, such a world is possible. Physicalism, however, is widely thought to be inconsistent with the possibility of such a world. If consciousness is composed entirely of physical parts and is nothing over and above those parts, then it must exist in all worlds that contain brains like ours (for some complications surrounding this point, see Chalmers, 2010). Hence, the possibility of a world that is in all physical respects identical to ours but differs in some phenomenal respect cannot be rendered consistent with physicalism (Chalmers, 1996, 2010; Kirk, 1974a, 1974b; Kripke, 1980). What such a possibility demonstrates is that there is more to consciousness than its physical components.

In the literature, one finds many different articulations of this sort of conceivability argument against physicalism. Nobody, however, has done more than David Chalmers to develop and defend this argument. For that reason, we focus our attention on Chalmers's presentation of the argument (Chalmers, 2002, 2010). Letting "*P*" stand for the conjunction of all physical truths about the world expressed in the fundamental (microphysical) vocabulary of a true and complete physical theory, "*T*" for a "that's all" claim stating that what is expressed in *P* is the complete description of our world, "*I*" for basic indexical information, and "*Q*" for any true claim about phenomenal states (cf. Chalmers & Jackson, 2001), a version of the argument can be presented as follows:

Premise 1. It is ideally conceivable that *PIT* & ~*Q*.
Premise 2. If it is ideally conceivable that *PIT* & ~*Q*, then it is possible that *PIT* & ~*Q*.
Premise 3. If it is possible that *PIT* & ~*Q*, then physicalism is false.
Conclusion. Physicalism is false.

We should note that our presentation of the argument somewhat simplifies Chalmers' position. Among other things, he formulates the argument using the resources of two-dimensional semantics and as such he distinguishes between primary and secondary conceivability and possibility. Although important for the argument, such a distinction can be put aside for present purposes. The point that we wish to make is that the first premise of the argument is another expression of the claim that the explanatory gap is permanent. If *PIT* & ~*Q* is ideally conceivable, then even if we know all that there is to know about physics, neuroscience, and biology,[1] then consciousness would still appear to be essentially disconnected from its physical (biological or neuronal) substratum. After all, *PIT* is not an expression of our current physical knowledge, but a massive (perhaps, infinitely long) conjunction of truths about the world expressed in physical language. *P* gives us *everything that we will ever be able to get* using physics (and perhaps all other sciences). Just like the knowledge argument, Chalmers's conceivability argument requires that the explanatory gap that proponents of physicalism face is a permanent one.[2]

What is more, many of the claims that Levine makes about the explanatory gap can be read in support of the permanent character of the explanatory gap. For instance, in his original (1983) formulation of the explanatory gap, Levine compares statements that are "fully explanatory" to ones that are not. For example, a statement like "Heat is the motion of molecules" is fully explanatory insofar as its acceptance leaves no questions unanswered about its subject matter. Once we come to understand the workings of molecules, we have explained all that there is to explain about heat.

However, when we turn our attention to psychophysical identifications—or more broadly, to statements that purport to account for the emergence of consciousness out of non-conscious material—"there is a 'gap' in the explanatory import of those statements" (p. 357). Why is this? According to Levine, all such statements or accounts of the connection between mind and brain leave the very connection that they purport to explain unexplained. They do not explain *why* the activation of a particular neurological assemblage feels a certain way. Instead, they simply posit that as a primitive fact. The claim, for example, "pain is neurological activation φ" does not explain *why* pain is a neurological phenomenon; it asserts it. Although Levine's claim can be understood as a description of our current situation with regard to consciousness (viz., we currently lack the means of accounting for why pain is a neurological phenomenon), it is tempting to read Levine's position as being committed to the claim that the explanatory gap is one that is a necessary feature of our scientific (and, for Levine, causal or functional) understanding of consciousness. Just like Nagel, Levine holds that even though our scientific theories can capture the causal or functional role of consciousness, they cannot explain the subjective (and qualitative) features of consciousness. Indeed, if scientific theories are committed to causal or functional accounts, then it follows, on Levine's view, that our scientific theories will always lack the means to account for the subjective or qualitative character of conscious experiences. The gap, in other words, is a permanent one.[3]

A fourth and final example of the view that the explanatory gap is permanent is found in Galen Strawson's argument in support of the conclusion that "real physicalism . . . entails panexperientialism or panpsychism" (2008, p. 71). Strawson does not mention the explanatory gap by name and, admittedly, his focus is metaphysical instead of explanatory or epistemic. Still, his argument is based on our inability to make sense of how consciousness (an experiential phenomenon) can emerge out of wholly non-experiential phenomena. Strawson deems that such an account of emergence is "incoherent" and thus the solution to the difficulty faced by physicalism requires one to accept that experience (in some form) is part of the basic fabric of reality. Such a contention makes clear that Strawson's position is one that requires an expansion of our fundamental ontological categories so that they include proto-experiential or experiential entities. The issue here is that the purported incoherence of the emergence of experiential phenomena from non-experiential phenomena will remain unless one gives up physicalism. In other words, for Strawson, physicalism is forever bound to an inability to understand the emergence of consciousness.

1.2. The Permanence of the Gap

If research program physicalism is successful, then the explanatory gap will eventually disappear. As was made clear in the previous section, arguments against physicalism are rooted precisely in the denial of such a claim. They do not simply maintain that there is an explanatory gap. Rather, and in order to be objections to physicalism, they postulate that physicalism will *always* face an unbridgeable explanatory gap.

But why is that? That is to say, what are the arguments in support of the view that the explanatory gap is, if one assumes the perspective of physicalism, permanent? Jackson's knowledge argument offers no explicit argument for the permanence of the explanatory gap. Instead, it more or less assumes such a feature of the explanatory gap (see also Churchland, 1996; Dennett, 2005). We are asked to accept the possibility of an ideal reasoner who although in possession of all physical knowledge somehow lacks knowledge about the subjective and qualitative character of consciousness. No amount of theorizing, we are told, allows Mary to come to know what it is like to experience red, for example, while she is still in her black-and-white room. As mentioned above, Mary's epistemic situation is an expression of the contention that the explanatory gap is permanent. Her situation is possible only under the assumption that complete physical knowledge does not suffice for complete phenomenal knowledge. But that means that one should accept the possibility of Mary only to the extent that one has reasons to think that the explanatory gap is permanent.

Perhaps one could object that the correct reading of the knowledge argument is not one according to which the acceptance of its key premise (viz., that Mary's epistemic situation is possible) requires the acceptance of the permanence of the explanatory gap. Rather, what the knowledge argument shows is that the fact that we find Mary's epistemic situation plausible is an indication that the explanatory gap is permanent. Understood in this way, the argument might not already presuppose the permanence of the explanatory gap, but it falls short of establishing it. The intuition that Mary's epistemic situation is possible (assuming that we do have this intuition) cannot be utilized to draw any final conclusions about the scope of scientific explanation. Mary's epistemic situation is alien to us and any intuition that we may have about it should not be taken at face value (Dennett, 2005).

If we turn to the conceivability argument, according to one reading of the argument, the permanence of the explanatory gap is also assumed. Recall the first premise of the argument: It is conceivable that there could be a world which is identical to the actual one in all physical respects, but differs in some phenomenal respect. The conceivability of such a scenario requires that phenomenal facts remain disconnected from physical facts, or that consciousness is somehow ungrounded in its physical substratum. If the explanatory gap were not permanent, then one could argue that although *PIT&~Q* is conceivable, it is only *prima facie* conceivable. It is conceivable now, given our limited comprehension of the nature of consciousness, but its conceivability is merely an illusion. The permanence of the explanatory gap is then presupposed by the conceivability argument, insofar as this claim about the nature of the explanatory gap is already built into the (ideal) conceivability premise. We should be quick to underscore that our diagnosis of the conceivability argument is not meant to suggest that proponents of the conceivability argument are incapable of offering independent arguments in support of the permanence of the explanatory gap and in doing so, of bolstering the conceivability premise. Rather, our point is that, by itself, the conceivability argument does not offer us any reasons to think that the explanatory gap is permanent. Additional considerations are needed.

What are then the reasons in support of the claim that physicalism faces a permanent explanatory gap? We identify and discuss four arguments in support of the gap's permanence: (1) *the argument from subjectivity;* (2) *the argument from intersubjectivity*; (3) *the argument from ignorance;* and (4) *the structure and dynamics argument.* The first two will be addressed in this chapter, the last two in the next. These are not the only arguments that one can offer in support of the claim that the explanatory gap is permanent. Still, an evaluation of these arguments and how they are related to the knowledge argument and to the conceivability argument provide a thorough treatment of the relevant philosophical terrain. Even if our treatment is not exhaustive, it is exhaustive enough to motivate the research program.

Although all of these arguments share a similar argumentative structure, they deserve separate treatments. In essence, they all conclude, on the basis of a perceived difference between facts (or presumed facts) about consciousness and facts about physical sciences, that there is an unbridgeable gap between the two. Proponents of the permanence of the explanatory gap do not maintain that we know all that there is to know about the mind and the brain and since there is an explanatory gap right now, the gap will always remain. Rather, they claim that despite our limited comprehension of physics, biology, and neuroscience, we know enough to know that we can never fully explain consciousness in terms of a physical or neurological basis. Obviously, this is a remarkable claim and it must be defended.

2. The Argument From Subjectivity

What we are calling "the argument from subjectivity" is an attempt to capture Nagel's skepticism regarding the prospects of physicalistic approaches to consciousness (see especially Nagel, 1974, p. 437). The argument can be presented in the following form:

> **Premise 1.** Science provides us only with objective truths about consciousness and the world.
> **Premise 2.** Certain truths about consciousness are subjective.
> **Premise 3.** One cannot derive subjective truths from objective truths.
> **Premise 4.** If one cannot derive subjective truths from objective truths, then an account of consciousness that is given solely in objective truths cannot (fully) explain consciousness.
> **Conclusion.** Science cannot (fully) explain consciousness.

What should one make of this argument? The argument is valid (assuming that we do not equivocate on any of our terms), so what remains to be seen is whether it is also sound. But before we can evaluate its soundness, we need to discuss how the subjective/objective distinction figures in the argument.

The subjective/objective distinction can be understood in different ways. It has been applied, for instance, to states (McClelland, 2013, p. 130) or features of the world (Pereboom, 2011, p. 121, n.48), to truths (Nagel, 1974; Stoljar, 2006), and even to theories (Howell, 2007). For the present purposes, the distinction will be understood as one that demarcates two types of truths. Furthermore, following Nagel, we take "objectivity [to be] a method of understanding" (1986, p. 4) and thus the distinction is one that signifies a difference in understanding truths. To wit, we hold that a subjective truth is one that its understanding necessarily requires the taking up of a specific perspective, whereas an objective truth is one for which such a requirement does not hold. Certain truths about consciousness, specifically those pertaining to the qualitative nature of conscious experiences, are subjective truths. To know, for example, what C# sounds like is to know a subjective truth. The same goes for knowing the painfulness of pain, the appearance of the color blue, or the felt roughness of a piece of sandpaper. To be in a position to know those truths is to be able to adopt a particular point of view. In other words, a truth is subjective if its understanding requires the tokening of a particular psychological state. An objective truth is one that denies such a requirement. This articulation of the subjective/objective distinction explains, for instance, why we cannot know, according to Nagel, what it is like to be a bat. We cannot understand (let alone know) truths about the qualitative character of the experience of bats because, insofar as they are subjective, they require the adoption of a perspective that is in principle unavailable to us. Although it is tempting to assimilate this idea of objectivity (as a method of understanding) to the notion of verifiability, we shall keep the two notions distinct (cf. Howell, 2007). The fact that a true sentence *S* is objective, does not guarantee that it is verifiable. Arguably, there are objective physical truths that cannot be verified even in principle. We discuss this issue in the following section where we examine whether verifiability could be used in support of the permanence of the explanatory gap.

Drawn in this way, the subjective/objective distinction forces us to accept premise 2. Consciousness is a vexing issue and it is not often the case that one can make a relatively uncontroversial pronouncement about its nature. But whatever consciousness is, it is a personal phenomenon. To be conscious is, among other things, to take up a (singular) perspective. Unless one is a radical eliminativist about consciousness, one has to accept that consciousness is a subjective phenomenon. Consequently, one has to accept that knowledge of consciousness requires knowledge of subjective truths.

Whereas truths about the phenomenal character of consciousness appear to be subjective, scientific claims and truths do not. Indeed, it seems that scientific claims, in virtue of the fact that they are scientific, are objective: "whatever else may be said of the physical, it has to be objective" (Nagel, 1974, p. 527, n.15). As a consequence, they can be entertained and understood through different perspectives. Such an explication of the distinction makes premise 1 hard to deny. To understand the workings of neurotransmission, for example, one does not have to take a specific perspective: that is to say, there is no *one* point of view—no singular experience, perceptual or imaginary—that allows one to grasp the workings of synaptic transmissions. One can understand neurotransmission by watching a video, by reading a description of its workings, or by listening to a lecture. In light of the foregoing considerations, the fate of the argument from subjectivity appears to rest on premises 3 and 4. But are those two premises true?

Let us start with premise 3. The premise states that subjective truths cannot be derived from objective truths. Any evaluation of this premise needs to articulate the meaning of "derive" as this figures in the premise. So, what do we mean when we say that a truth can be derived from another truth? Although there is no agreed-upon meaning of "derive," it seems appropriate to suggest that, in the context of the argument, "derive" is intended to mean something akin to logical deduction. Accordingly, one can derive phenomenal truths (truths about consciousness' qualitative character) from objective truths if and only if the latter logically or a priori entail the former. Anti-physicalist arguments make much of the claim that no logical connections exist between the two realms. However, in the present context one cannot use those arguments to *argue* for the lack of logical or conceptual connections. The argument from subjectivity is meant to establish the permanence of the explanatory gap, a claim that, as we argued above, is needed both by the knowledge argument and the conceivability argument.

What is more, not everyone agrees that there are *no* logical connections between subjective truths of consciousness and objective (physical or biological) truths. For instance, so-called a priori physicalists and logical behavioralists both deny that there is an explanatory gap between phenomenal truths and physical truths and hold that the two sets of truths are logically connected. Although both of these positions reject premise 3, one cannot cite them as reasons to reject the premise: Not only are they contentious philosophical positions, but to assume them in this context is to beg the question against the proponent of the argument from subjectivity.

A different source of resistance to premise 3 comes from Daniel Stojar's treatment of the notion of objectivity in his *Ignorance and Imagination* (Stoljar, 2006, p. 157). Stoljar argues that there are in fact logical connections between phenomenal truths and what we have been calling "objective" truths. He defends this by offering counterexamples to the purported logical or conceptual independence between subjective (in this case, phenomenal) and objective truths. According to Stoljar, there are statements that connect phenomenal truths to physical truths (or vice versa) and which can be known a priori. Consider, for example, the following two conditional statements:

(1) If Oliver is not alive, then Oliver does not experience pain.
(2) If x is a number, then x is not a red sensation.

If one is already in possession of the relevant concepts (PERSON, PAIN, BEING ALIVE, NUMBER, and SENSATION), then one can come to know the truth of conditionals (1) and (2) without any appeal to experience. But if the previous conditionals are taken to be a priori, then given the operative understanding of the notion of derivation, it is false to hold that no subjective claims can be derived from objective claims.

There is little doubt that Stoljar is correct to maintain that (1) and (2) can be known a priori. Still, the question that Stoljar's position faces is not one about the apriority of those conditionals. Rather, what is at stake are the consequences that one can draw from granting the apriority of conditionals (1) and (2). Specifically, we ought to examine whether it is correct to maintain that the apriority of conditionals (1) and (2) demonstrates that there are logical connections between subjective truths and objective truths that permit us to derive the former from the latter. In other words, can one use Stoljar's examples as an objection to premise 3?

There are at least two reasons that speak against using (1) and (2) as an objection to the argument from subjectivity. First, one could argue that the apriority of the two conditionals does not show that there are logical connections between subjective truths and objective truths because the consequents of the two conditionals do not involve subjective truths. Rather, the objection continues, the consequents involve the negation of a subjective truth, which is itself *not* a subjective truth. Second, one could accept that the apriority of conditionals (1) and (2) demonstrates the existence of some logical connections between subjective truths and objective truths. However, one could add that such logical connections are insufficient to warrant the conclusion that any *interesting* subjective truths can be derived from objective truths. To wit, what examples like (1) and (2) demonstrate is either the existence of certain necessary conditions that connect objective truths to subjective truths (e.g., it is necessary to be alive in order to experience pain) or certain sufficient conditions that connect objective truths to *negative* subjective truths (e.g., being a number suffices for not being a red sensation). The fact that such connections can be known a priori is beside the point. In the context of arguing for the plausibility of a physicalistic explanation of consciousness, one needs to show how *positive* phenomenal truths can be derived (*a priori* entailed or deduced) from objective truths. Conditionals (1) and (2) do nothing of that sort (Diaz-Leon, 2008; Balog, 2009).

We will not engage in a detailed evaluation of these two objections against the use of Stoljar's examples to undermine premise 3. For even if such responses are successful, one still needs to offer reasons as to why there are no a priori connections between objective truths and subjective truths. And it is important to remember that such reasons ought to be independent of the usual anti-physicalist arguments and must amount to more than mere appeal to intuitions. The fact that subjective and objective claims involve different conditions for knowledge does not warrant us to conclude that premise 3 is true.

At this point in the dialectic, it is important to emphasize that the discussion of premise 3 has proceeded so far at a level of abstraction that only benefits the proponents of the argument from subjectivity. When one asks, "Can subjective truths be derived from objective truths?", one is phrasing the issue in a way that makes it hard to see how an affirmative answer could be provided. What subjective truths does one have in mind? And what is exactly the phenomenon that they describe? Our attempts to deal with the explanatory gap cannot afford to leave our explanandum underspecified. As Robert van Gulick notes in his discussion of the explanatory gap, "the more we can articulate the structure within the phenomenal realm, the greater the chances for physical explanation; without structure we have no place to attach our explanatory 'hooks'" (1997, p. 565). Thus, in order to determine whether an aspect of our conscious life can be explained in physical terms, one must first take care to describe it in sufficient detail. For example, we might not currently be in a position to see how complex visual experiences arise out of physical processes, yet we have made great progress in explaining certain (simpler) features of our visual experience in terms of neuronal activity. As mentioned in Chapter 1, perception scientists regularly offer mechanistic explanations of visual illusions (Eagleman, 2001). Clearly, illusions count as subjective phenomena. Thus, to the extent that we have successful explanations of aspects of visual illusions such as Mach bands, the Hermann grid, and many others, we have explanations of subjective truths in terms of objective ones.

A similar observation holds in the case of pain. An appreciation of the phenomenal complexity of pain, allows us to concentrate on specific features of the experience and to investigate how they arise in virtue of the workings of the brain. To give just one example, it is a well-known phenomenon that some kinds of tissue damage give rise to two temporally separated experiences of pain: There is a sharp and localized pain that is followed by a dull and more diffuse pain. The ordering of these two pain experiences can be explained by citing differences in the physiological properties of the two primary afferent fibers (PAFs), A-delta and C, which are responsible for carrying information about the presence of noxious stimuli to the central nervous system. Given their axonal diameter (2–6 μm) and the fact that they are covered with myelin, A-delta fibers have a higher conduction velocity than C fibers that have thinner (0.4–1.2 μm) unmyelinated axons. Thus, even though both fibers respond to the presence of noxious stimuli, A-delta fibers are responsible for the first, sharp experience of pain, whereas C fibers are responsible for the second, temporally delayed, dull experience of pain.

The foregoing considerations do not demonstrate that one can derive subjective truths from objective truths, but they do underline the need for specificity. The more we know about the phenomena that we are called to explain, the better our chances are for explaining them in terms of their physical components. Such an attitude towards the phenomena that are in need of an explanation is an integral part of our version of physicalism. As an interdisciplinary, ongoing research program, physicalism attempts to bridge the explanatory gap not only by developing our biological and neuroscientific theories, but also by requiring us to acknowledge the complexity of our phenomenal experiences. Our attempt to render the physical nature of conscious phenomena intelligible demands that we proceed both bottom-up and top-down. Physicalism, as we understand it, assumes neither that we have a satisfactory understanding of the presumed physical (biological and neuronal) nature of consciousness nor that we are in possession of a perfect (and thus fixed) understanding of consciousness itself—far from it.

Thus, an important difference between Stoljar's (2006) ignorance hypothesis and our position emerges. For Stoljar, what is missing from a complete understanding of the place of consciousness in nature is a type of non-experiential but experience-relevant truth. The research program makes no such assumption. It is consistent with the research program that further non-experiential *and* experiential truths (i.e., truths pertaining to the phenomenal character of consciousness) are needed in order to finally bridge the explanatory gap. To use again Van Gulick's (1997) term, such experiential truths might be the explanatory or conceptual "hooks" that currently escape us. To presuppose that the only truths missing are non-experiential is to accept that our present understanding of phenomenal consciousness is more or less complete—no substantial changes will come about. From the perspective of research program physicalism, such a view is unacceptable for it contradicts its basic methodology. Of course, physicalism as a research program does not insist that a profound change in our understanding of consciousness is forthcoming; nor does it demand that such a change is required in order to bridge the explanatory gap. Research program physicalism merely maintains that it is a mistake to try to settle this issue a priori.

In addition to its commitment to a flexible, co-evolutionary approach in the study of consciousness, our version of physicalism brings something else to the table. Research program physicalism neither demands that there are logical connections between subjective truths and objective truths nor denies it. This issue is irrelevant from the perspective of the research program. What it denies however is that an explanation of consciousness requires logical deduction of some sort. Stated otherwise, although research program physicalism neither endorses nor rejects premise 3, it does reject the truth of premise 4, *if derivation is understood as involving logical deduction*. Research program physicalism rejects that a physicalistic explanation of consciousness is available only if truths about consciousness can be a priori deduced from truths about consciousness' neurological substratum and function. As we argued in the previous chapter, a compositional explanation is not subject to such a requirement. Although a compositional explanation of consciousness explains it in terms of the interaction of its components, it does not require that one is able to deduce claims about consciousness from claims about its components. The choice between no explanation or an explanation that involves a priori entailment is a false choice, one abetted by an outdated model of scientific explanation, overly demanding metaphysical claims, or both.

Once we give up the idea that an explanation of consciousness requires that subjective truths of consciousness are a priori entailed by objective, physical truths, then the subjective/objective distinction ceases to be an insurmountable obstacle to physical explanations of consciousness. Although it is still the case that the physical (compositional) explanation of consciousness will be given in purely objective truths, such objective truths can give rise to subjective truths about consciousness. Subjective truths might not be the logical consequences of our physical explanations but they will follow from them nonetheless. If a compositional explanation of consciousness is achieved, then consciousness is shown, in an explanatory sense, to be nothing over and above its components. Consciousness' place in nature is rendered intelligible by explaining the workings of its parts. Thus, if we have sufficient reason to think that we have given a compositional explanation of consciousness, then we have shown how objective truths amount to subjective truths. Subjectivity will be one of those "novel" features that the whole has but the parts lack (see previous chapter). To be clear, the research program does not insist that a compositional explanation is guaranteed. But as long as there are no decisive reasons to think that the explanatory gap is permanent, the research program has a license to operate. In sum, because of the research program's commitment to compositional explanations as these are found in *actual* scientific practice, it does not require that phenomenal (subjective) truths must be a priori entailed by physical (objective) truths. As a result, premise 4 can be rejected and the subjective/objective distinction does not by itself put a stop on the research program.[4]

We are expecting, of course, pushback. Anti-physicalists (and perhaps even some physicalists) would object that without metaphysical (or logical) connections, one could never be sure that consciousness is nothing over and above the physical. For instance, if it is possible that there could be a world with brains like ours but without consciousness, then consciousness is not *just* physical. However, if there are metaphysical (or logical) connections between truths of consciousness and truths about its physical substratum, then such a scenario is not possible. Metaphysical (or logical) connections is the presumed glue that binds the mind to matter and in doing so renders the former nothing over and above the latter.

Such a response, we contend, fails to take seriously the research program approach. There are two claims that are important for the research program and unappreciated by this response. First, the research program does not require a metaphysical reduction of the mental to the physical. As we have discussed in Chapter 2, it is unclear whether there is a way of showing that the mental is nothing over and above the physical, if the notion of nothing-and-over-and-aboveness is articulated in metaphysical terms. Instead, the research program utilizes an explanatory notion of nothing-over-and-aboveness: Consciousness is nothing over and above the physical if it can be given a compositional explanation in which its components are physical entities. Since an explanatory approach is ubiquitous in science, we are warranted to believe that it also applies in the case of consciousness. Or at the very least, we are warranted to investigate the possibility of offering a compositional explanation of consciousness.

Second, and relatedly, by shifting the focus from the metaphysical (or the conceptual) to the explanatory, research program physicalism also changes its relationship to non-physicalist, competitor views. Precisely because research program is not a metaphysical position, it is not directly affected by certain metaphysical views or assumptions that traditionally have been thought to be antithetical to physicalism (when understood as a metaphysical view). Indeed, contrary to the widely held belief that physicalism is committed to either a metaphysical or logical relationship between the physical and the mental *in order* for physicalism to be distinguished from dualism, research program physicalism denies the need for either type of relationship. Research program physicalism requires that in the actual world we can offer a compositional explanation of consciousness. Because the demands of research program physicalism are restricted to the actual world, it posits only nomological connections between the physical and the mental. Dualism is, of course, consistent with nomological connections between the two. All the same, the two positions can be meaningfully distinguished. From the perspective of research program physicalism, dualism is understood to be a competing research program: a different interdisciplinary approach that aims to explain our place in nature. Consequently, the two can be distinguished and contrasted on the basis of their assumptions and goals as research programs. The superiority of physicalism (as a research program) over dualism (as a research program) will not be demonstrated by the discovery of a priori or metaphysical connections between the physical and the mental. Scientific explanations, we argued, do not postulate such connections. Instead, if research program physicalism is to be chosen over dualism (understood as a research program), it would be on the basis of its virtues qua research program. Ultimately, research program physicalism will win over research program dualism if consciousness no longer figures as something for which we have no physical (compositional) explanation. The same point applies, *mutatis mutandis*, to research program physicalism's relationship to strong emergentism and Russellian monism (see Chapter 8).

3. The Argument From Intersubjectivity

Whereas the argument from subjectivity argues that consciousness cannot be physically explained because of the subjective/objective distinction, the argument from intersubjectivity aims to establish the same conclusion by utilizing a different distinction. It maintains that although truths about the world and our brains are intersubjectively verifiable, truths about the phenomenal nature of our consciousness are not. Precisely because such truths cannot be intersubjectively verified, we can never have a science of consciousness. The argument from intersubjectivity can be presented in the following premises-conclusion form:

Premise 1. Any scientific explanation of a phenomenon must consist of only intersubjectively verifiable statements.
Premise 2. True statements about the phenomenal character of consciousness are not intersubjectively verifiable.
Conclusion. There cannot be a scientific explanation of consciousness.

Some clarifications are in order. First, we shall assume that statements are the entities that, properly speaking, are intersubjectively verifiable or not. Phenomena (or states of affairs) can be said to be intersubjectively verifiable but only derivatively: they are so only insofar as the statements that accurately describe them are intersubjectively verifiable. Second, a statement *S* is said to be intersubjectively verifiable just in case it is possible for two or more subjects to share all evidence that is relevant to the determination of the truth-value of *S*. Stated otherwise, for every *S* that is intersubjectively verifiable, there must be evidence which is sufficient to allow an appropriately informed subject to determine whether the statement is true or false and that evidence must be, at least in principle, accessible to more than one agent.[5] Finally, a statement can be said to be intersubjectively verifi*able* even if it cannot be, as a matter of fact, intersubjectively verifi*ed*. The statement "Jeanne d'Arc sneezed 24 hours before her death" is an intersubjectively verifiable statement even if, let us assume, it cannot be verified.

By and large scientific claims are intersubjectively verifiable. Indeed, a great many of them are ones that have been already verified. Whereas almost all scientific statements are intersubjectively verifiable, no statement about the phenomenal character of our experiences appears to possess this feature. By necessity, it seems, statements about the phenomenal character of consciousness describe something that is first-personal and inaccessible to anyone other than the subject of that consciousness. Consequently, even if we can verify (intersubjectively) whether one's brain is being stimulated in such-and-such manner, we cannot intersubjectively verify that one experiences a certain experience.

What is to be made of this argument? Let us begin by noting that both premises of the argument can be met with skepticism. Against premise 1 one can argue that it is false to maintain that *necessarily* scientific explanations consist of only intersubjectively verifiable statements. There are at least two reasons in support of such a contention. First, one could argue that there could be a science of consciousness, even if this science consists of only first-personal statements. Edmund Husserl, for instance, conceived of phenomenology as a science that aimed to offer a systematic elucidation of the contents and structures of human experience from the first-person perspective. Phenomenology includes its own laws and generalizations (e.g., laws of genesis) and can carry its own methodological principles (e.g., eidetic variation) (Husserl, 1913/1983, 1966/2001).

Second, one could point out that even certain branches of physics contain statements that cannot be intersubjectively verifiable. Cosmology is a case in point. The existence of a multiverse has been presented as a *scientific* solution to the problem of fine-tuning. For instance, Steven Weinberg (1987, 2007) employs the multiverse hypothesis in order to explain the value of the cosmological constant Λ. (For other uses of multiverse, see Rees, 2001.) Weinberg argues that the existence of gravitationally bound systems (galaxies and larger globular clusters) is necessary for the existence of observers. Such a condition sets an upper bound for possible values of Λ: Any value greater than that bound would not permit the existence of gravitationally bound systems. At the same time, there is a lower bound for Λ—if Λ is assigned a large negative number then because it contributes to Einstein's field equations like matter, it would lead to a model of the universe that collapses before the arrival of any observers. Weinberg argues that the expected value of Λ should be the mean of the values of Λ suitable for life. Weinberg's prediction leads to a positive value of Λ within two orders of magnitude of the currently accepted values, compared to estimates by particle physics that are off by up to 120 orders of magnitude (Smeenk, 2013). Weinberg's argument for the calculation of Λ can be used as evidence for the existence of multiverse (Weinberg, 2007; Livio & Rees, 2005). First, Λ can be understood as a random variable whose a priori probability distribution is determined by the laws of physics according to inflationary cosmology. Second, the same mechanism that is thought to be responsible for creating our universe could have given rise to a plurality of "pocket" universes—i.e., universes that are causally isolated from other universes—with different characteristics (e.g., Guth, 2007; Ellis, Kirchner, & Stoeger, 2004). Thus, the proposed existence of a multiverse is related both to a remarkably successful application of the anthropic reasoning and to cosmological inflation. Yet, multiverse proposals cannot be verified, not even in principle. If such universes exist, they stand in causal isolation from each other (Ellis, 2007).

One does not need to entertain exotic possibilities such as the existence of a multiverse to find limits of verification in cosmology. As discussed in detail in papers by George Ellis and others, relativistic cosmology is bound to make assumptions that are unverifiable (see, e.g., Ellis, 1980). For one, cosmological models assume that the laws of physics apply throughout the universe. Yet, such an assumption is unverifiable. Furthermore, the Friedmann-Lemaître-Robertson-Walker metric (FLRW), which is a solution of Einstein's relativistic field equations, starts with the assumption that the universe is spatially homogeneous and isotropic.[6] Most cosmologists accept that the universe is well described by some *model* of the universe that relies on the FLRW metric (Debono & Smoot, 2016). If so, then (standard) cosmological modeling is founded upon assumptions regarding the global structure of the universe that cannot be verified and that are even inductively suspect (Wald, 1984; Norton, 2011).[7] Indeed, drawing upon the work of Clark Glymour (1977) and David Malament (1977), John B. Manchak (2009, 2011) has argued that in almost every space-time obeying general relativity (causally bizarre space-times notwithstanding), no amount of observational data that we could ever amass could force us to accept one and only cosmological model. This is an important result because it holds even if we assume (a) that our physical theories apply universally, (b) that the full metric structure of our local space-time is determined, and (c) that there are eternal observers (see Butterfield, 2014; Malament, 1977). Finally, given what we know about the geometry and the rate of the expansion of our universe, there are parts of the universe that will never enter into our observable universe: They are currently beyond our particle horizon and will stay that way. Still, cosmology contains statements about the unobservable universe.

What can a proponent of the argument from intersubjectivity say in response to these two objections to premise 1? In response to the first objection, the proponent could deny that Husserlian phenomenology—and indeed any other first-personal study of consciousness—is, properly speaking, a science. Note, however, that the proponent of the argument cannot conclude that such an enterprise is not scientific merely on the grounds that the enterprise deals with the nature of consciousness. Such a response already presupposes the conclusion of the argument. The proponent of the argument thus has to provide independent considerations—ones that do not directly relate to the fact that consciousness is the object of study—that demonstrate that first-personal investigations into the nature of consciousness are unscientific. It is not clear, however, that such criteria are readily available (Chalmers, 1996, Ch. 6).

Alternatively, the proponent of the argument could offer a weaker response. That is, one need not deny that first-personal investigations into the nature of consciousness are scientific. Rather, one only needs to maintain that they are not scientific in the sense that is of relevance here. In other words, the issue is not whether there can be a systematic investigation of the nature of consciousness and the immanent structures of our experience from the first person perspective, but whether consciousness can be explained by a physical theory. Husserlian phenomenology or other first-personal studies of consciousness do nothing to support the latter claim. Such a response is of course correct in maintaining that first-personal studies of consciousness do not offer a *physical* explanation of consciousness. Still, this fact does not exclude them from being either a part of a physical explanation of consciousness or compatible with such an explanation. In other words, the fact that an investigation of a target phenomenon may involve intersubjectively unverifiable statements does not ipso facto render it unscientific. And although the existence of such statements may not provide immediate help for the physicalists' cause, they certainly do not hurt it.

In response to the second objection, the proponent can deny that intersubjectively unverifiable statements should be included in our scientific theories. Although available, such a dialectical move is ultimately unattractive. First, in the case of cosmology, it would render large parts of our scientific edifice unscientific. Such an attitude might perhaps be acceptable when it comes to the hypothesis of a multiverse. However, it will be met with resistance when it comes to various assumptions that govern our cosmological FLRW model—especially in light of the predictive power of such a model and the observational evidence that we have amassed in favor of it (see Smeenk, 2013). Second, the attitude of rendering intersubjectively unverifiable statements unscientific rests on a positivist conception of science that clashes with contemporary practice. Consider, for example, the following claims:

> The test of a physical theory is not that everything in it should be observable and every prediction it makes should be testable, but rather that enough is observable and enough predictions are testable to give us confidence that the theory is right.
>
> (Weinberg, 2007, p. 39)

> [I]f a theory has testable and falsifiable predictions in the observable parts of the universe, we should seriously consider and be prepared to accept its predictions in parts of the universe (or multiverse) that are not accessible to direct observation.
>
> (Livio & Rees, 2005, p. 1023)

The attitudes expressed by Weinberg and Livio and Rees are not uncommon amongst physicists. Yet, they are hard to reconcile with premise 1. Thus, if scientists are willing to accept claims that are not testable as part of their theories, then the scientific status of such claims is not determined by whether they are verifiable or not.

In light of such difficulties, the proponent of the argument could offer a different and somewhat more conciliatory response. The proponent could allow that *some* scientific statements are intersubjectively unverifiable and still insist that this admission does nothing to ameliorate the force of the argument from intersubjectivity. Statements about the phenomenal character of consciousness are *all* intersubjectively unverifiable—they are so by their very nature—but the vast majority of scientific statements are not. There is still an important dissimilarity between the two classes of statements, and this suggests, the proponent can hold, that consciousness cannot be explained in physical terms.

Whatever the merits of the previous responses may be, it is clear, we think, that the proponent of the argument cannot state premise 1 as if it is a premise that meets catholic acceptance. But of course premise 1 is not the sole premise of the argument. So, even if the proponent of the argument could respond to objections to premise 1, it still remains to be seen whether the proponent could also succeed in defending premise 2. And such a premise is faced with an obvious worry: It appears to be false that we cannot intersubjectively verify claims about the character of one's phenomenal character. Don't we know, for instance, that anesthesia induces lack of consciousness? Don't we know that certain type of peripheral stimulation brings about the experience of pain?

It may appear that the proponent of the argument has an obvious response to this objection. The proponent can insist that the objection just offered misunderstands the argument. To object to premise 2 by noting that one can intersubjectively verify a true sentence about the phenomenal experience of a subject through physical means is to misuse the notion of intersubjective verification. What one can intersubjectively verify, the proponent of the argument would point out, is only that a certain type of neural stimulation or activation occurs. What one cannot intersubjectively verify is whether and how the pain is experienced by the subject. The required evidence that would render such a statement about one's experience verifiable is unique and accessible only via one perspective. By the very nature of the phenomenon that they seek to describe, true statements about one's phenomenal consciousness are intersubjectively unverifiable.

Although such a response blocks the initial objection, it paves the way for a different one. Recall that the aim of the argument is to demonstrate that the explanatory gap that we are facing is a permanent one. The argument's method of establishing this claim is by showing that there cannot be a proper science of consciousness because claims about consciousness are not intersubjectively verifiable. But now it seems that in order for the argument to go through the notion of intersubjective verifiability has to be understood in a manner that renders the argument circular: It has to already presuppose the permanence of the explanatory gap. Let us explain.

If intersubjectively verifiable is used as the proponent of the argument intends it, then statements about the phenomenal character of one's experience turn out to be intersubjectively unverifiable only if first-personal evidence for the occurrence (or character) of an experience *E* is not epistemically (or explanatorily) on a par to neurophysiological evidence for the occurrence (or character) of the same experience *E*. In other words, premise 2 is committed to the claim that the first-person perspective offers to a subject an evidential status that it can never be captured by a third-person description of the situation. Such a claim, however, is a tacit acceptance of the permanence of the explanatory gap. One is already assuming that the nature of consciousness can never be fully captured by a physical description. Consequently, if the notion of intersubjective verifiability already contains the idea that first-person evidential grounds are not only unique and irreducible to third-person evidential grounds but also the only grounds that can justify true phenomenal statements, then of course the explanatory gap is not going to be bridged. But given that the argument from intersubjectivity is offered as a way of demonstrating the permanence of the explanatory gap, the suggested understanding of intersubjective verification turns out to be unacceptable. Initial appearances to the contrary, the argument offers us no reasons to accept the claim that the explanatory gap is a permanent one.

Notes

1. For ease of explication, and only for that reason, we are assuming here that truths of neuroscience and biology can be deduced from truths of physics and thus one can consider them to be a part of *P*. Although we do not hold this position (see Elpidorou, 2014), we are not begging any questions by assuming it. In fact, if truths of biology cannot be a priori entailed by the true statements contained in *P*, then the conceivability argument, by itself, would be incapable of demonstrating the falsity of physicalism. If there is an epistemic (or explanatory) gap between truths of microphysics and truths of biology but no corresponding ontological gap, then an epistemic (or explanatory) gap between physical truths and phenomenal truths cannot be taken as indicative of an ontological gap between physical entities (or matter) and consciousness.
2. To state that the argument requires that the explanatory gap is permanent does not mean that it assumes it. For a discussion of an argument in support of the permanence of the gap that is usually given in the context of the conceivability argument, see Chapter 6, Section 3.
3. The claim here is not that Levine is necessarily committed to the permanence of the explanatory gap. Rather, the claim is that an understanding of the explanatory gap as permanent seems to be a natural extension of his position. Indeed, some of Levine's remarks elsewhere lend credence to extending his view in such a way. For instance, in his review of Stoljar's *Ignorance and Imagination* he writes the following: "I see the conceivability and knowledge arguments as symptoms of our not knowing how to even go about empirically studying conscious experience, and thus it is the 'empirical problem'—a very deep philosophical problem as well—that is the core problem of experience" (2008, pp. 229–230). Although Levine does not explicitly embrace the permanence of the explanatory gap in this passage, one could argue that if we do not know "how to even go about empirically" to study consciousness, then the problem of consciousness is not one that will be going away. Perhaps more tellingly, when discussing Jackson's knowledge argument in *Purple Haze*, Levine accepts that Mary, despite her impressive knowledge, would still not be in a position to explain the character of her colored experience in terms of physical processes (2001, p. 77). See also 2001, pp. 7–8 and 93–96.
4. There is at least another possible understanding of the notion of derivation that one may choose to employ in in this context. By "derive" one could mean that one can ***both*** generate and justify subjective truths on the basis of objective truths. That is, somehow by entertaining objective/physical truths, one can generate the subjective/phenomenal truths that follow as a logical consequence. If "derive" is understood in this manner, then premise 3 has to be accepted as true. It is not the case (or at any rate, it does not appear to true) that by *simply* entertaining the claims of science, one will get to the subjective facts of consciousness. The concepts needed to understand subjective claims are not already included in objective claims. But such a reading of premise 3 does not help the argument: It makes premise 4 all the more improbable. No other science places a similar requirement

on the nature of explanation. To offer a compositional explanation of some chemical phenomenon in terms of its physical components one needs to be in possession of the relevant concepts, both at the chemical and physical level. One does not somehow and miraculously proceed from the physical to the chemical.

5. Derk Pereboom discusses a related notion based on Feigl (1958). He writes: "X *is rationally intersubjectively accessible* just in case X's existence and defining properties (or essence) can be known either directly through observations that any subject with a reasonably powerful sensory apparatus could make, or indirectly through deduction, or abduction from such observations and background conditions" (Pereboom, 2011, p. 118).
6. The assumption that the universe is both homogeneous and isotropic is often called the "Cosmological Principle" and follows from the Copernican Principle which holds that we are not privileged observers in the universe (Ellis, 1984, p. 98).
7. There are alternative models that do not assume that the universe is homogeneous. For a discussion of those models, see Debono and Smoot (2016).

References

Balog, K. (2009). Phenomenal concepts. In B. McLaughlin, A. Beckermann, & S. Walter (eds.), *The Oxford handbook in the philosophy of mind* (pp. 292–312). New York, NY: Oxford University Press.

Butterfield, J. (2014). On under-determination in cosmology. *Studies in History and Philosophy of Science Part B: Studies in History and Philosophy of Modern Physics*, 46, 57–69.

Chalmers, D. J. (1996). *The conscious mind: In search of a fundamental theory*. New York: Oxford University Press.

Chalmers, D. J. (2002). Does conceivability entail possibility? In T. Gendler & J. Hawthorne (eds.), *Conceivability and possibility* (pp. 145–200). Oxford, UK: Oxford University Press.

Chalmers, D. J. (2010). The two-dimensional argument against materialism. In *The character of consciousness* (pp. 141–207). Oxford, UK: Oxford University Press.

Chalmers, D. J., & Jackson, F. (2001). Conceptual analysis and reductive explanation. *The Philosophical Review*, *110*(3), 315–360.

Churchland, P. S. (1996). The hornswoggle problem. *Journal of Consciousness Studies*, *3*(56), 402–408.

Debono, I., & Smoot, G. F. (2016). General relativity and cosmology: Unsolved questions and future directions. *Universe*, *2*(4), 23. doi: 10.3390/universe2040023

Dennett, D. (2005). *Sweet dreams: Philosophical obstacles to a science of consciousness*. Cambridge, MA: MIT Press.

Diaz-Leon, E. (2008). Defending the phenomenal concept strategy. *Australasian Journal of Philosophy*, *86*(4), 597–610.

Eagleman, D. M. (2001). Visual illusions and neurobiology. *Nature Reviews Neuroscience*, *2*(12), 920–926.

Ellis, G. F. R. (1980). Limits to verification in cosmology. *Annals of the New York Academy of Sciences*, *336*(1), 130–160.

Ellis, G. F. R. (1984). Cosmology and verifiability. In R. S. Cohen & M. W. Wartofsky (eds.), *Physical sciences and history of physics (Boston studies in the philosophy of science, volume 82)* (pp. 93–114). Dordrecht: D. Reidel.

Ellis, G. F. R. (2007). Issues in the philosophy of cosmology. In J. Butterfield & J. Earman (eds.), *Handbook of the philosophy of physics* (pp. 1183–1286). Oxford: Elsevier.

Ellis, G. F. R., Kirchner, U., & Stoeger, W. R. (2004). Multiverses and physical cosmology. *Monthly Notices of the Royal Astronomical Society*, *347*(3), 921–936.

Elpidorou, A. (2014). Blocking the a priori passage. *Acta Analytica*, *29*(3), 285–307.

Feigl, H. (1958). The "mental" and the "physical." In H. Feigl, M. Scriven, & G. Maxwell (eds.), *Concepts, theories and the mind-body problem: Minnesota studies in the philosophy of science* (Vol. 2, pp. 370–497). Minneapolis, MN: University of Minneapolis Press.

Glymour, C. (1977). Indistinguishable space-times and the fundamental group. In J. Earman, C. Glymour, & J. Statchel (eds.), *Foundations of space-time theories, Minnesota studies in the philosophy of science* (Vol. 8, pp. 50–60). Minneapolis: University of Minnesota Press.

Guth, A. H. (2007). Eternal inflation and its implications. *Journal of Physics A: Mathematical and Theoretical*, *40*(25), 6811–6826. doi: 10.1088/1751-8113/40/25/S25

Howell, R. J. (2007). The knowledge argument and objectivity. *Philosophical Studies*, *135*(2), 145–177.

Husserl, E. (1913/1983). *Ideen zu einer reinen Phänomenologie und phänomenologischen Philosophie. Erstes Buch: Allgemeine Einführung in die reine Phänomenologie*, K. Schuhman (ed.), Hua III, 1976, The Hague: Martinus Nijhoff, 1976; *Ideas I: Ideas for a pure phenomenology and phenomenological philosophy* (F. Kersten, Trans.). Dordrecht: Springer.

Husserl, E. (1966/2001). *Analysen zur passiven Synthesis. Aus Vorlesungs-und Forschungsmanuskripten, 1918–1926*, M. Fleischer (ed.), Hua XI, The Hague: Martinus Nijhoff; *Analyses concerning passive and active synthesis* (A. J. Steinbock, Trans.). Boston: Kluwer Academic Publishers.

Jackson, F. (1982). Epiphenomenal qualia. *Philosophical Quarterly*, *32*(127), 127–136.

Jackson, F. (1986). What Mary didn't know. *The Journal of Philosophy*, *83*(5), 291–295.

Kirk, R. (1974a). Sentience and behaviour. *Mind*, *83*(329), 43–60.

Kirk, R. (1974b). Zombies v. materialists. *Proceedings of the Aristotelian Society*, *48*(Suppl.), 135–152.

Kripke, S. (1980). *Naming and necessity*. Cambridge, MA: Harvard University Press.

Levine, J. (1983). Materialism and qualia: The explanatory gap. *Pacific Philosophical Quarterly*, *64*(4), 354–361.

Levine, J. (2001). *Purple haze: The puzzle of consciousness*. New York, NY: Oxford University Press.

Levine, J. (2008). Daniel Stoljar: Ignorance and imagination: The epistemic origin of the problem of consciousness. *Mind*, *117*(465), 228–231.

Livio, M., & Rees, M. J. (2005). Anthropic reasoning. *Science*, *309*(5737), 1022–1023.

Malament, D. (1977). Observationally indistinguishable space-times. In J. Earman, C. Glymour, & J. Statchel (eds.), *Foundations of space-time theories, Minnesota studies in the philosophy of science* (Vol. 8, pp. 61–80). Minneapolis: University of Minnesota Press.

Manchak, J. B. (2009). Can we know the global structure of spacetime? *Studies in History and Philosophy of Science Part B: Studies in History and Philosophy of Modern Physics*, *40*(1), 53–56.

Manchak, J. B. (2011). What is a physically reasonable space-time? *Philosophy of Science*, *78*(3), 410–420.

McClelland, T. (2013). The neo-Russellian ignorance hypothesis a hybrid account of phenomenal consciousness. *Journal of Consciousness Studies*, *20*(3–4), 125–151.

Nagel, T. (1974). What is it like to be a bat? *The Philosophical Review*, *83*(4), 435–450.

Nagel, T. (1986). *The view from nowhere*. New York, NY: Oxford University Press.

Norton, J. D. (2011). Observationally indistinguishable spacetimes: A challenge for any inductivist. In G. J. Morgan (ed.), *Philosophy of science matters: The philosophy of Peter Achinstein* (pp. 164–176). Oxford, UK: Oxford University Press.

Pereboom, D. (2011). *Consciousness and the prospects of physicalism*. Oxford, UK: Oxford University Press.

Rees, M. (2001). *Our cosmic habitat*. Princeton, NJ: Princeton University Press.

Smeenk, C. (2013). Philosophy of cosmology. In R. Batterman (ed.), *The Oxford handbook of philosophy of physics* (pp. 607–652). Oxford, UK: Oxford University Press.

Stoljar, D. (2006). *Ignorance and imagination: The epistemic origin of the problem of consciousness*. Oxford, UK: Oxford University Press.

Strawson, G. (2008). *Real materialism and other essays*. Oxford, UK: Oxford University Press.

van Gulick, R. (1997). Understanding the phenomenal mind: Are we all just armadillos? Part I: Phenomenal knowledge and explanatory gaps. In N. Block, O. Flanagan, & G. Güzeldere (eds.), *The nature of consciousness: Philosophical debates* (pp. 559–566). Cambridge, MA: MIT Press.

Wald, R. (1984). *General relativity*. Chicago: University of Chicago Press.

Weinberg, S. (1987). Anthropic bound on the cosmological constant. *Physical Review Letters*, *59*(22), 2607–2610. doi: 10.1103/PhysRevLett.59.2607

Weinberg, S. (2007). Living in the multiverse. In B. Carr (ed.), *Universe of multiverse?* (pp. 29–42). Cambridge, UK: Cambridge University Press.

6 Ignorance and Knowledge

In the previous chapter, we considered two attempts to establish the permanence of the explanatory gap both of which employed a distinction between truths about consciousness and truths about the physical. Those attempts, we argued, are unsuccessful: They fail to demonstrate that the explanatory gap will necessarily persist. But even if the shortcomings of those two attempts are acknowledged, our job is not complete. There are additional ways in which one could attempt to establish the permanence of the explanatory gap. And if any of those are successful, then physicalism as a research program would be in jeopardy.

The aim of this chapter is to continue our investigation into potential reasons for thinking that the explanatory gap is permanent. As mentioned in Chapter 5, we shall address two additional arguments. These are the argument from ignorance and the argument from structure and dynamics. The label "the argument from ignorance" will not be used to refer to any specific argument but to a family of arguments all of which embody the following two-fold argumentative structure: first, they argue that we are chronically ignorant of some truths about the world; and, second, on account of this ignorance, they conclude that the explanatory gap cannot be bridged. In Sections 1 and 2 of the present chapter, we will examine the prospects of the argument from ignorance by focusing on and evaluating three different versions of the argument.[1] Whereas the argument from ignorance is premised on an irremediable ignorance about some aspect of the world, the argument from structure and dynamics adopts a different strategy. It holds that we know enough about the nature of the physical sciences to know that such sciences will never explain consciousness. The argument from structure and dynamics is presented and evaluated in Section 3.

1. Cognitive Closure and Consciousness

Colin McGinn (1989) has argued that, as human beings, we are cognitively closed with respect to a theory that will make the relationship between mind and brain intelligible. To be cognitive closed with respect to a theory *T* means to be incapable of ever forming the concepts that will allow one to understand *T*. Although McGinn insists that there is a scientific theory, "that describes the link between consciousness and the brain in a way that is no more remarkable (or alarming) than the way we now describe the link between the liver and bile," such a theory is in principle inaccessible to us. McGinn's position is remarkable. Not only does he maintain that we are incapable of ever coming to grips with a solution to the mind-body problem, he also thinks that there is a solution that is, as he puts it, "natural and prosaic" (1989, p. 362). Startling as it may be, McGinn's latter claim is not to the point. What we are concerned with presently is why he thinks that a solution to the mind-body problem is beyond our reach.

McGinn offers the following argument in support of his conclusion:

Premise 1. "[T]here exists some property *P*, instantiated by the brain, in virtue of which, the brain is the basis of consciousness. Equivalently, there exists some theory *T*, referring to *P*, which fully explains the dependence of conscious states on brain states."

(p. 353)

Premise 2. "There seem to be [only] two possible avenues open to us in our aspiration to identify *P*; we could try to get to *P* by investigating consciousness directly [i.e., via introspection], or we could look to the study of the brain for *P*."

(p. 354)

Premise 3. Introspection cannot deliver *P*.

Premise 4. *P* is neither a perceptual property (i.e., a property that we can come to know through perceptual means) nor is it a property that we can conceive of using inference from what is perceived. In other words, we are both perceptually and cognitively closed with respect to *P* and thus the study of the brain will not deliver *P*.

Lemma. We cannot identify *P*.

Premise 5. If we cannot identify *P*, then we can never bridge the explanatory gap.

Conclusion. We can never bridge the explanatory gap.

Although there is much that can be said about McGinn's argument (Flanagan, 1991; Rowlands, 2001; Stoljar, 2006), we will be succinct. We shall restrict our attention to how his argument affects our version of physicalism. Consider first premise 1. Research program physicalism accepts premise 1 with two important qualifications. First, premise 1 must be relaxed to allow for the possibility that *P* might not be a brain property. McGinn's argument presupposes that consciousness is a phenomenon constituted by the brain. However, there is nothing physicalistically untoward with the possibility that the vehicles of consciousness do not reside entirely within the brain. Research program physicalism is consistent with both an internalist and an externalist (embodied or enactive) understanding of consciousness. Second, the research program accepts premise 1 (in this more relaxed form) but not insofar as it takes it to be a fact that can be established by a priori considerations. We understand physicalism not as a metaphysical thesis but as an ongoing research program. As a result, the research program allows premise 1 because the premise is an expression of the program's ultimate end. It would be deeply irrational for the research program to persist in light of a rejection of premise 1.

We also grant premise 2, as long as premise 2 permits for a co-evolutionary approach and leaves room for contributions from the body and external environment. In other words, our reading of premise 2 allows for an investigation into the nature of consciousness that simultaneously examines the problem of consciousness both from the physical (biological, neuronal, or bodily) and the mental (or phenomenal) perspective (Lycan, 1996; P.S. Churchland, 1986; P. M. Churchland, 1995; Flanagan, 1992). Premise 3 is also accepted. The research program is committed to a compositional explanation of consciousness and although first-personal investigations of consciousness could help to direct our physical science, it is highly unlikely that the components themselves and their workings will be accessible from the first-person perspective. Introspection puts us in touch with consciousness and not, it seems, with its working components. The research program takes issue primarily with premise 4.

McGinn claims that we are both perceptually and cognitively closed with respect to *P*. From the perspective of the research program, such a contention is truly astounding—it asserts that no amount of empirical or theoretical advancement about the workings of the brain will ever allow us to infer the constitutive mechanisms of consciousness. What is McGinn's defense of this claim? First, McGinn argues that *P* is not a property that is perceptually accessible by us: Whatever *P* turns out to be, it will not be something that we will be able to observe by looking at the brain or at an instrument. It is of the essence of our perceptual systems, McGinn maintains, that they represent spatial properties. But according to McGinn, *P* is not a spatial property and thus we are perceptually closed to it. Second, McGinn holds that no form of inference from what is perceived will lead us to *P*. For McGinn, our introduction of theoretical concepts is (necessarily) governed by a principle of "homogeneity." That is, our theoretical concepts must be homogenous with our perceptual concepts. McGinn says very little as a way of explicating the operative notion of homogeneity that governs the introduction of theoretical concepts. What he does say is that (i) theoretical concepts are formed "by a sort of analogical extension of what we observe" (p. 358) and (ii) if *P* cannot be represented by experience (p. 357), then no analogical extension on observational entities is such that will ever allow us to form a concept that represents *P*. Thus, his conclusion that we are cognitively closed with respect to *P* makes use of the following two assumptions: Our senses are restricted to representing only spatial entities, and our theoretical concepts are limited by observation insofar as their introduction is made (necessarily) on the basis of some analogical extension on what we can observe.

McGinn's argument in support of cognitive closure is unsuccessful. In fact, a closer examination of premise 4 shows that it is faced with a dilemma and the acceptance of either horn causes trouble for McGinn's position. The dilemma arises because either the senses only represent spatial properties or they do not. If not, then the fact that *P* is *not* a spatial property, as McGinn assumes, provides us with no reason to think that we are perceptually closed to *P*. Indeed, there seem to be many non-spatial properties, including pitch, odor, time, and hunger, to name a few, that are represented by our perceptual systems. Each of these properties has receptors and modality-specific subsystems dedicated to their processing. A defender of McGinn might respond that the perception of such properties arises in response to objects and events that occur in space (or perhaps more felicitously, space-time) and as such, they ought to be considered spatial. Whether or not it is possible to broaden the definition of spatial property so that it encompasses all perceptual states but rules out consciousness in a non-question begging way (given that the core issue is whether or not consciousness is a physical phenomenon) remains to be seen. Even if this were possible, though, McGinn's argument would be impaled by the second horn of the dilemma. If the senses only represent spatial properties, then McGinn's requirement that all theoretical concepts have to be *homogeneous* to observational concepts has to be either denied or relaxed so much that it loses its force. It is clear that we have many concepts that do not represent entities as spatial. In what way are our concepts of GROUNDING, BEAUTY, CAUSE, EFFECT, IDENTITY, JUSTICE, and many others *merely* spatial? The homogeneity requirement is false (because the aforementioned concepts are not homogenous to observational concepts) or such concepts are homogenous to observational concepts but in such a lose way that there is no reason to think that we will not be able to form a theoretical concept of *P* that is homogenous to our observational concepts. Without a strict homogeneity restriction in place, McGinn's claim that we are cognitive closed with respect *P* is robbed of any plausibility.

Before we conclude this section, we would like to raise an additional point regarding McGinn's position. In discussing the claim that we are cognitively closed with respect to *P*, McGinn offers what might be taken to be a different argument in support of his position. Consider the following passage in which McGinn argues that *P* cannot be discovered (or postulated) by an inference to the best explanation:

> If our data, arrived at by perception of the brain, do not include anything that brings in conscious states, then the theoretical properties we need to explain these data will not include conscious states either. Inference to the best explanation of purely physical data will never take us outside the realm of the physical, forcing us to introduce concepts of consciousness. Everything physical has a purely physical explanation.

> So the property of consciousness is cognitively closed with respect to the introduction of concepts by means of inference to the best explanation of perceptual data about the brain.
>
> (p. 358)

In this passage, McGinn argues that an inference to the best explanation will be incapable of postulating *P* because what we aim to explain is the physical data. But since the physical data can be explained without an appeal to consciousness (consciousness, he writes, is "theoretically epiphenomenal" [p. 359]), then we will have no need to posit *P* in order to explain our physical data. McGinn's argument turns on an overly narrow notion of "physical data." If by "physical data" one means only the neurological and biological properties of the brain, then, yes, *P* will not be needed in order to explain that data. But that is not what "physical data" means. Or better, this is not how the research program understands "physical data." In fact, the phenomenal character of consciousness will count, at least by the research program, as physical data, the same way that the solidity of a diamond is a piece of physical data: both of which call for an explanation.[2] The character of consciousness is clearly what ought to be explained and thus an inference to the best explanation will, inevitably, require us to postulate some kind of property that compositionally accounts for consciousness. Such an understanding of physical data does not in any way settle the issue in favor of the research program. The research program holds that consciousness is part of our physical data only insofar as consciousness is something that demands an explanation. Such an attitude determines the target of the research program, but not its success. Whether the research program turns out to be successful or not depends on whether it is capable of offering a compositional explanation of consciousness.

Finally, McGinn's position rests on an intuitive empiricism that can itself be questioned. It depends on our ability to clearly demarcate perceptual data from the theoretical inferences drawn from that data and our antecedent theoretical commitments. Certainly, a number of philosophers of science have questioned the idea of theory-neutral observation (Duhem, 1996; Quine, 1951; Sellars, 1963). Furthermore, evidence from the psychological and brain sciences suggest that distinguishing the perceptual from the inferential may not be a simple task. On the one hand, several aspects of perception appear to be cognitively penetrable (P.M. Churchland, 1988; Lyons, 2011; Macpherson, 2012; Pylyshyn, 1999; Raftopoulos, 2001, 2009; Siegel, 2012; Stokes, 2013; Zeimbekis & Raftopoulos, 2015); on the other hand, an emerging body of evidence suggests that cognition may depend in part on perceptual mechanisms (Barsalou, 1999, 2008; Fischer & Zwaan, 2008; Gallese & Lakoff, 2005; Kemmerer, 2010; Kiefer & Pulvermüller, 2012). McGinn's empiricism may be correct in the end, but it is far from established. Given this, it seems premature to assume that it is true and should serve as the basis for concluding that we can never have an adequate theory of consciousness.

In sum, McGinn fails to show that we are cognitively closed with respect to the type of property the discovery of which can solve the mind-body problem. As such, McGinn's version of the argument from ignorance does not show that the explanatory gap is permanent.

2. Humility: Kantian or Ramseyan

The second argument from ignorance that we will consider is an argument that is inspired (but not entailed) by the work of both Rae Langton (1998) and David Lewis (2008) on (epistemic) humility. Through different means, Langton and Lewis present a metaphysical picture of the world according to which we are chronically ignorant about certain aspects of our world. The version of the argument from ignorance that we will evaluate is one that goes beyond Langton and Lewis's expressed aims, so it is not meant to reflect their views. Still, the articulation of their respective positions and the reasons that they provide in support of epistemic humility are germane to present considerations. If there are reasons to think that we are chronically ignorant about certain features of our world and those features turn out to be pertinent to an explanation of consciousness, then it follows that we will be incapable of ever offering a satisfactory explanation of consciousness. In its most general form, this version of the argument from ignorance proceeds as follows:

Premise 1. There are aspects of the world about which we are chronically ignorant.
Premise 2. Knowledge of those aspects of the world about which we are chronically ignorant is necessary for explaining consciousness.
Premise 3. If there are aspects of the world that are necessary for explaining consciousness but which we can never know, then the explanatory gap is permanent.
Conclusion. The explanatory gap is permanent.

We take premise 3 to be definitional so we shall put it aside. We shall instead focus on premises 1 and 2. It is important to note from the outset that premise 1 does double duty. Not only does it assert that we are ignorant of certain aspects of our world, but it also maintains that we have reasons to think that those aspects exist despite our ignorance. For ease of explication, we will restrict our attention to properties and suppose that our (purported) ignorance concerns a specific class of properties. Accordingly, premise 1 claims that we have reasons to think that such properties are instantiated in our world even though we cannot know anything about their nature. Premise 1, thus, is the conjunction of the following two statements:

Premise 1.1. We are ignorant of the nature of certain properties.
Premise 1.2. We have reasons to think that the properties of whose nature we are ignorant are instantiated in the actual world.

Both Langton and Lewis offer different defenses for premise 1. We consider them in order.

2.1. *Langton on Kant on Intrinsic Properties*

Langton's presentation of premise 1 is the product of her engagement with Immanuel Kant's claim that we have no knowledge of things in themselves. According to Langton, such an epistemological claim should be understood as being tantamount to the claim that we have no knowledge of the *intrinsic* properties of things. In her discussion of Kant's position, she presents an intriguing argument in support of the contention that such an epistemological claim ("Kantian Humility") is the consequence of certain Kantian theses. Specifically, Langton argues that for Kant the only knowledge that we have of mind-independent entities is knowledge of how such entities are *related* to other entities and to us. We can thus know their relational characteristics yet when it comes to their non-relational (intrinsic) nature we are in the dark. In what follows, we will not be concerned with the historical or textual accuracy of Langton's interpretation of Kant nor with determining whether the argument that Langton attributes to Kant is a valid one (see Van Cleve, 2011). Our aim is a different one: we seek to investigate whether Kantian Humility of this sort is a live possibility and to draw out its consequences for our version of physicalism.

Before we explicate the Kantian view and articulate Kant's argument (as presented by Langton) in support of premise 1, it is imperative to clarify the distinction between intrinsic and extrinsic properties. The literature on intrinsic and extrinsic properties is not only contentious but also plurivocal (Humberstone, 1996; Francescotti, 1999; Langton & Lewis, 1998; Lewis, 2001; Sider, 1993; Vallentyne, 1997; Weatherson & Marshall, 2017). For our purposes, we follow Langton's understanding of intrinsic and extrinsic properties. According to Langton, if *P* is an intrinsic property, then *P* is both "compatible with loneliness and lawlessness" and if a property *P* is compatible with loneliness and lawlessness then *P* is intrinsic (1998, p. 119; but see also pp. 18–19). Hence, being compatible with loneliness and being compatible with lawlessness are jointly sufficient, but independently necessary, for being an intrinsic property. *P* is compatible with loneliness just in case *P* is a property that an entity could possess even if that entity were lonely (i.e., the only entity existing in the world) (p. 19). And *P* is compatible with lawlessness just in case *P* is a property an entity could have even in the absence of laws (p. 119). Extrinsic properties are then defined as those properties that are incompatible either with loneliness or lawlessness. Consequently, extrinsic properties are properties an entity has in virtue of how such an entity is related to other things in the world. *Being the last person standing* or *being parked 12 feet away from a fire hydrant* are both extrinsic properties.

Kant's claim, as interpreted by Langton, is that we have no knowledge of intrinsic properties. Although the details of Langton's reading of Kant's view are largely inconsequential for our purposes, it is still instructive to consider why Kant held, according to Langton, such a view. As Langton argues, Kant held on to a physical theory that committed him to the claim that matter is constituted by forces, which, according to Kant, are the *extrinsic* properties of substances—that is, relational properties that substances have in virtue of how they are related to other entities. Such an understanding of matter leads Kant to conclude that all knowledge of matter is knowledge of relations. He writes:

> What presents itself in this or that location, or, beyond this change of location, what activities occur within the things themselves, is not given through these relations, Now through mere relations one cannot be acquainted with a thing as it is in itself. We may therefore conclude that since external sense gives us nothing but representations of mere relations, this sense can contain in its representation only the relation of an object upon the subject, and not the intrinsic properties that belong to the object as it is in itself.
>
> (Kant, B67; cited in Langton, 1998, p. 42)

We must note the following two points. First, Kant's conception of matter, and more broadly his view of physical phenomena, is admittedly outdated and thus contemporary philosophers and physicists will not agree that our physical sciences teach us only about the extrinsic properties of substances. Still, as Langton and others have noted, contemporary physics is Kantian in spirit insofar as it teaches us about properties *only* in terms of their relations and causal features. Charge, mass, spin, and whatever other properties we might take as fundamental (or near-fundamental) are ones that we are acquainted with in virtue of their causal roles. Not only does physics tell us that charge, for example, is that which plays the charge role but it also seems that advances in physics are unlikely to go beyond the postulation of some or other causal role. As Simon Blackburn puts it, "[s]cience finds only dispositions all the way down" (1990, p. 62; see also Ney, 2007 for a helpful discussion on this point).

Second, even if we accept that we know physical entities in virtue of their relations (and extrinsic properties), this does not show that we can have no knowledge of their intrinsic properties—should such properties exist. In other words, it does not follow from the premise that our knowledge of material substances is knowledge of relations, that we are ignorant of their intrinsic properties. And the conclusion is not reached even if we add the Kantian assumption that human sensory knowledge is receptive (Van Cleve, 2011). Something is still missing in order for the inference to be rendered valid—something that guarantees that we cannot acquire knowledge of intrinsic properties from knowledge of their relational features. Langton argues that what is missing is a claim about the irreducibility of relational properties of substances to their intrinsic properties. Whether this is a claim that contemporary proponents of Kantian Humility would accept is beside the point. What is worth noting is that an acceptance of the view that contemporary physics describes the world in terms of relations is not a sufficient reason to embrace Kantian Humility.

But of course the matter does not end here. As mentioned previously, even if one were to show that we are ignorant of certain features of the world (say, intrinsic properties), such a demonstration would only carry us half way. To complete our support of premise 1, we need also to show that such intrinsic properties are in fact instantiated.

There are different proposals in support of the existence of intrinsic properties. First, there is the suggestion that the existence of extrinsic properties entails the existence of intrinsic properties—the former could not exist without the latter as their grounds. Second, there is a Kantian reason in support of premise 1.2 that Langton develops in her discussion. According to Langton, if there are substances, then substances must have intrinsic properties. That is because whatever substances are, they must be compatible with loneliness and lawlessness. But since there are no substances without any properties, substances must have *some* properties that are compatible with loneliness and lawlessness. Thus, substances, if they exist, must have intrinsic properties. A third reason in support of the existence of intrinsic properties is found in Alyssa Ney's (2007) discussion of physicalism and intrinsic properties. Ney holds that if it is possible that a substance has *P* and *P* is intrinsic, then *not-P* is also an intrinsic property. The idea here is that if the having of a property does not depend on anything other than the entity that has the property in question, then lacking the property should likewise not depend on anything other than the entity. Thus, if it is possible for there to be any intrinsic property *P*, then the bearer of this property must either have *P* or lack *P* (have non-*P*) *intrinsically*. (Ney attributes this argument to Ted Sider.) A fourth reason for the existence of intrinsic properties stems from Lewis's notion of duplication (Lewis, 1983). The very idea that *x* is a duplicate of *y* requires that there are certain properties common in both *x* and *y* that can persist even if *x* and *y* do not share all of their properties and even if their respective worlds differ. But if duplicates must share certain properties and these properties do not depend on the world, then such properties appear to be, given our definition of intrinsicness, intrinsic.

Each of the four reasons can be developed in much more detail. And additional reasons can be adduced. All the same, the foregoing brief presentation suffices for our purposes. What it is evident even from the sketches of those positions offered earlier is that premise 1.2 is a substantial philosophical claim. Consequently, proponents of the argument from ignorance have to do important work in order to motivate it. For example, the first argument that posits intrinsic properties as the grounds of extrinsic properties (or dispositions) will be opposed by causal structuralism (Hawthorne, 2001; Swoyer, 1982; Shoemaker, 1984, 1998) that holds that fundamental properties (or properties posited by our best physical science) are individuated exhaustively in terms of their causal profiles.[3] Thus, if causal structuralism is a live option (Hawthorne, 2001), then one is not forced to countenance intrinsic properties. There is nothing more to a property than its causal profile. Causal structuralism is also an argument against the Kantian and Lewisian reasons: it militates against the existence of lonely substances[4] and against properties that will necessarily remain constant upon duplication.[5] The argument offered by Ney cannot be so easily dismissed. However, from the perspective of the research program metaphysical arguments in support of the existence of unknowable intrinsic properties will have to be judged on the basis of the work that such intrinsic properties are thought to be doing. But what motivates us to accept premise 1.1, namely, the practice of science, is also that which motivates us to *reject* premise 1.2 (see also Ney, 2007). If our best science has and will have no use for intrinsic properties, then we ought to think twice before allowing them into our ontological inventory. This sentiment is echoed by John Hawthorne who maintains that such considerations constitute in fact the best argument in support of causal structuralism. He writes:

> All scientific knowledge about negative charge is knowledge about the causal role it plays. Science seems to offer no conception of negative charge as something over and above "the thing that plays the charge role." If there were a quiddity that were, so to speak, the role filler, it would not be something that science had any direct cognitive access to, except via the reference fixer "the quiddity that actually plays the charge role." Why invoke what you don't need? . . . Why posit from the armchair distinctions that are never needed by science?
>
> (2001, pp. 368–369)

In 1844 Michael Faraday made use of a similar methological principle to argue that physics has no need for properties other than causal properties.

> If, in the ordinary view of atoms, we call the particle of matter away from the powers *a*, and the system of powers or forces in and around it *m* . . . [then] the *a* or nucleus vanishes, and the substance consists of the powers or *m*; and indeed what notion can we form of the nucleus independent of its powers? all our perception and knowledge of the atom, and even our fancy, is limited to ideas of its powers: what thought remains on which to hang the imagination of an *a* independent of the acknowledged forces? . . . why then assume the existence of that of which we are ignorant, which we cannot conceive, and for which there is no philosophical necessity
>
> (Faraday, 1844, pp. 396–397; the passage is cited in Langton, 1998, p. 181)

Hawthorne's suggested methodological principle is one that is readily accepted by the research program. And even if one does not want to use such a principle in arguing for causal structuralism, one can still use it against the use (if not the existence) of intrinsic properties. In other words, research program physicalism is best described as agnostic about the existence of intrinsic properties. It is after all not a metaphysical doctrine but an explanatory project. But if the reasons for accepting premise 1.1 are such that guarantee that intrinsic properties serve no *explanatory* purpose and thus statements about them cannot serve as explanans for worldly phenomena, then physicalism as a research program is free to ignore them. As Langton herself admits, "the intrinsic properties of which we have no knowledge deserve the name 'idlers' because they are actually instantiated, but they play no active part in nature" (2004, p. 133). Explanatory projects must make do only with explanans. Given that intrinsic properties are not part of our available explanans, they are, from the perspective of the research program, otiose.

To summarize: We have been focusing on premise 1 from the argument from ignorance. Following Langton's reading of Kant, we construed this premise as one that posits the existence of unknowable intrinsic properties. We have showed that such a premise is in fact a double premise and that both parts of the premise are subject to difficulties and objections. Importantly, an acceptance of premise 1.1 is a reason to be skeptical of premise 1.2. Research program physicalism is thus not threatened by the argument from ignorance at least when this is understood as pertaining to intrinsic properties of physical entities.

2.2. *Lewis on Humility, Ramsey, and Quidditism*

In "Ramseyan Humility" (2008), Lewis argues that even if we had a final and complete theory of our world, such a theory would unavoidably leave out important information about our world. What we are and would be ignorant of, according to Lewis, is the underlying nature of many of the fundamental properties that play an active role in our world.[6] When we postulate a property we do so by describing its causal role, but, as Lewis points out, "it is one thing to know that a role is occupied, another thing to know what occupies it" (2008, p. 204). What a fundamental theory tells us is that various causal roles are occupied. It is silent as to what are the properties that occupy those roles.

Lewis's argument is complex and depends on a number of contentious assumptions. Still, we can present the main idea in the following, somewhat simplified manner. First, suppose that there is a final and complete theory T of our world. T both introduces and implicitly defines theoretical terms, which name, according to Lewis, all fundamental properties that play an active role in our world.[7] T will not include two types of fundamental properties, if such properties exist: "idlers," i.e., fundamental properties that play no active role, and "aliens," i.e., properties that are fundamental but are not actually instantiated. Second, in addition to T there is our old language

("O") that suffices, for Lewis, to describe all of our possible observations. The language of T would involve both T-terms and O-terms: The former are those defined implicitly by T, the latter are those terms which are part of our old language and have meaning independently of T. Third, we can write T as a single, long conjunctive sentence and replace our T-terms with variables. The result is the open sentence "$T(x_1, x_2, x_3, \ldots, x_n)$" and any n-tuple of properties that satisfies this sentence is a realization of T. Four, if we existentially quantify the open sentence, we get the Ramsey sentence of T—"$\exists x_1 \exists x_2 \exists x_3 \ldots \exists x_n T(x_1, x_2, x_3, \ldots, x_n)$." The Ramsey sentence of T states that there is at least one actual realization of T: the n-tuple of fundamental properties that satisfies T in the *actual* world. Five, the Ramsey sentence implies, Lewis holds, all and only the O-language sentences that are the theorems of T. What this means is that "any predictive success for T is equally a predictive success for the Ramsey sentence of T" (p. 207). Consequently, any evidence in support of T is also evidence for the Ramsey sentence. But here is where the issue of humility arises: If T can be multiply realized, then we cannot know which realization is actual.

To make this point clear, suppose that the ordered n-tuple of fundamental properties $\langle P_1, P_2, P_3, \ldots P_n \rangle$ realizes T in the actual world and that P_1 and P_2 are properties of the same category and adicy. Lewis argues that we could permute P_1 and P_2 while keeping everything else fixed. The roles occupied by P_1 (causal, locational, etc.) would be occupied by P_2 and vice versa. This permutation would give rise, according to Lewis, to a *distinct* possible realization of T. But we would never be in a position to tell the two realizations apart. Any evidence in support of the actual realization of T is evidence in support of the possible realization of T, and vice versa. Lewis offers an additional argument in support of his conclusion—the "replacement argument"—but for present purposes we can safely ignore it: Not only does it rest on what we take to be more contentious assumptions, but what we will say about the permutation argument applies, *mutatis mutandis*, to the replacement argument.

What should we make of Lewis's argument as an argument in support of premise 1? First, the argument rests on a number of assumptions that are not universally shared. There are the semantic assumptions about T and O—e.g., that T-terms are implicitly defined by T, that O-terms do not name fundamental properties "except as occupants of roles" (Lewis, 2008, p. 206), and that O is rich enough to account for any possible observation (see Leuenberger, 2010). There is also the assumption that T is a complete and final theory. And then there are the metaphysical assumptions governing possibility and the nature of properties that Lewis employs. Permuting P_1 with P_2 is possible, we are told, because possibility is governed by the Principle of Recombination, which holds, according to Lewis, that "anything can coexist with anything else, at least provided they occupy distinct spatio-temporal positions" (Lewis, 1986, p. 88). Of course, Lewis's argument does not just require that this permutation is possible but also that it is a *distinct* possibility—after all, the possible realization is distinct from the actual realization. What guarantees that permuting P_1 and P_2 gives rise to two distinct possibilities is the claim that *quidditism* is true, i.e., the view that it is possible for a fundamental property to realize any causal role of appropriate adicy and category (Locke, 2008, 2012).[8] Thus, one could take issue with one or more of the governing assumptions of Lewis's argument.

We will not do that here. There is an issue that is much more relevant to our version of physicalism that needs to be discussed. This is the nature of ignorance that is supposed to follow from Lewis's argument. In particular, one can ask how damning or problematic is Ramseyan Humility for the research program? On reflection, it seems rather innocuous. First, despite Lewis's claim, one could argue that we have knowledge of intrinsic properties—or better, we have all the knowledge about intrinsic properties that we would ever want.[9] We know that they are the occupiers of some roles; we know what those roles are; and we know how they relate to the roles of other properties. What we do not know is their exact, intrinsic nature. We do not know what is that which fills the role. But that is a type of ignorance with which we can easily live. What we are lacking is, as Stoljar put it, "(mere) *quiddistic* ignorance; that is, ignorance of the numerical identity of the properties in question, and about nothing else" (2013, p. 26). Lacking knowledge of the numerical identity of the properties in question does not seem particularly worrisome. Indeed, even if we had such knowledge, it would be explanatorily epiphenomenal.

A second, related reason that Ramseyan Humility is not particularly problematic for our version of physicalism is that T is not only a final theory but also a *complete* theory. As such, it explains all that there is to be explained. If T is a physicalist theory—this is not Lewis's claim but it is not inconsistent with his position—then research program physicalism would be vindicated. If it is really a complete theory, then it must be such that accounts for all phenomena that need to be explained. And consciousness, presumably, is one of them. Thus, if there is a residual and irremediable ignorance, then such ignorance is one that is no way a hindrance to the research program. After all, the knowledge that we cannot have according to Ramseyan Humility is *useless*—it is not knowledge that we could ever use in our scientific (explanatory) projects. Research program physicalism and Ramseyan Humility can thus coexist (but see note!).[10]

2.3. *Premise 2: Ignorance and Consciousness*

Recall the argument from ignorance:

> **Premise 1.** There are aspects of the world about which we are chronically ignorant.
>
> **Premise 2.** Knowledge of those aspects of the world about which we are chronically ignorant is necessary for explaining consciousness.

Premise 3. If there are aspects of the world that are necessary for explaining consciousness but which we can never know, then the explanatory gap is permanent.

Conclusion. The explanatory gap is permanent.

So far, we have been concerned with evaluating premise 1. However, before we can conclude our assessment of the argument of ignorance, we also have to examine premise 2. Even if we were to accept premise 1, in order for the argument to go through, one would have to demonstrate the truth of premise 2. But premise 2 is one that it is hard to motivate in the context of this argument. The reason is this. We are told by premise 1 that there are features of the world about which we are chronically ignorant. Premise 2, however, requires that those features are ones that are necessary in explaining consciousness. The problem here is that if we accept premise 1, then we have little or no reason to accept premise 2. After all, if we are truly ignorant of certain features of the world (e.g., intrinsic properties), then what reasons would we have to think that intrinsic properties are relevant to an explanation of consciousness? We cannot simply assume their relevance. This would be begging the question against the research program. To do so, we would be assuming the permanence of the explanatory gap. Furthermore, any reason in support to premise 2 cannot be scientific. Science, we are assuming, cannot tell us anything about those properties. Nor can such a reason be one that we acquire on the basis of observation. Ramseyan Humility is one that survives any type of observation. So, for instance, someone who thinks that qualia are fundamental properties because of some features that they possess would not be able to use Lewis's argument. That is because, arguably we *have* access to qualia and thus we are not ignorant of them. The dialectical space for a defender of premise 2 gets uncomfortably narrow.

The problem for the defender of premise 2 can be summarized as follows. On the one hand, if we know that intrinsic properties are related in an explanatory way to consciousness, then knowledge of their explanatory role ought to be part of T and thus we will not be ignorant of it. To deny that knowledge of their explanatory role is part of T while accepting that they do play such a role is to deny that T is the complete theory of our world. On the other hand, if T does not include the role that intrinsic properties play in explaining consciousness, then we are forever ignorant of such a role—T is final and complete after all. As a result, we have no reason to accept premise 2. To be clear, we do not wish to claim that the argument from ignorance is necessarily beyond repair. We have only been focusing on the prospects of premise 2 given certain conditions found in Langton and Lewis's arguments. So, the conflict might turn out to be more apparent than real once we relax some of those conditions. Such a qualified conclusion still suffices for present purposes: We have shown that the argument from ignorance as presented in this chapter offers no convincing a priori reasons to think that the research program cannot be successful.

3. The Structure and Dynamics Argument

The fourth and final argument in support of the permanence of the explanatory gap that we wish to consider is one that has recently received a considerable amount of attention. What we are calling "the structure and dynamics argument" is an argument found in Chalmers (1996 and 2003/2010a), but the basic idea of the argument is one that has a rich philosophical lineage and is connected in some ways to the argument from ignorance. In its simplest form, the argument maintains that physical truths (and for the purposes of this chapter, we are assuming that biological and neuroscientific truths fall under the extension of the term "physical") are truths of structure and dynamics. But because truths about consciousness involve truths that are not *just* about structure and dynamics, then physical truths cannot fully explain consciousness.[11] In David Chalmers's words:

> First: Physical descriptions of the world characterize the world in terms of structure and dynamics. Second: from truths about structure and dynamics, one can only deduce further truths about structure and dynamics. And third: Truths about consciousness are not [just] truths about structure and dynamics.
>
> (2010a, p. 120)

If successful, the argument would undermine research program physicalism. It would show that the explanatory gap is permanent because no progress in either the "south" or "north" pole of the mind-body problem would ever be capable of showing how the mind could be physicalistically explainable.

In addition to being an obstacle to our preferred variety of physicalism, the argument plays an important, albeit underappreciated, role in the relevant literature. In our previous discussion we argued that both the knowledge argument and (at least a version of) the conceivability argument demand, in order to motivate their premises, an acceptance of the permanence of the explanatory (or epistemic) gap. That is because if the gap is merely temporary then intuitions about what Mary cannot know and about conceivability (what appears to be possible) cannot be trusted. The argument from structure and dynamics offers much-needed support to those two arguments. If the argument is correct in holding that all physical truths are truths about structure and dynamics, then even though we are in no position either to comprehend *P* (the complete physical or microphysical description of the world) or ascertain Mary's purportedly complete physical knowledge, we still know that both—P and Mary's knowledge—are nothing but descriptions of structure and dynamics. Thus, if consciousness cannot be captured by structure and dynamics, then we have a reason to accept that *PIT&~Q* is ideally (and not just prima facie) conceivable. Likewise, if truths about consciousness are not just truths about structure and dynamics, then Mary could know all that there is to know about the physical nature of our world, without knowing everything about consciousness (see also Alter,

2016, p. 5). Anti-physicalist arguments have been accused of appealing to ignorance when drawing their conclusions (P. S. Churchland, 1996; Stoljar, 2006). By focusing on what we do not know or cannot currently understand, they illegitimately conclude, the objection goes, that consciousness can never be explained. The argument from structure and dynamics can be thought as a response to such an objection to anti-physicalist arguments. With the help of the argument from structure and dynamics, anti-physicalist arguments are shown not to be based on ignorance but on knowledge. That is, such arguments emphasize the fact that structure and dynamics can never suffice for an explanation of consciousness. In other words, anti-physicalist arguments are means by which one attempts to show that we know enough to know that we cannot physicalistically explain consciousness. The structure and dynamics argument is thus doubly important: Not only does it pose a threat to research program physicalism, it also provides important (and perhaps, indispensible) support to popular anti-physicalist arguments.

The plan for this section is as follows. First, we present the structure and dynamics argument in a premises-conclusion form and discuss its premises. Second, by consulting the existing literature on the argument, we present three different ways of understanding the claim that physical truths are structural-dynamic truths and evaluate whether the argument, in any of its forms, is successful.

3.1. The Argument

The argument from structure and dynamics can be presented in the following form:

Premise 1. All physical truths are either truths about structure, dynamics, or both (for short, "structural-dynamic truths").
Premise 2. From purely structural-dynamic truths one can only deduce further purely structural-dynamic truths.
Premise 3. There are truths about consciousness that are not purely structural-dynamic.
Lemma. There are truths about consciousness that cannot be deduced from physical truths.
Premise 4. If there are truths about consciousness that cannot be deduced from physical truths, then consciousness cannot be explained by physical truths.
Conclusion. Consciousness cannot be explained by physical truths.

In *Conscious Mind*, Chalmers summarizes this argument in the following way: "physics only gives us structure and dynamics, and structure and dynamics does not add up to phenomenology" (1996, p. 165). Our formulation of the argument is an expansion of this basic idea, one that is faithful to how Chalmers presents the argument in a later work (see, e.g., Chalmers

[2003/2010a]). Let us examine the reasons why Chalmers thinks the premises of the argument have to be accepted. We will focus on premises 1 and 2.

Premise 1

Chalmers draws support for premise 1 from the practice and nature of physics. For Chalmers, physics aims to offer a comprehensive description of the basic physical systems that exist in our world and to specify their workings and interactions. What is needed in order for such a goal to be achieved is a complete specification of the structure and dynamics of the basic components of the world. A specification of the *structure* of such components would amount to a characterization of "their spatiotemporal properties and properties such as mass, charge, and quantum wave function state," the latter of which will have to be characterized "in terms of spaces of states that have a certain abstract structure (e.g., the space of continuously varying real quantities or of Hilbert space states)" (2010a, p. 120). A specification of the *dynamics* of the basic systems would require a description of how such systems (and their components, in case they are not simple) change over time. Admittedly different physical descriptions and theories will invoke different types of structure and dynamics. See, for instance, Figure 6.1 for various mathematical structures currently employed in physics. Still, all such attempts are deemed to be importantly similar in so far as they specify in their own ways the structure and dynamics of various basic systems. In fact, as Chalmers makes clear, premise 1 is one that we should accept despite the fact that our current physics is incomplete.

> But here we do not need to have a complete physics. We simply need the claim that physical descriptions are in terms of structure and dynamics. This point is general across physical theories. Novel theories such as relativity and quantum mechanics may introduce new structure and new dynamics over those structures, but the general point (and the gap with consciousness) remains. . . . Novel physical properties are postulated for their potential in explaining existing physical phenomena, themselves characterized in terms of structure and dynamics, and it seems that structure and dynamics always suffice here.
>
> (ibid.; Alter, 2009, p. 760 repeats this point)

What happens if physics does not progress in this business-as-usual (i.e., structural-dynamic) way? Chalmers does not rule out this possibility. Yet, he holds that such a possibility is not one that will be welcomed by physicalists. The business-as-usual model may cease to apply when consciousness is itself postulated as a fundamental property, one that cannot be explained in any physical way. Such a result goes against the spirit of physicalism and would be a demonstration of the failure of physicalism as a research program.

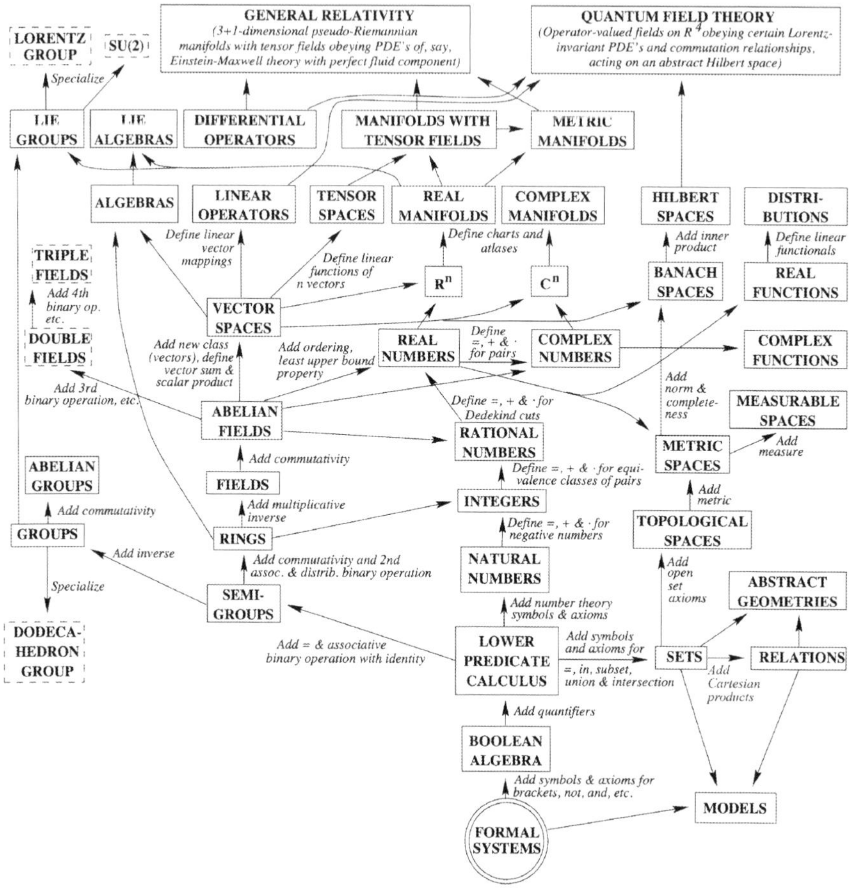

Figure 6.1 Various Relationships Between Different Mathematical Structures. The presence of arrows indicates addition of symbols or axioms and arrows that meet indicate the combination of structures.

The figure is reproduced here from Tegmark (1998) with kind permission from the publisher (Elsevier).

Another related possibility is that we end up with a future theory that is different than Lewis's T theory: in addition to characterizing properties (and entities) in terms of their causal roles and thus relationships to other properties (and entities) within a spatiotemporal structure, the theory also offers an account of the intrinsic nature of these properties (and entities). In offering a description of the intrinsic nature of existent properties (and entities), the theory will in essence characterize the grounds of the various structural and dynamic relationships *currently* studied by our physical theories. As such, the future theory under consideration would go beyond structure and dynamics. It is unclear why a theory, especially a *scientific* theory, would have a need to postulate intrinsic properties (or grounds) of fundamental physical properties (and entities), but one possibility is that it would do so in order to account for consciousness (Chalmers, 1996; Lockwood, 1989; Maxwell, 1979; Montero, 2010; Russell, 1927; Strawson, 2008; Stoljar, 2001, 2006). If by "physical truths" one includes both truths about structure and dynamics and truths about the intrinsic nature of existent properties and entities, then truths about consciousness may be entailed by such a broader physical basis. However, the proposed extension of our current physical theory is at odds with physicalism in general and with research program physicalism in particular. If consciousness arises out of the intrinsic grounds of the properties postulated by physics, then consciousness is not nothing over and above the physical properties entities studied by physics and would not be compositionally explained by them.

In sum, Chalmers holds that physics is currently committed to offering structural-dynamic descriptions of the world. Extensions of physics that are amenable to physicalism will be versions of physics that include more structural-dynamics descriptions. And extensions of physics that go beyond structure and dynamics are ones that pose difficulties for physicalists.

Premise 2

From a purely structural-dynamic description we can only infer or deduce further structural-dynamic descriptions. Chalmers appears to think that premise 2 is prima facie plausible. In fact, when presenting the premise in his (2003/2010a) paper, Chalmers does not so much defend as state it:

> [W]hat can be inferred from this sort of description in terms of structure and dynamics? A low-level microphysical description can entail all sorts of surprising and interesting macroscopic properties, as with the emergence of chemistry from physics, of biology from chemistry, or more generally of complex emergent behaviors in complex system theory. In all of these cases, however, the complex properties that are entailed are nevertheless structural and dynamic . . . from structure and dynamics, one can infer only structure and dynamics.
>
> (p. 121)

What could Chalmers's reasoning be in support of this premise? As we highlighted before, we do not think that he can appeal to one of the usual anti-physicalist arguments (the knowledge argument or the conceivability argument) in order to support it. If our foregoing assessment is correct, then such arguments presuppose the premise in question.[12] The fact that a functional account of consciousness appears to leave out something important from consciousness (namely, its phenomenal character) requires that functional descriptions (descriptions that are purely structural-dynamic) never yield anything other than structure and dynamics. The same applies to an appeal to the distinction between the "easy" and "hard" problems of consciousness (Chalmers, 1995). The very distinction is based on the assumption that functional explanations cannot suffice to solve the "hard" problem of consciousness, i.e., they will not offer an explanation of the phenomenal character of consciousness. Once again, such reasoning depends on premise 2 and cannot be assumed. The point here is not to suggest that Chalmers assumes the truth of this premise. Far from it—see, e.g., Chalmers (1996, pp. 73–81) and (2012). Rather, we wish to highlight that support for this premise ought to come from sources that are independent of the typical anti-physicalist arguments.

What is more, Stoljar offers a simple counterexample to premise 2 (Stoljar, 2015, p. 329 n. 11). Suppose that S_1 is both true and a purely structural-dynamic sentence. Further, suppose that S_2 is not a purely structural-dynamic sentence. S_1 entails the disjunction of the two sentences, S_1 or S_2, but the disjunction is not itself purely structural-dynamic. Therefore, premise 2 is false. Torin Alter offers a response to Stoljar on behalf of Chalmers (Alter, 2016). By introducing the notion of *weaker-than-structural* he suggests a reformulation of the argument that is immune to Stoljar's objection. According to Alter, a sentence *S* is *weaker-than-structural* if and only if *S* is a priori entailed by a purely structural true sentence but does not a priori entail such a true sentence. Utilizing this notion, Alter suggests that we can allow that some weaker-than-structural truths are entailed by purely structural truths, but deny that all truths about consciousness are either purely structural truths *or* weaker-than-structural truths.[13]

Although it is possible to refine the argument in a way that avoids Stoljar's objection, we think that it is best to re-orient the argument in a way that eschews an explicit appeal to deduction or a priori entailment. Although Chalmers appears to be committed to premise 2 as stated above, it is possible to reconstruct a version of the argument that is free from such a commitment and thus targets research program physicalism directly. Recall that research program physicalism does not require a priori or conceptual connections between physical truths and truths about consciousness in order for the former to explain the latter. As we argued in Chapter 4, to demand that explanations require a priori entailment or deduction is to operate on an outdated (and thus, in our minds, unscientific) model of explanation. The structure and dynamics argument, we think, persists even in the absence of premise 2. A form of the argument that does not depend on premise 2 is in fact given by Chalmers a few pages before he explicitly develops the argument that we summarized above. He presents it in the following way:

1. Physical accounts explain at most structure and function.
2. Explaining structure and function does not suffice to explain consciousness.

---

3. No physical account can explain consciousness.

(Chalmers, 2010a, p. 106)

Reformulating this argument using the language of structure and dynamics, instead of function, we get the following version of the argument from structure and dynamics:

> **Premise 1*.** Physical accounts explain at most structure and dynamics.
> **Premise 2*.** Explaining structure and dynamics does not suffice to explain consciousness.
> **Conclusion.** No physical account can explain consciousness.

This argument is closely related to the explanatory gap argument (Levine, 1983). However, a virtue of expressing the argument in this form is that we have made explicit where the problem with physicalist explanations of consciousness is supposed to lie. Physical accounts are limited insofar as scientific explanans can only involve structural-dynamic descriptions. The point of the argument is thus to show that such explanans do not suffice to explain an explanandum that is not purely structural-dynamic, namely, consciousness. What we said about premise 1 also applies to premise 1*. Physical accounts of the world that are amenable to physicalism are such that appear to be restricted to structure and dynamics. However, as we shall see in what follows, not every explication of the notions of structure and dynamics is one that can be used in the argument for not every explication of those notions is in agreement with scientific practice. Furthermore, we shall argue that regardless of how one understands structure and dynamics, the argument from structure and dynamics fails to demonstrate the permanence of the explanatory gap.

3.2. *If Not Just Structure and Dynamics, Then What Else?*

According to premise 2*, there is something about consciousness that cannot be captured by any amount of structural-dynamic descriptions. To see what that might be, we need to explain how structure and dynamics are understood in this context. In what follows, we follow the literature in focusing primarily on the notion of structure and taking dynamics to be changes of structural properties over time. In the relevant literature, one finds three different explications of the notion of structure (see Stoljar, 2013, 2015). We examine all three in what follows.

3.2.1. *Structure (and Dynamics) as Relations*

In a number of places, Stoljar considers whether structure could be understood in terms of either mathematical/logical or metaphysical structure (Stoljar, 2013, 2015; see also Newman, 1928). The first suggestion, however, is quickly shown to be at odds with the practice of science. If "structure" is understood as synonymous to "mathematical/logical structure," then, under the assumption that physical truths are structural (and dynamical), physics is restricted to merely logical or mathematical descriptions. Without question, physics is mathematical. Yet, it is much more than just that (Newman, 1928; Demopoulos & Friedman, 1985). It tells us what exists (the various properties that are instantiated in the world, e.g., subatomic particles, fields, or strings) and how those properties change with the passage of time (e.g., the laws of thermodynamics, wave equations of quantum mechanical systems, principles of relativity). Logical and mathematical descriptions cannot suffice to capture the descriptions offered by physics.

If logical or mathematical structure is an inappropriate way of capturing the notion of structure as it figures in premise 1, can we do better by understanding it as metaphysical structure? By "metaphysical structure", Stoljar means "a system (any system) of relations (i.e., *n*-place properties, where $n>1$)" (Stoljar, 2013, p. 34). There are problems with this suggestion as well. To begin with, many phenomenal truths appear to be structural in precisely this relational sense. A particular painful experience can be more or less painful than a different painful experience. The experience of seeing orange is more similar to the experience of seeing yellow than to the experience of hearing a window smashing. But if truths about consciousness are relational, then they are structural and consequently, they are the type of truths that are amenable to a physical explanation. One could, of course, point out that *not* all phenomenal truths are structural in this relational sense. Therefore, even if physical truths are relational, physics (and related structural-dynamic sciences) would still leave some aspects of consciousness unexplained (Alter, 2009; Alter and Nagasawa, 2012 raise such a concern). Such a response is a good one, but its success is limited. Even if we assume that some truths about consciousness are not relational, one would still need to show why a relational description could never explain a non-relational feature or property. Shape is often taken to be a paradigmatic case of a non-relational property. Yet, relational descriptions can explain why a system has the shape that it has. So, even if consciousness is a non-relational property, it is unclear why we could not explain it from a rich enough set of relational (structural-dynamic) descriptions. Lastly, this notion of structure as relational overly restricts the domain of physics. Is physics exclusively committed to claims that are relational? As Stoljar (2006, 2013) notes, physics also tells us about non-relational (i.e., one-place) properties. According to the Standard Model, fermions have the property of having spin ½, a property which many take to be intrinsic. Whatever the fate of the Standard Model might be, the point is that physics is not in principle opposed to the practice of postulating non-relational truths.

3.2.2. *Structural vs. Absolutely Intrinsic*

A second understanding of structure implicates the notion of *absolutely intrinsic property*. The notion of an absolutely intrinsic property comes from Derk Pereboom (2011, 2013, 2015). Utilizing this notion, one can formulate a different version of the argument from structure and dynamics: Physical descriptions are not descriptions (and thus truths) about absolutely intrinsic properties; an explanation of consciousness requires truths that are about absolutely intrinsic properties; ergo, physical truths cannot explain consciousness.

Even though the basic idea of argument is relatively straightforward, the notion of an absolutely intrinsic property is unfortunately obscure. First, Pereboom contrasts it both to the notion of an intrinsic property and to the notion of a purely extrinsic property. An intrinsic property is a property an object has solely in virtue of how the object is in itself and not in virtue of how it is in relation to other things. In offering a definition of absolutely intrinsic property, Pereboom writes: "P is an *absolutely intrinsic* property of X just in case P is an intrinsic property of X, and P is not necessitated by purely extrinsic properties of parts of X" (Pereboom, 2013, p. 51). And then we are told that a property P is purely extrinsic "just in case P is an extrinsic property of X and P has no intrinsic components" (p. 50).[14] Pereboom's definition of absolutely intrinsic property offers a more demanding notion of intrinsicness than the standard one. If a property were merely intrinsic and not *absolutely* intrinsic, then such a property could follow from relational (or extrinsic) properties. Pereboom gives the example of compositional properties as intrinsic but not absolutely intrinsic properties. He writes: "if objects *x* and *y* compose object *z*, then it is possible to derive intrinsic properties of *z* from relational properties of *x* and *y*" (p. 57). In the context of the structure and dynamics argument, a merely intrinsic (what Pereboom calls "comparatively intrinsic") property could be captured by relational (structural-dynamic) descriptions. Thus, even if consciousness were intrinsic, it would still be possible to explain consciousness using relational and thus physical descriptions. However, the notion of an *absolutely* intrinsic property precludes such a possibility. If truths about (phenomenal) consciousness are truths about absolutely intrinsic properties, then given the definition of an absolutely intrinsic property, we will be incapable, it seems, of explaining consciousness in terms of structural (i.e., relational or extrinsic) descriptions.

Should Pereboom's proposed articulation of non-structural property as an absolutely intrinsic property be accepted? Pereboom offers not one but two arguments in support of his conclusion. Still, both arguments are unconvincing. His first argument is a variation of the conceivability argument against physicalism. He writes:

> if we let PRP be any epistemically possible description of the world that features only purely relational properties, the intuition that "PRP and ~Q" is ideally, primarily, and positively conceivable will be very strong. If from this we can conclude that the phenomenal truths are not necessitated by or derivable from the purely relational truths, we can also conclude that the phenomenal truths are not truths exclusively about purely relational and merely comparatively intrinsic properties.

> And this in turn would entail that the phenomenal truths are at least partly about intrinsic properties and/or absolutely intrinsic aspects of properties.
>
> (Pereboom, 2013, pp. 58–59)

Pereboom's idea here (simplifying a bit) is that we could know all that there is to know about the structural features of the world and we would still fail to see any logical connection between truths about structural features of the world and truths about consciousness. In other words, according to Pereboom, there is nothing logically inconsistent with supposing that the world could be structurally the same but phenomenally different. But if such possibility is accepted, then it would seem that structural explanations leave something out—they fail to capture the nature of consciousness.

Pereboom's argument is successful only if PRS&~Q is ideally conceivable. No substantial conclusion can be drawn if PRS&~Q is only prima facie conceivable. So, we must ask: Can Pereboom justify the claim that PRS& ~Q is not just prima facie but also ideally conceivable? We do not see how. To be in a position to draw this conclusion one already needs to know that consciousness is such that its truth involves absolutely intrinsic properties and that descriptions of such properties cannot be captured by physical descriptions. But this claim is exactly what the conceivability argument was set to demonstrate. (See also Stoljar [2015, p. 337] for a similar response.)

Alter responds to this objection by pointing out that there is nothing illegitimate in invoking conceivability arguments in the context of the structure and dynamics argument. Thus, Pereboom is not guilty of begging the question. Alter writes the following:

> conceivability argument proponents . . . tend to advance the premise that zombies are conceivable on direct, intuitive grounds without invoking absolute intrinsicness or structural-dynamic considerations.
>
> (2016, p. 804)

Previously, we argued that the conceivability argument rests precisely on structural-dynamic considerations—in fact, Chalmers himself seems to appeal to such considerations when defending the claim that zombies are ideally conceivable and not just prima facie conceivable (see note 12). So, we are skeptical of the accuracy of Alter's description of the dialectical situation. Having said that, we are happy to allow Alter's claim. That is because all that it shows is that the conceivability argument, when divorced from structural-dynamic considerations, is based on one's intuitions. The research program has no problem accepting either that such anti-physicalist intuitions exist or that they are even ubiquitous among us. It does, however, insist that these intuitions are mere *intuitions* and thus cannot be taken to reflect the fundamental reality of the world. Whether these intuitions are accurate representations of reality is a question that, according to the research program, ought to be settled by science.

In sum, Pereboom tries to defend the claim that truths about consciousness involve truths about absolutely intrinsic properties by using a conceivability argument. However, either such an argument is question-begging in the present context because its key premise presupposes the conclusion of the structure and dynamics argument, or it is not question-begging and the argument has little or no force against the research program physicalism.

Pereboom offers an additional argument in support of the claim that truths about consciousness involve truths about absolutely intrinsic properties. According to Pereboom, it is plausible to maintain that introspection represents phenomenal qualities as primitive. But if such qualities are not only primitive but also intrinsic, then they will turn out to be *absolutely* intrinsic properties. What is a primitive property?

> a primitive property is (i) one whose entire qualitative nature or essence is revealed in our sensory or introspective representation of it, and thus is not identical to a property with a qualitative nature distinct from what is revealed by the representation, and (ii) one that is metaphysically simple and thus not constituted by a plurality of other properties.
> (Pereboom, 2013, p. 59)

Thus, if introspection gives us grounds to think that phenomenal qualities are primitive and if we also have grounds to think, as Pereboom claims, that phenomenal qualities are intrinsic, then they must be absolutely intrinsic.

The argument is again unconvincing. First, one could deny that phenomenal qualities are absolutely intrinsic. In fact, many have done precisely that. Proponents of representationalism, e.g., maintain that the phenomenal character of experience is intimately related to representational content and as such it is not absolutely intrinsic (Dretske, 1995; Harman, 1990; Hill, 2009; Lycan, 1996; Tye, 1995, 2009). Second, one could deny the epistemological role that the preceding argument assigns to introspection (Elpidorou, 2016). Is it really the case that introspection gives us insight into the fundamental nature of consciousness? Does introspection reveal to us that phenomenal properties are metaphysically simple? We find that hard to believe. Of course, what matters here is not our opinion on this matter but rather the point that one cannot assume such a demanding claim about introspection. One has to show it. But any argument in support of such a claim will be, it seems, rather contentious. Last, the very definition of a primitive property is one that denies the possibility of a compositional explanation of consciousness. If phenomenal properties are primitive insofar as they are metaphysically simple, then one could never explain them in terms of their components. Such an articulation of phenomenal qualities/properties proves (by *assumption*) that the research program physicalism can never succeed. Such a result, however, should give us pause. It renders the argument from structure and dynamics superfluous—the conclusion is reached directly in virtue of our supposition that phenomenal properties are primitive. And it rules out via fiat the prospects of any physicalist explanation of consciousness. Indeed, it threatens to rule out more than that. Coupled with the assumption that phenomenal qualities are intrinsic, Pereboom's position rules out any attempt (physicalistic or otherwise) to offer an explanation of consciousness that treats phenomenal qualities as merely intrinsic (i.e., comparatively intrinsic and not absolutely intrinsic). Ultimately, for Pereboom, introspection reveals much more than merely the falseness of physicalism, and yet he offers us no convincing reasons to accept that truths about consciousness involve truths about absolutely intrinsic properties.

3.2.3. Structure (and Dynamics) and Ramsey Sentences

A third and final suggestion as to how to understand structure and dynamics comes from Chalmers (2010a). Chalmers's understanding of structure and dynamics should be distinguished from the foregoing two attempts to articulate those notions. For Chalmers, structural-dynamic truths are not truths about relational (or extrinsic) *properties*. As he notes, "claims about intrinsic properties play no role in the argument I have given" (p. 121, n. 18). Instead, a structural and dynamic description is one that is equivalent to a Ramsey sentence whose O-terms include, in addition to logical and mathematical expressions, *at most* nomic and spatiotemporal expressions (Chalmers, 2010a, p. 120, n. 17). Using this understanding of structural-dynamic truths, we can interpret the argument from structure and dynamics as follows: Every physical truth is equivalent to a Ramsey sentence of the previously stated sort; not every truth about consciousness is equivalent to such a Ramsey sentence; if a truth is not equivalent to such a Ramsey sentence, then it cannot be explained by truths that are equivalent to the Ramsey sentence in question; therefore, physical truths cannot fully explain consciousness.

We must begin by considering whether it is correct to maintain that physical truths are equivalent to Ramsey sentences that involve only logical, mathematical, nomic, and spatiotemporal expressions (or terms). Neither physics nor other physical sciences obviously offer us such Ramsey sentences in their descriptions and theories. Still, such an observation is not a concern for Chalmers's proposal. The issue here is not whether science actually offers such sentences but rather whether scientific statements (let us focus on the statements that physics provides) are ones that are equivalent to the relevant Ramsey sentences. For the present purposes, we follow Stoljar (2015, p. 329, n.10) and hold that a sentence S_1 is equivalent to sentence S_2 if the bi-conditional "S_1 is true iff S_2 is true" can be known a priori. So, the question becomes: Is it correct to maintain that every physical truth is equivalent (in this a priori sense) to some Ramsey sentence? Before we can answer this question, we need to discuss the terms that are involved in the relevant Ramsey sentences.

The assumption that the Ramsey sentences include both logical and mathematical terms appears to be unproblematic because physical sentences and truths also include such terms. One would not be able to express the totality of physical truths in the absence of such vocabulary. The values of physical constants and lawful generalizations are two examples of physical truths that require, respectively, mathematical and logical vocabulary. Here we are not interested in determining whether logical or mathematical terms can somehow be deduced by a more primitive vocabulary—that is, it does not matter whether quantified truths can be deduced from nonquantified truths, nor is it important to examine how many connectives we need and if the required mathematics can be stated in set theory (for some of these issues, see Chalmers, 2012). All that it matters is whether our physical sciences make use of such vocabulary. And the answer appears to be "yes."

A similar argument holds for the case of nomic terms. Under the assumption that physical truths set out to describe the dynamics of basic systems, then physical truths would need to have the means of describing how such systems *change* over time. Physics (and other sciences) describe dynamical changes by explicit appeal to certain laws (e.g., the laws of thermodynamics). Thus, the claim that the Ramsey sentences include nomic terms appears to be consistent with the practice of science.

What about spatiotemporal terms? What are those terms and in what sense do they figure in physical truths? This question of the nature of spatiotemporal terms has received attention both by proponents and detractors of the structure and dynamics argument. In fact, Chalmers (2012) offers a detailed discussion of the character of those terms and it would be beneficial to draw upon that discussion.

Chalmers distinguishes between two ways of understanding spatiotemporal terms. We can hold either that spatiotemporal terms are derivable from some other vocabulary or that they are primitive. Chalmers conceives of the first option as being committed to a functionalist analysis of those terms—that is, "spatiotemporal concepts are concepts of those properties that play a certain functional role" (2012, p. 325). As both Stoljar (2015) and Alter (2016) note in their discussions of the argument from structure and dynamics, the pertinent question to ask in the case of a functionalist analysis is whether consciousness plays any type of role in determining the extension of those terms. If yes, then we are led to phenomenal spatiotemporal functionalism; if no, then we have non-phenomenal spatiotemporal functionalism. Before turning to functionalism, in its two forms, let us discuss briefly the prospects of primitivism.

According to the primitivist view, "spatial [and temporal] concepts involve some sort of direct grasp of spatial [and temporal] properties, and that they are not analyzable in functional terms, especially not in terms of relations to anything mental" (2012, p. 325).[15] The primitivist view, at least as articulated by Chalmers, is a non-starter when considered as a way of explicating the structure and dynamics argument. Chalmers takes primitive properties to be "Edenic," namely, properties and relations which are instantiated in a fictional place where "[o]bjects were simply presented to us without causal mediation, and properties were revealed to us in their true intrinsic glory" (2006, p. 49). He writes:

> In spatial experience, I think we are presented with certain primitive spatial properties, such as Edenic squareness (although probably not with Edenic absolute lengths). Just as experience confers a grasp of a certain qualitative properties associated with colors, it also confers a grasp of a certain qualitative properties associated with space. These properties might have been instantiated in the garden of Eden, and perhaps in a classical Newtonian world. But I think that there is little reason to think that they are instantiated in our world. Certainly, it is not easy to see how there could be Edenic squareness in a relativistic world, or in a string-theoretic world in which any spatial properties are complex and derivative. In such a world, the status of primitive spatial properties is much like the status of primitive color properties in a post-Galilean world.
>
> (Chalmers, 2012, p. 333)

Abstracting from the details of Chalmers's account, the issue that arises for the primitivist account is, we think, clear. A scientific account of the world appears to have no need for primitive spatial concepts because our spatial properties are *not* Edenic. If our world does not instantiate such properties, then our science will neither postulate them nor demand the use of (primitive) terms that refer to them.

It is of course possible that there are alternative primitivist views that do not involve Edenic properties and which could be used by the proponents of the structure and dynamics argument. Such a supposition, however, is no more than a promissory note and without a detailed articulation of the nature of those terms one cannot motivate the structure and dynamics argument. Recall what is at issue here. According to the version of the structure and dynamics argument that we are currently considering, every physical truth is structural-dynamic insofar as it is expressible by a Ramsey sentence that includes only nomic, spatiotemporal, logical, and mathematical vocabulary. But how can we determine whether physical truths are equivalent to such sentences if such sentences not only involve primitive terms but we are not even told what those terms are? Indeed, in the absence of a detailed articulation of the nature of spatiotemporal terms, we would be incapable of judging whether sentences that involve such terms are capable of explaining consciousness.

What is more, according to the research program, whether we should postulate primitive spatial concepts is a question that ought to be addressed through the lens of science. Even if this is not an issue that can be entirely determined via scientific means, it is still one that makes important use of science. Thus, according to research program physicalism, one cannot assume primitivism. In fact, one cannot even assume the falsity of primitivism. Rather, one should examine how our best sciences understand spatiotemporal properties. For instance, if physics progresses in such a way that it is able to explain spatial properties in terms of *non-spatial* properties, then we would have good reasons to give up primitivism. Indeed, there are accounts of spatial (and even temporal) properties that take them to be non-fundamental (Merali, 2014; Seiberg, 2007). But if spatial (and temporal) properties turn out to be derivative, then it puts pressure on the idea that our *concepts* of those properties are, as primitivism demands, primitive. What such considerations show is that proponents of the structure and dynamics argument cannot simply assume a primitivist (or a functionalist, for that matter) account of spatiotemporal terms. They have to motivate their account of choice and say enough to clarify the nature of spatiotemporal terms.

In contrast to the primitivist view, the functionalist view is not barred from offering an explication of spatiotemporal terms in a different vocabulary. According to Chalmers, if phenomenal functionalism is correct, then:

> spatial concepts pick out that manifold of properties that serves as the normal causal basis of a corresponding manifold of properties in our spatial experience. Temporal concepts pick out that manifold of properties that serves as the normal causal basis of a corresponding manifold of properties in our temporal experience. On a view of this sort, spatial and temporal truths are a priori scrutable from phenomenal and causal truths, along with other uneliminated background truths.
>
> (2012, p. 335)

Regardless of the merits of such a view about spatiotemporal terms, it is clear that it is not one that can be used by proponents of the structure and dynamics argument. Assuming the truth of phenomenal functionalism, then physical truths because of their use of spatiotemporal terms turn out to involve phenomenal truths (see also Stoljar, 2015). If so, then one can no longer make a case that physical truths cannot explain consciousness because the former are purely structural-dynamic whereas the latter are not. Under the assumption that spatiotemporal terms implicate consciousness in some way, then a clear distinction between physical and phenomenal truths cannot be maintained: Physical truths are no longer *purely* structural-dynamic (where the qualification "purely" serves as a way to contrast structure and dynamics to the phenomenal).

It seems then that, in the present context, if one is a functionalist about spatiotemporal terms, then one has to be a *non-phenomenal* functionalist. This means that spatiotemporal terms are derivable from, or analyzable in, terms that do not involve reference to our experiences. If non-phenomenal functionalist is accepted, then the Ramsey sentence with which we began can do away with spatiotemporal terms: It only needs logical, mathematical, and nomic vocabulary.

Stoljar argues that such a construal of structural truths gives us "a very implausible account of what physical truths are" (2015, p. 341). According to Stoljar, physical truths involve more than what such Ramsey sentences can offer us. Alter (2016) disagrees. He writes:

> Theoretical physicists tend to describe their theories in highly abstract terms. Some of those theories might well be nomic-Ramsifiable, and perhaps one of them will also provide the information needed to do the relevant deduction. In any event, ruling out that possibility seems incongruous with type-C materialism.
>
> (2016, p. 809)

We are not interested in adjudicating the prospects of non-phenomenal functionalism here. If Stoljar is right, then non-phenomenal functionalism is not an appropriate account of the nature of spatiotemporal terms, and thus if one would want to run the argument from structure and dynamics one would need to offer an alternative account. If Alter is correct, then non-phenomenal functionalism is an appropriate account and can be used to explicate the notions of structure and dynamics. Still, the question as to whether consciousness can be explained by physical truths that are equivalent to Ramsey sentences that involve nomic, mathematical, and logical terms remains open. And that is all that research program physicalism requires. Research program physicalism does not claim that a compositional explanation of consciousness in terms of its physical components is certain. Our version of physicalism cannot determine that a priori. Rather, it holds that one ought to strive for such a compositional explanation and that the research program would be successful just in case it has succeeded in giving such an explanation.

Lastly, it is important to repeat that research program physicalism rejects the account of explanation that has been imposed on physicalists by anti-physicalists: A deductive-nomological model is neither the only available account of explanation nor the most appropriate one. Thus, even if structural-dynamic truths fail to a priori entail truths about phenomenal consciousness, this does not show that our physical sciences cannot explain consciousness. Such a realization emphasizes a need both for a more flexible and indeed more scientifically accurate understanding of explanation and for an expansion of our permissible understandings of physicalism. As we argued in previous chapters, an appeal to compositional explanation retains physicalism's core commitment that consciousness is nothing over and above the physical while relaxing physicalism's reliance on epistemic notions. Our revisionist understanding of physicalism turns out to be much more resilient than traditional characterizations of physicalism. Just like the previous two, this last version of the structure and dynamics argument does not offer any reasons that arrest the research program.

4. A Fresh Start

In this chapter and the previous one, we critically examined four arguments that attempt to establish the permanence of the explanatory gap: the argument from subjectivity, the argument from intersubjectivity, the argument from ignorance, and the argument from structure and dynamics. Each of these arguments falls short—that is, none manages to demonstrate that the gap will persist. In other words, none is able to rule out research program physicalism before it starts.

In a way, this should not be surprising. Philosophy has a poor track record when it comes to demarcating the limits of science. Past efforts to establish the inherent specialness of life, disease, or the heavens did not fare well. Why should consciousness be any different? The impetus for research program physicalism is the empirically informed hunch that it not. Two caveats are warranted though. The first caveat is that all we have shown is that extant arguments for a permanent explanatory gap do not work. Clearly, this does nothing to remove or ameliorate our current epistemic and explanatory situation. Worse, it does not establish that the gap will ever be closed or that the research program will succeed. Indeed, the possibility of failure is built into our conception of physicalism. Admittedly, we see this as a great benefit of our approach. Indeed, we would go further and claim that an advantage that research program physicalism has over other reconstructive approaches is that there is a clear sense in which it could fail. Having said this, it is important not to celebrate too early. This brings us to our second caveat: None of what we have said so far provides an explanation of the explanatory gap as it exists today. Why does consciousness appear so special? Why do we have such trouble conceptualizing consciousness as something nothing over and above the physical? In many ways, each of the arguments outlined previously builds on this appearance and conceptual difficulty. In the next chapter, we offer an explanation for them. We propose that, due to fundamental features of our psychology, it may very well be the case that this appearance and conceptual difficulty would persist even in the face of a successful compositional explanation of consciousness.

Notes

1. In its different forms, the argument from ignorance should be clearly distinguished from Stoljar's ignorance hypothesis. Although Stoljar's position is committed to the fact that we are ignorant of a non-experiential (but experience-relevant) truth, his position does not depend on the chronic character of such ignorance. In fact, Stoljar is explicit that whether ignorance is chronic or not is irrelevant for his purposes (see Stoljar, 2006, p. 93). For that reason, we are excluding Stoljar's position from this category of arguments.
2. McGinn repeats this narrow conception of his understanding of physical data in the following passage: "To explain the observed physical data we need only such theoretical properties as bear upon those data, not the property that explains consciousness, which does not occur in the data. Since we do not need consciousness to explain those data, we do not need the property that explains consciousness" (1989, p. 359).

3. The causal profile of property *P* consists both in the collection of conditional properties that *P* would confer on its bearer and in all the causal features that can bring about its instantiation. See, however, Shoemaker (2011). According to causal structuralism, the causal profile of *P* is both necessary and sufficient for *P*. Causal structuralism appears to be committed to the view that the profile of a property is just its causal profile. However, it has been argued that it is best to expand the profile of a property to include not only its causal features (i.e., the causal relations that it bears to other properties) but also certain higher-order mathematical features. For an elaboration and defense of this point, see Berestain (2016). Causal structuralism should be distinguished from dispositional essentialism (Locke, 2012). The latter view holds that all fundamental properties are (simply or purely) dispositions (Bird, 2007; Mellor, 1974, 1982).
4. Suppose that *O* is a lonely substance with a single property *P*. Property *P* bears no relations to other substances or properties—in this hypothetical situation, there are no other properties—and thus its causal profile is the null set. Thus, assuming the truth of causal structuralism, *P* does not exist and, contrary to our initial assumption, there cannot be a lonely substance with a single property. If, however, *O* is a lonely substance that has more than one property, then causal structuralism does not rule out its existence. The properties of *O* would be intrinsic because they will depend on nothing "external" to the substance. However, if such properties are related to other intrinsic properties, then they would still be instantiated according to causal structuralism. In other words, each intrinsic property of *O* would bear some relationship to some other intrinsic property. Although such a view about intrinsic properties would allow for the existence of lonely substances with a plurality of properties, it would render their existence both explanatorily otiose and completely mysterious.
5. Supposing that *P* and *Q* are fundamental properties, then if such properties have different associated causal profiles then they will be *distinct* properties. That is because causal structuralism requires that *P* is a duplicate of *Q* only if *P* and *Q* share their causal profiles.
6. In §6 of his essay, Lewis argues that our ignorance spreads to (most) non-fundamental properties. Such properties supervene on fundamental properties and ignorance of the identity of fundamental properties would lead, Lewis holds, to ignorance of the identities of the more complex properties that are constructed out of fundamental properties. He writes: "So, if Humility applies to some or all of the fundamental properties, it applies also to very many more properties" (2008, p. 215). We will not be concerned with the question of whether Lewis's argument also applies to non-fundamental properties. For a worry about this extension of scope, see Whittle (2006, pp. 464–465).
7. Such properties are simple; they "are not at all disjunctive, or determinable, or negative" nor are they "conjunctive or structural" (2008, p. 204).
8. Lewis's point is one that both Bertrand Russell and Grover Maxwell raised before. For instance, Maxwell agrees with Lewis when he says that scientific terms refer to intrinsic properties and yet science "leave[s] us completely ignorant as to *what* these intrinsic properties *are*" (1979, p. 397). In fact, Maxwell seems to accept *quidditism*: "It is (logically) possible for different causal networks to have the same causal structure; or, in other words, one and the same causal structure may be realized in a number of different ways" (1979, p. 390). See also Russell (1927).
9. For a different development of this point, see Langton (2004), Whittle (2006), and Schaffer (2005). For a response, see Locke (2008).
10. Obviously, there will be tension between the two positions *if* intrinsic properties turn out to be phenomenal in some way. We address this point in the following section.
11. For the purposes of evaluating this argument, we are grouping together, on the one hand, physical truths, and on the other, biological and neuroscientific truths.

First, both types of truths appear to be truths about structure and dynamics and thus if the argument applies to physical truths, it should also apply to biological and neuroscientific truths. Second, proponents of the argument are likely to accept that biological and neuroscientific truths are a priori entailed by physical truths. If so, then biological and neuroscientific truths come for free: Armed with the necessary biological and neuroscientific concepts, one can deduce them from a rich enough collection of physical truths. We think that proponents of the argument are committed to both of these reasons. On the one hand, a denial of the first reason renders the conclusion of the argument false: If biological and neuroscientific truths are not structural or dynamic, then, given that we have physical explanations of biological and neuroscientific phenomena, it is not true that we cannot explain non-structural, non-dynamical truths using only structural-dynamic truths. On the other hand, if proponents of the argument do not accept that biological and neuroscientific truths are a priori entailed by physical truths, then even if the argument is sound, it would still not show that the explanatory gap is permanent. Even if consciousness cannot be given an explanation in terms of physics, it could still be the case that we can explain consciousness using a broader explanatory basis, one that includes in addition to the truths of physics those of biology and neuroscience. What is more, a rejection of the claim that biological and neuroscientific truths are a priori entailed by physical truths would undermine the main motivation behind anti-physicalist arguments. If there is an epistemic gap between biological truths and physical truths but no corresponding ontological gap, then the fact (assuming that it is one) that phenomenal truths are not a priori entailed by physical truths, should not lead one to any ontological conclusions about the status of consciousness.

12. See Chalmers's (2010b) "Two Dimensional Argument Against Materialism." In his defense of the claim that *PIT&~Q* is not merely prima facie conceivable but also ideally conceivable, he appeals to the structure and dynamics argument. Jackson's presentation of the knowledge argument does not appeal to considerations about structure and dynamics. However, if premise 2 were false, then it becomes much harder to insist that Mary lacks certain knowledge while in her black-and-white room.
13. In presenting this response to Stoljar, Alter focuses only on structure and not also on dynamics, but his notion of *weaker-than-structural* can be expanded to accommodate both. That is, whereas a sentence *S* is weaker-than-structural if and only if *S* is a priori entailed by a purely structural true sentence but does not a priori entail such a true sentence, a sentence S is *weaker-than-dynamical* if and only if *S* is a priori entailed by a purely dynamical true sentence but does not a priori entail such a true sentence. Consequently, premise 3 should now hold that the truths about consciousness cannot be exhausted by any combination of purely structural truths, purely dynamical truths, weaker-than-structural truths, and weaker-than-dynamical truths.
14. For some issues with the notion of a purely extrinsic property, see Stoljar (2015, p. 333).
15. Or as Stoljar describes the primitivist view: "the primitivist account . . . treats these expressions not as a priori equivalent to definite descriptions of a certain form but as instead as names for a certain class of properties and relations" (2015, p. 342).

References

Alter, T. (2009). Does the ignorance hypothesis undermine the conceivability and knowledge arguments? *Philosophy and Phenomenological Research*, 79(3), 756–765.

Alter, T. (2016). The structure and dynamics argument against materialism. *Noûs*, *50*(4), 794–815.

Alter, T., & Nagasawa, Y. (2012). What is Russellian monism? *Journal of Consciousness Studies*, *19*(9–10), 67–95.

Barsalou, L. W. (1999). Perceptual symbol systems. *Behavioral and Brain Sciences*, *22*, 577–609.

Barsalou, L. W. (2008). Grounded cognition. *Annual Review of Psychology*, *59*, 617–645.

Berestain, N. (2016). What a structuralist theory of properties could not be. In A. Marmodoro & D. Yates (eds.), *The metaphysics of relations* (pp. 157–176). Oxford, UK: Oxford University Press.

Bird, A. (2007). *Nature's metaphysics*. Oxford, UK: Oxford University Press.

Blackburn, S. (1990). Filling in space. *Analysis*, *50*(2), 62–65.

Chalmers, D. J. (1995). Facing up to the problem of consciousness. *Journal of Consciousness Studies*, 2(3), 200–219.

Chalmers, D. J. (1996). *The conscious mind: In search of a fundamental theory*. New York: Oxford University Press.

Chalmers, D. J. (2003). Consciousness and its place in nature. In S. P. Stich & T. A. Warfield (eds.), *The Blackwell guide to philosophy of mind* (pp. 102–142). Malden, MA: Blackwell. Revised version in Chalmers, 2010, pp. 103–140.

Chalmers, D. J. (2006). Perception and the fall from Eden. In T. S. Gendler & J. Hawthorne (eds.), *Perceptual experience* (pp. 49–125). Oxford, UK: Oxford University Press.

Chalmers, D. J. (2010a). *The character of consciousness*. New York: Oxford University Press.

Chalmers, D. J. (2010b). The two-dimensional argument against materialism. In *The character of consciousness* (pp. 141–207). Oxford, UK: Oxford University Press.

Chalmers, D. J. (2012). *Constructing the world*. Oxford, UK: Oxford University Press.

Churchland, P. M. (1988). Perceptual plasticity and theoretical neutrality: A reply to Jerry Fodor. *Philosophy of Science*, *55*, 167–187.

Churchland, P. M. (1995). *The engine of reason, the seat of the soul*. Cambridge, MA: MIT Press.

Churchland, P. S. (1986). *Neurophilosophy*. Cambridge, MA: MIT Press.

Churchland, P. S. (1996). The hornswoggle problem. *Journal of Consciousness Studies*, *3*(5–6), 402–408.

Demopoulos, W., & Friedman, M. (1985). Bertrand Russell's the analysis of matter: Its historical context and contemporary interest. *Philosophy of Science*, *52*(4), 621–639.

Dretske, F. (1995). *Naturalizing the mind*. Cambridge, MA: MIT Press.

Duhem, P. (1996). *Essays in history and philosophy of science*. (R. Ariew & P. Barker, eds.). Indianapolis, IN: Hackett.

Elpidorou, A. (2016). A posteriori physicalism and introspection. *Pacific Philosophical Quarterly*, 97(4), 474–500.

Faraday, M. (1844). A speculation touching electric conduction, and the nature of matter. *Journal of the Franklin Institute*, *37*(6), 392–399.

Fischer, M. H., & Zwaan, R. A. (2008). Embodied language: A review of the motor system in language comprehension. *Quarterly Journal of Experimental Psychology*, *6*, 825–850.

Flanagan, O. (1991). *The science of the mind*. Cambridge, MA: MIT Press.
Flanagan, O. (1992). *Consciousness reconsidered*. Cambridge, MA: MIT Press.
Francescotti, R. (1999). How to define intrinsic properties. *Noûs*, *33*, 590–609.
Gallese, V., & Lakoff, G. (2005). The brain's concepts: The role of the sensory-motor system in reason and language. *Cognitive Neuropsychology*, *22*, 455–479.
Harman, G. (1990). The intrinsic quality of experience. *Philosophical Perspectives*, *4*, 31–52.
Hawthorne, J. (2001). Causal structuralism. *Noûs*, *35*(s15), 361–378.
Hill, C. S. (2009). *Consciousness*. Cambridge, UK: Cambridge University Press.
Humberstone, I. L. (1996). Intrinsic/extrinsic. *Synthese*, *108*, 205–267.
Kemmerer, D. (2010). How words capture visual experience: The perspective from cognitive neuroscience. In B. Malt & P. Wolff (eds.), *Words and the world: How words capture human experience* (pp. 289–329). Oxford, UK: Oxford University Press.
Kiefer, M., & Pulvermüller, F. (2012). Conceptual representations in mind and brain: Theoretical developments, current evidence, and future directions. *Cortex*, *48*, 805–825.
Langton, R. (1998). *Kantian humility: Our ignorance of things in themselves*. Oxford, UK: Oxford University Press.
Langton, R. (2004). Elusive knowledge of things in themselves. *Australasian Journal of Philosophy*, *82*(1), 129–136.
Langton, R., & Lewis, D. (1998). Defining "intrinsic." *Philosophy and Phenomenological Research*, *58*, 333–345.
Leuenberger, S. (2010). Humility and constraints on O-language. *Philosophical Studies*, *149*(3), 327–354.
Levine, J. (1983). Materialism and qualia: The explanatory gap. *Pacific Philosophical Quarterly*, *64*(4), 354–361.
Lewis, D. (1983). New work for a theory of universals. *Australasian Journal of Philosophy*, *61*(4), 343–377.
Lewis, D. (1986). *On the plurality of worlds*. Malden, MA: Blackwell Publishing.
Lewis, D. (2001). Redefining "intrinsic." *Philosophy and Phenomenological Research*, *63*, 381–398.
Lewis, D. (2008). Ramseyan humility. In D. Braddon-Mitchell & R. Nola (eds.), *Conceptual analysis and philosophical naturalism* (pp. 203–222). Cambridge, MA: MIT Press.
Locke, D. (2008). A partial defense of Ramseyan humility. In D. Braddon-Mitchell & R. Nola (eds.), *Conceptual analysis and philosophical naturalism* (pp. 223–242). Cambridge, MA: MIT Press.
Locke, D. (2012). Quidditism without quiddities. *Philosophical Studies*, *160*(3), 345–363.
Lockwood, M. (1989). *Mind, brain, and the quantum*. New York, NY: Oxford University Press.
Lycan, W. (1996). *Consciousness and experience*. Cambridge, MA: MIT Press.
Lyons, J. (2011). Circularity, reliability, and the cognitive penetrability of perception. *Philosophical Issues*, *21*(1), 289–311.
Macpherson, F. (2012). Cognitive penetration of color experience: Rethinking the issue in light of an indirect mechanism. *Philosophy and Phenomenological Research*, *84*(1), 24–62.
Maxwell, G. (1979). Rigid designators and mind-brain identity. *Minnesota Studies in the Philosophy of Science*, *9*, 365–403.

McGinn, C. (1989). Can we solve the mind-body problem? *Mind*, *98*(391), 349–366.

Mellor, D. H. (1974). In defense of dispositions. *The Philosophical Review*, *83*, 157–181.

Mellor, D. H. (1982). Counting corners correctly. *Analysis*, *42*, 96–97.

Merali, Z. (2014). In search of time's origin. *Nautilus*, (9). http://nautil.us/issue/9/time/in-search-of-times-origin

Montero, B. (2010). A Russellian response to the structural argument against physicalism. *Journal of Consciousness Studies*, *17*(3–4), 70–83.

Newman, M. H. A. (1928). Mr. Russell's causal theory of perception. *Mind*, *37*, 137–148.

Ney, A. (2007). Physicalism and our knowledge of intrinsic properties. *Australasian Journal of Philosophy*, *85*(1), 41–60.

Pereboom, D. (2011). *Consciousness and the prospects of physicalism*. Oxford, UK: Oxford University Press.

Pereboom, D. (2013). Russellian monism and absolutely intrinsic properties. In U. Kriegel (ed.), *Current controversies in philosophy of mind* (pp. 40–69). New York, NY: Routledge.

Pereboom, D. (2015). Consciousness, physicalism, and absolutely intrinsic properties. In T. Alter & Y. Nagawasa (eds.), *Consciousness in the physical world: Perspectives on Russellian monism* (pp. 300–323). Oxford, UK: Oxford University Press.

Pylyshyn, Z. W. (1999). Is vision continuous with cognition? The case for cognitive impenetrability of visual perception. *Behavioral and Brain Sciences*, *22*, 341–423.

Quine, W. V. O. (1951). Two dogmas of empiricism. *The Philosophical Review*, *60*(1), 20–43.

Raftopoulos, A. (2001). Reentrant neural pathways and the theory-ladenness of perception. *Philosophy of Science*, *68*(S3), S187–S199.

Raftopoulos, A. (2009). *Cognition and perception: How do psychology and neural science inform philosophy?* Cambridge, MA: MIT Press.

Rowlands, M. (2001). *The nature of consciousness*. Cambridge, UK: Cambridge University Press.

Russell, B. (1927). *The analysis of matter*. London, UK: Kegan Paul Ltd.

Schaffer, J. (2005). Quiddistic knowledge. *Philosophical Studies*, *123*, 1–32.

Seiberg, N. (2007). Emergent spacetime. In D. Gross, M. Henneaux, & A. Sevrin (eds.), *The quantum structure of space and time*, proceedings of the 23rd Solvay conference on physics, Brussels, Belgium, 1–3 December, 2005 (pp. 163–178). Singapore: World Scientific.

Sellars, W. (1963). *Science, perception and reality*. London, UK: Routledge & Kegan Paul Ltd.

Shoemaker, S. (1984). Causality and properties. In *Identity, cause, and mind* (pp. 206–233). Cambridge, UK: Cambridge University Press.

Shoemaker, S. (1998). Causal and metaphysical necessity. *Pacific Philosophical Quarterly*, *79*, 59–77.

Shoemaker, S. (2011). Realization, powers, and property identity. *The Monist*, *94*(1), 3–18.

Sider, T. (1993). Intrinsic properties. *Philosophical Studies*, *83*, 1–27.

Siegel, S. (2012). Cognitive penetrability and perceptual justification. *Noûs*, *46*(2), 201–222.

Stokes, D. (2013). Cognitive penetrability of perception. *Philosophy Compass*, *8*(7), 646–663.

Stoljar, D. (2001). Two conceptions of the physical. *Philosophy and Phenomenological Research*, *62*(2), 253–281.

Stoljar, D. (2006). *Ignorance and imagination: The epistemic origin of the problem of consciousness*. Oxford, UK: Oxford University Press.

Stoljar, D. (2010). *Physicalism*. New York, NY: Routledge.

Stoljar, D. (2013). Four kinds of Russellian monism. In U. Kriegel (ed.), *Current controversies in philosophy of mind* (pp. 17–39). New York, NY: Routledge.

Stoljar, D. (2015). Russellian monism or Nagelian monism? In T. Alter & Y. Nagawasa (eds.), *Consciousness in the physical world: Perspectives on Russellian monism* (pp. 324–345). Oxford, UK: Oxford University Press.

Strawson, G. (2008). *Real materialism and other essays*. Oxford, UK: Oxford University Press.

Swoyer, C. (1982). The nature of natural laws. *Australasian Journal of Philosophy*, *60*, 203–223.

Tegmark, M. (1998). Is "the theory of everything" merely the ultimate ensemble theory? *Annals of Physics*, *270*(1), 1–51.

Tye, M. (1995). *Ten problems of consciousness*. Cambridge, MA: MIT Press.

Tye, M. (2009). Representationalist theories of consciousness. In A. Beckermann, B. P. McLaughlin, & S. Walter (eds.), *The Oxford handbook of philosophy of mind* (pp. 253–267). Oxford, UK: Oxford University Press.

Vallentyne, P. (1997). Intrinsic properties defined. *Philosophical Studies*, *88*, 209–219.

van Cleve, J. (2011). Epistemic humility and causal structuralism. In J. Roessler, H. Lerman, & N. Eilan (eds.), *Perception, causation, and objectivity* (pp. 82–91). Oxford, UK: Oxford University Press.

Weatherson, B., & Marshall, D. (2017). Intrinsic vs. extrinsic properties. In E. N. Zalta (ed.), *The Stanford encyclopedia of philosophy*. https://plato.stanford.edu/archives/fall2017/entries/intrinsic-extrinsic/

Whittle, A. (2006). On an argument for humility. *Philosophical Studies*, *130*(3), 461–497.

Zeimbekis, J., & Raftopoulos, A. (eds.). (2015). *The cognitive penetrability of perception: New philosophical perspectives*. Oxford, UK: Oxford University Press.

7 The Psychological Turn

Let us take stock of where we are and how we got here. We began in Chapter 2 with a discussion of the significant challenges facing attempts to offer an effective metaphysical account of the nothing-over-and-above relationship central to most forms of physicalism. Although many philosophers would likely respond that their favorite approach overcomes these challenges, we proposed that a reconsideration of physicalism is warranted. In Chapter 3, we highlighted an additional problem for physicalism, Hempel's Dilemma, which threatens to undermine its connection to the physical sciences. As others have before, we argued that a reconstructive account is needed in order to address this dilemma. Building on previous attempts, we developed the idea that physicalism should be viewed as a research program. In Chapter 4, we then argued that this research program should seek to offer a physically based compositional explanation of consciousness, and we explicated the demands of such a type of explanation. Lastly, in Chapters 5 and 6 we responded to arguments meant to show that the explanatory gap that we face with respect to consciousness can never be overcome. We argued that research program physicalism is not threatened by theoretical or a priori attempts to establish the permanence of the explanatory gap.

For physicalists who are looking for an alternative to traditional metaphysical conceptions of physicalism, the news is good. The research program offers an explanation-first account of physicalism with the following characteristics: It avoids Hempel's Dilemma, is not undermined by traditional anti-physicalist arguments, and is attuned to scientific practice insofar as the notion of explanation that it employs is one that figures prominently in successful scientific explanations.

1. The Persistence of an Appearance

Despite its promise, research program physicalism might still be met with suspicion. That is because even after all that has been said and done, consciousness continues to *appear* other than physical. While in and of itself the appearance of a difference between physical processes and consciousness may not serve as a direct refutation of the goals or ambitions of the research program, its persistence ought to concern us. Previously, we have tried to undermine attempts meant to establish that the explanatory gap is permanent. Yet, we have not addressed the appearance of consciousness' uniqueness. Doesn't consciousness appear to be different or distinct from physical entities and processes? Doesn't it appear to be something other than the physical? And more importantly, won't it continue to appear as such even in the face of great biological and neuroscientific progress? The challenge that the appearance of consciousness' uniqueness poses to the research program is different, we contend, than the challenges considered in Chapters 5 and 6. In those chapters, we examined arguments against the possibility of offering an explanation of consciousness. But the appearance of consciousness' uniqueness, one may hold, could persist even if we have (compositionally) explained consciousness. That is, even if we have specified the components that we take to be constitutively responsible for the presence of consciousness, one might insist that consciousness will persist to seem to us as something over and above its components. If so, then how could the research program succeed? Wouldn't the appearance demonstrate the limited reach of physical explanation?

Among those who support an empirical approach to the question of consciousness, it has become standard to push back against the notion that consciousness' status or nature is remarkable or somehow special (e.g., P. S. Churchland, 1986; Daniel, 1991). The general idea behind this response is simple: Consciousness is no more special than other complex phenomena. A prominent criticism of the purported uniqueness of consciousness points out that such an appearance of uniqueness might simply be the result of a failure of the imagination. After all, isn't the whole point of science to overcome ignorance and offer explanations for striking and previously mysterious phenomena? Didn't magnetism, the movement of celestial bodies, and existence of life seem similarly puzzling and unexplainable? Defenders of the severity of the problem of consciousness often respond that there are compelling reasons to think that the problem of consciousness is vexing in a way that these other problems were not. This feeds into a second and related criticism of consciousness' purported uniqueness. This criticism uses the historical failures of analogous arguments made in relation to the specialness of life or planetary motion to undermine the current claim about the specialness of consciousness. We too make use of these analogies. Indeed, as discussed in Chapter 3, these analogies help shape the core of the research program. However, an important caveat needs to be made: The success of the research program physicalism does not require that the appearance of uniqueness be extinguished; it only requires that we find a successful compositional explanation of consciousness.[1] While we do not deny that the appearance of uniqueness may ultimately fade, our account does not require this particular outcome.

Hence, although we advocate an empirically oriented conception of physicalism, we also accept that consciousness appears different than ordinary physical processes and entities. The important question then becomes: What does such an appearance reveal? The answer favored by most anti-physicalists is that such an appearance of uniqueness is symptomatic of consciousness' ontological status. To wit, the reason why consciousness appears to be unique is because it is, ontologically speaking, *sui generis*: Consciousness is not physical. The research program is, of course, antithetical to such an account of consciousness' appearance of uniqueness. In fact, as we argued in detail in the previous chapters, we are confident in the prospects of a research program that aims to offer a compositional explanation of consciousness. But in light of our assessment that we do not have any good reasons to think that the explanatory gap is permanent, the need to offer an alternative account for the obstinacy of this appearance becomes all the more pressing. In this chapter, we aim to do precisely that. We offer an explanation for the apparent uniqueness of consciousness that is fully compatible with research program physicalism: We argue that our perception of consciousness' uniqueness is the result of basic features of human psychology.

The psychological turn that we take in this chapter shares much with a popular defense of physicalism within analytic metaphysics referred to as "the Phenomenal Concept Strategy" (PCS).[2] The research program is *not* however a version of PCS. Research program physicalism is after all incompatible with a key premise of PCS. The latter holds that even though the explanatory gap remains, it is still incorrect to infer on the basis of such a gap an ontological gap. In other words, even though we will never have a physical explanation of consciousness, consciousness is still physical according to PCS. It is physical because our inability to bridge the explanatory gap is a consequence of our conceptual capacities. Therefore, the presence of the explanatory gap is indicative of a fact about human psychology and not of a metaphysical fact about the ontological status of consciousness.

From the perspective of research program physicalism, PCS combines a good idea with two problematic ones. The good idea is that presumed facts about consciousness ought to be examined *psychologically*—we need to empirically investigate our attitudes towards consciousness, especially if these play a prominent role in anti-physicalist arguments. Yet, PCS takes two wrong turns that render it an unattractive and a deeply problematic position. First, PCS accepts an unscientific and overly demanding model of explanation—it requires that a successful physical explanation of consciousness is one that demonstrates the a priori deducibility of phenomenal truths from physical truths. Second, in light of the difficulties in offering an a priori deduction from the physical to the phenomenal, PCS maintains that although consciousness cannot be physically explained, physicalism demands no such explanation. Physicalism, PCS holds, is consistent with the presence of a permanent explanatory gap.[3] Such an admission, however, robs PCS of its plausibility as a *physicalist* view. An explanation is necessary in order to render consciousness' place in our world intelligible. In the absence of such an explanation, the anti-physicalist has every right to conclude that consciousness is something over and above the physical.

Research program physicalism insists that it is a grave mistake to demand such a strong conception of explanation. And by eschewing this notion of explanation, our version of physicalism can draw a distinction between an explanation and our attitudes towards it. The presence of a compositional explanation does not ipso facto render the explained phenomenon ordinary or humdrum; it need not dispel any residual feelings of uneasiness or puzzlement. Nor is a sense of satisfaction ("seeing" how everything fits together) a necessary condition for a good explanation. Explanation is one thing; our subjective understanding of explanation is another. It is thus perfectly consistent with research program physicalism that a compositional explanation of consciousness may still give rise to the psychological appearance that consciousness is different than its components. The contention that a sense of understanding or intelligibility is neither a necessary nor a sufficient condition of an adequate explanation is not original with us (de Regt, 2009; Rowlands, 2001; Trout, 2002; Wright, 2007). Still, in this chapter, we offer support for this contention by considering the nature of our conceptual capacities when thinking about physicalist explanations of consciousness. We argue that bridging the explanatory gap does not require that consciousness cease to appear other than physical. We establish this by offering a speculative account of this appearance that is inspired by current research on concepts. While this account leaves some questions unanswered, it illustrates the possibility of a plausible empirical explanation of this appearance.

Even though a compositional explanation of consciousness would explain consciousness by specifying how it arises out of the workings of its components, the intuition (or appearance) that consciousness is something more than its parts might not go away. But precisely because this appearance is a product of our psychological makeup, it carries no real epistemic weight—it fails to establish that the explanatory gap is permanent and does not threaten the research program.

Previously we mentioned that the research program sees the problem of consciousness similarly to how non-vitalistic biology viewed life: Just like life, consciousness is a phenomenon that calls for a compositional explanation. Although this is true, there still may be an important difference between the two cases. Examinations of consciousness are, in an important sense, impredicative: Consciousness itself is implicated in explanations of consciousness. In other words, we use consciousness in order to grasp our explanation of consciousness. Because of this feature of consciousness, an investigation of the nature of consciousness and its place in the world may require an examination not only of its objective reality but also of our subjective understanding of that reality. Therefore, in addition to a physical (compositional) explanation of consciousness, one may also need to offer a psychological account of why consciousness continues to appear different than, or over and above, its physical components. The work of research program physicalism may not be complete until we have addressed the psychology of a physicalist explanation of consciousness.

2. The Problem and a (Proposed) Solution

Psychological attitudes toward consciousness have often been cited as reasons to doubt the prospects of physicalism. Perhaps the most famous use of such attitudes occurs in the concluding pages of Saul Kripke's *Naming and Necessity*. Let us agree that "pain of type Φ" (hereafter abbreviated as "pain Φ") and "neural activity Ψ"[4] are both rigid designators and that pain Φ, according to identity theorists, is identical to neural activity Ψ. The statement "pain Φ is neural activity Ψ," if true, must be true necessarily. Yet, the statement appears to be contingent: We can conceive of a possible world[5] in which pain Φ occurs but there is no neural activity Ψ, and we can conceive of a possible world in which there is neural activity Ψ without the occurrence of pain Φ. This appearance of contingency is at odds with the purported metaphysical status of the proposition expressed by the identity statement. If "pain Φ is neural activity Ψ" is true necessarily, then there can be no possible world in which pain Φ is not neural activity Ψ and in which neural activity Ψ is not pain Φ. Identity theorists thus owe us a story as to how an identity claim can appear to be contingent even though it is not. As Kripke puts it:

> Someone who wishes to maintain an identity thesis [say, "*A* is identical to *B*," where "*A*" names the sensation of pain and "*B*" names a brain state] cannot simply *accept* the Cartesian intuitions that *A* can exist without *B*, that *B* can exist without *A*, that the correlative presence of anything with mental properties is merely contingent to *B*, and that the correlative presence of any specific physical properties is merely contingent to *A*. He must explain these intuitions away, showing how they are illusory.
>
> (Kripke, 1980, p. 148)[6]

The problem with the mind-brain identity thesis is that there seems to be no obvious way of explaining *away* the appearance of contingency (see also Kripke, 1971). Unlike other *a posteriori* necessary identity statements (e.g., "water is H_2O" or "heat is molecular motion"), the appearance of contingency in mind-brain identity statements is persistent.[7] Or so Kripke holds.

In recent years, many physicalists have offered a response to Kripke's challenge. According to them, mind-brain identity statements should not be thought to be analogous to ordinary *a posteriori* identity statements of the sort "heat is molecular motion," for even though we can explain away the appearance of contingency in the latter case, the appearance of contingency in the former remains. Yet, this persistence of the appearance of contingency raises no insurmountable difficulties for physicalism. That is because proponents of physicalism can offer a physicalistically acceptable explanation of both the appearance of contingency and its persistency. Kripke's challenge is thus met not by explaining *away* the appearance of contingency, but by explaining why the appearance fails to go away.

In trying to account for the appearance and persistency of contingency, the following approach, which is integral to most versions of the PCS, has gained prominence. First, a distinction between two different ways of thinking about conscious experiences is drawn. Accordingly, one can think of experiences both *physically* and *phenomenally*. One thinks of experiences (one's own or others') physically if one thinks about them in terms of either their material constitution or their functional/behavioral profiles. In doing so, one picks out experiences as external, physical (or functional) properties, and does so via the use of what are often called "physical concepts."[8] At the same time, one can also think of experiences in terms of their phenomenological character. In this case, one thinks of experiences from within, so to speak, and in doing so one employs phenomenal concepts. Phenomenal concepts are the concepts that we use when, but arguably not only when, we introspectively notice or focus on the phenomenological character of our experiences. They refer to phenomenological properties (or qualities) and they do so in a first-personal and direct (non-relational) manner. Different proposals specifying the nature of these concepts can be found in the literature.[9] However, as long as such accounts are enlisted in the service of physicalism, they must all hold that the referents of phenomenal concepts are ultimately physical. In other words, although phenomenal concepts may conceive of or present their referents phenomenally, they must still denote physical states or properties.

It is precisely on the basis of the distinction between physical and phenomenal concepts that many proponents of the PCS have found a way to respond to Kripke's challenge. More specifically, they have offered the following explanation for the appearance of contingency in mind-brain identity statements:

> **Difference in Introspective Phenomenology (DIP):** Mind-brain identity statements involve both physical and phenomenal concepts. Entertaining such statements, therefore, requires the exercise of both physical and phenomenal concepts. But the exercise of those two different kinds of concepts brings about a difference in introspective phenomenology. The exercise of phenomenal concepts typically involves a distinctive experience, viz., one that is similar or identical to the referent of the phenomenal concept deployed, whereas the exercise of physical concepts does not. It is precisely this difference in phenomenology that gives rise to the appearance of contingency. Example: Thinking about patterns of neural activity Ψ does not involve the same type of phenomenology that thinking about pain Φ involves. On account of this difference in phenomenology, we are misled to think that the concepts PAIN Φ and NEURAL ACTIVITY Ψ do not necessarily co-refer.

DIP can be traced back to Nagel's (1974, fn. 11) famous distinction between *sympathetic* and *perceptual* imagination. Note, however, that whereas Nagel's distinction is meant to explain the appearance of contingency in *imaginative* acts, DIP applies to ways of thinking about mind-brain identity statements that occur without the explicit engagement of imagination. Furthermore, Nagel's proposed model for explaining the appearance of contingency is often thought to require a distinction between two psychological mechanisms or faculties of the imagination (Doggett & Stoljar, 2010, pp. 128–130). DIP requires no such distinction. Still, both DIP and Nagel's explanation of the appearance of contingency are premised on the existence of a difference in introspective phenomenology between thinking of or imagining mental states, on the one hand, and thinking of or imagining brain states, on the other.

Although a version of DIP can also be found in Lycan (1987, pp. 76–77), it is Loar (1990 and 1997) and Papineau (1993) that appear to be the first proponents of physicalism to have defended DIP in the form given previously (see also Hill, 1984 and Jackson, 1980 for the earliest expressions of PCS or something near enough). For example, in his "Phenomenal States," Brian Loar writes:

> A phenomenal concept exercised in the absence of the phenomenal quality it stands for often involves not merely a recognitional disposition but also an image. And so, as a psychological state in its own right, a phenomenal concept—given its intimate connection with imaging—bears a phenomenological affinity to a phenomenal state that neither state bears to the entertaining of a physical-theoretical concept. When we then bring phenomenal and physical-theoretical concepts together in our philosophical ruminations, those cognitive states are phenomenologically so different that the illusion may be created that their references must be different. It is as though antiphysicalist intuitions rest on a resemblance theory of mental representation, as though we conclude from the lack of resemblance in our phenomenal and physical-functional conceptions a lack of sameness in the properties to which they refer.
>
> (1997, p. 302)[10]

David Papineau's discussion of the "antipathetic fallacy" reiterates Loar's diagnosis of the appearance of contingency (Papineau, 1993). In his *Thinking about Consciousness*, Papineau develops DIP even further:

> [E]xercising a phenomenal concept will *feel* like having the experience itself. When you think imaginatively about a pain, or about seeing something red—or even more, when you think introspectively about these experiences while having them—versions of these experiences themselves will be present in you. . . . Now compare the exercise of

> some material concept which might refer to just the same conscious state. No similar feelings there. . . . So there is an intuitive sense in which exercises of material concepts "leave out" the experience at issue. They "leave out" the pain and the technicolour phenomenology, in the sense that they don't activate or involve these experiences. Now, it is all too easy to slide from this to the conclusion that, in exercising material concepts, we are not thinking about the experiences themselves.
>
> (2002, p. 170)

> There is a sense in which material concepts do "leave out" the feelings. They do not use the experiences in question—they do not activate them, by contrast with phenomenal concepts, which do activate the experiences. . . . This then offers a natural account of the intuitive feeling that conscious experiences must be distinct from any material states. This feeling arises because we have a special way of thinking about our conscious experiences—namely, by using phenomenal concepts. We can think about our conscious experiences using concepts to which they bear a phenomenal resemblance. And this then creates the fallacious impression that other, material ways of thinking about those experiences fail to refer to the felt experiences themselves.
>
> (p. 171; compare this to Papineau, 1993 but also to Papineau, 2007, §4)[11]

In addition to Nagel (1974), Lycan (1987), Loar (1990 and 1997), and Papineau (1993 and 2002), other proponents of physicalism have thought that introspective phenomenology is crucial in offering a response to Kripke's challenge (see, e.g., Tye, 1999, p. 712f. and 2003, p. 100; §17; Balog, 2012, pp. 29–30; cf. Hill, 1997; Sturgeon, 1994, pp. 231–232; Levin, 2007b).[12]

It is important to note that the fact that DIP has been traditionally used in support of PCS and metaphysical accounts of physicalism does not necessarily restrict its application to such views. Indeed, it is easy to see how DIP can be of value to the research program. Even though the research program is not directly threatened by Kripke's conceivability-style argument (see Chapters 5–6), Kripke's challenge is one that has to be taken seriously: If, as we maintain, consciousness is physical, then why does it appear to be otherwise? An answer to this question is needed. It should be clear, however, that within the context of the research program DIP will not be offered as a way of explaining the appearance of contingency—the research program is not a metaphysical thesis and as such it does not concern itself with metaphysically possible scenarios. Rather, within the context of the research program, DIP will be employed as a way of accounting for the psychological fact that consciousness persists to appear other than physical even as we amass more and more facts about its physical nature.

Our objective in this chapter is to evaluate DIP in light of recent empirical research on concepts. If it is true that consciousness appears to be distinct from (or over and above) the physical, then such an attitude is first and foremost a *psychological* fact: It is a fact about how the human mind operates when it entertains certain statements. But if it is a psychological fact, then psychology and cognitive science are poised to help us to understand the nature of this appearance of consciousness' uniqueness and to evaluate whether DIP offers the correct explanation. Given the importance of DIP, it is surprising that proponents of physicalism have generally advanced it on intuitive grounds and largely without consulting empirical findings regarding the nature of conceptual representations.

We are not alone in recognizing this omission. Nicholas Shea (2014) offers an attack on DIP that rests on the claim that empirical psychology fails to support the very idea of a meaningful phenomenological distinction between physical concepts and phenomenal concepts. In particular, he makes an appeal to the large body of evidence suggesting that our concepts are often embodied and thus grounded in sensorimotor systems. Roughly put, he argues that conceptual embodiment excludes DIP because physical concepts also contain experiential representations and their deployment can bring about a certain type of introspective phenomenology. Intrigued by this argument and somewhat surprised by its conclusion, we endeavor to examine the relationship of embodied cognition to DIP. What we find is ultimately more complicated and, to our minds, more interesting than we initially expected. While it is true that embodiment threatens most traditional formulations of DIP that focus on the special features of phenomenal concepts, it is possible to formulate a new version of DIP that is thoroughly in keeping with embodied cognition and focuses on the features of physical concepts.

3. Conceptual Embodiment

Concepts are important building blocks of human cognition. Cognitive scientists view them as bodies of knowledge that are stored in long-term memory and used in higher cognitive activities such as categorization, decision-making, and language processing.[13] Traditionally, researchers have assumed that concepts were handled by an amodal representational system that was independent of the modality-specific systems associated with our experiences of the world (Anderson, 1983). Recently, though, this assumption has been challenged and there has been a general movement away from a disembodied view of concepts towards an embodied one in which they are significantly grounded in sensory and motor systems.

A diverse and ever increasing body of evidence supports the thesis that action, emotion, and perception systems play an instrumental role in many types of conceptual processing (for extensive reviews, see Barsalou, 2008; Fischer & Zwaan, 2008; Kemmerer, 2010). Because a full accounting of this evidence would take too long, we will limit ourselves to a brief description of some representative behavioral, brain imaging, and neuropsychological studies that provide an initial indication that our concepts are tightly intertwined with sensorimotor systems. For the sake of space and ease of presentation, we will focus on perceptual and action systems.

A number of behavioral studies implicate perceptual systems in semantic tasks. To give an example, Pecher, Zeelenberg, and Barsalou (2003) found a modality-switching cost associated with a property verification task. Participants verified verbally expressed facts involving one modality (such as the fact that *leaves rustle*) more rapidly after verifying a fact involving the same modality (such as the fact that *blenders make noise*) than after verifying a fact involving a different modality (such as the fact that *cranberries are tart*). More recently, van Dantzig, Pecher, Zeelenberg, and Barsalou (2008) found a similar modality-switching cost when participants alternated between a perceptual detection task and a property verification task.

Neuroimaging data provide further evidence of embodiment. Martin, Wiggs, Ungerleider, and Haxby (1996), for example, compared neural responses in a naming task to line drawings of animals and tools. In addition to shared areas of activation, the animal drawings selectively activated early visual areas and the tools selectively activated premotor areas. Some caution is warranted because subsequent studies have generated inconsistent results with these categories (Gerlach, 2007). Fortunately a number of studies have found links between conceptual processing and activation in sensory areas. For instance, reading odor-related words (e.g., *cinnamon*, *garlic*, and *jasmine*) elicits increased activation in the primary olfactory cortex relative to neutral control words (Gonzalez et al., 2006). In a carefully constructed study combining functional magnetic resonance imaging (fMRI) and recordings of event-related potentials (ERP), visual words with acoustic conceptual features activated auditory brain areas approximately 150 ms after stimulus presentation (Kiefer, Sim, Herrnberger, Grothe, & Hoenig, 2008). The rapidity and selectivity of this response suggests that is automatic and unconscious. Further support for conceptual embodiment involving perception systems is provided by clinical studies indicating that damage to perceptual areas can lead to conceptual deficits (Simmons & Barsalou, 2003). Damage to the somatosensory cortex, for example, may impair the visual recognition of facial expressions (Adolphs, Damasio, Tranel, Cooper, & Damasio, 2000) and damage to the left auditory association cortex may impair the perceptual and conceptual processing of sounds linked to everyday objects (Trumpp, Kliese, Hoenig, Haarmeier, & Kiefer, 2013).

Behavioral studies also implicate action systems in cognitive tasks. Glenberg and Kaschak (2002) uncovered an "Action-Sentence Compatibility Effect." Reaction times in a sensibility task decreased when response direction (a button pressed either away/toward the body) and the implied direction of action sentences (e.g., *Andy gave you the pizza/You gave Andy the pizza*) were congruent. Borghi, Glenberg, and Kaschak (2004) found a similar effect when participants were instructed to decide whether or not a word that followed a sentence named a part of the object mentioned in the sentence. Half of the selected parts occurred in the upper-portion of the object and half occurred in the lower-portion of the objects. Responses were faster when the direction of the key press movement (upward or downward) matched the part location.

One of the more striking examples of research implicating the motor system in semantic processing involves effector-specific activations in motor areas during language tasks (Kemmerer, 2010; Willems & Casasanto, 2011). Scorolli and Borghi (2007), for instance, found such an effect when they asked their participants to judge the sensibility of simple sentences containing a verb that referred to an action typically performed with the mouth, hands, or the feet. Subjects responded by pressing a pedal or speaking into a microphone. Response times with the microphone were fastest with "mouth-sentences," and response times with the pedal were fastest with "foot-sentences." This somatopic specificity fits with the findings of a number of brain imaging studies. Hauk, Johnsrude, and Pulvermüller (2004) had participants read similar action words and each type produced increased activation in the cortical regions associated with performing the relevant movements. Increased activation in effector-specific premotor and motor areas has been observed when participants heard action-related sentences (Tettamanti et al., 2005). Right- and left-handers have exhibited increased activation in the premotor areas that were contralateral to their dominant hands (Willems, Hagoort, & Casasanto, 2010). Buccino et al. (2005) demonstrated that listening to action-related sentences affected activity in the motor system. Motor evoked potentials (MEPs) recorded from hand and foot muscles were selectively modulated by hand-related and foot-related action sentences respectively. Pulvermüller, Hauk, Nikulin, and Ilmonlemi (2005) carried out a repeated Transcranial Magnetic Stimulation (TMS) study in which they weakly stimulated different parts of the motor system while participants performed a lexical decision task on arm- and leg-related action words. Response times increased with arm-related words when there was weak stimulation of left hemisphere areas associated with arm-movement and with leg-related words when there was weak stimulation of motor areas associated with leg-movement. Response times were not modulated in a control condition with a faux stimulation.

Admittedly, there have been some criticisms of embodied cognition. These fall into three broad types. The first questions the relative scope of the role played by sensorimotor systems in our concepts. Some have pointed out that most of the evidence for embodiment involves concrete concepts (Chatterjee, 2010; Dove, 2009; Mahon & Caramazza, 2008; Weiskopf, 2007) and suggest that it is reasonable to doubt the inference that all concepts are equally embodied. The second proposes that the engagement of the sensorimotor systems is epiphenomenal, perhaps the result of something like spreading activation (Mahon & Caramazza, 2008; Weiskopf, 2007). The third questions the methodological assumptions behind this research. For example, it is often pointed out that many of the studies merely indicate a correlation between sensorimotor activation and conceptual processing and thus fail to exclude alternative explanations for this activation (Machery, 2007; Mahon, 2015).

Clearly, these issues are substantial and resolving them is beyond the purview of this chapter. We offer some initial responses to each, though, in order to establish the plausibility of our approach and show that it does not require adopting an overly radical form of the embodiment thesis. We contend that, despite the existence of controversies surrounding how to properly characterize embodiment (Meteyard, Cuadrado, Bahrami, & Vigliocco, 2012; Shapiro, 2011), the claim that concepts are embodied to some nontrivial extent is well supported. With respect to the question of scope, we suggest that a reasonable interpretation of the extant evidence is that it supports the proposition that many concepts (particularly concrete ones) are dependent on experiential systems (Dove, 2011; Louwerse & Connell, 2011; Markman & Brendl, 2005).[14] With respect to the question of causal relevance, we suggest that the rapidity and apparently automatic nature of the observed effects throws into doubt the claim that they are epiphenomenal (Kiefer et al., 2008; although for a contrary view see Mahon, 2015). It is also worth noting that some of the evidence outlined above, such as that provided by neuropsychological case studies and TMS interventions, more directly implicates a causal role for sensorimotor systems. Finally, with respect to the question of methodology, we suggest that an embodied approach is supported by a defeasible inference to the best explanation. As should be the case with any empirical theory, time will tell.

In the end, the notion that some concepts—importantly, some *non-phenomenal* concepts—are embodied is supported by a robust body of evidence (for reviews of this evidence, see Bergen, 2012; Fischer & Zwaan, 2008; Kemmerer, 2010; Kiefer & Pulvermüller, 2012; Meteyard et al., 2012). Although the theoretical implications of conceptual embodiment are not fully settled, there is good reason to think that experiential representations employed during our interactions with the world are often reactivated during many cognitive tasks (Barsalou, 2008; Gallese & Lakoff, 2005; Hesslow, 2012). This re-activation appears to be fast and automatic. Different theories may provide different accounts of the functional role of this engagement of perceptual, motor, and emotion systems—for example, viewing it in terms of simulations (Barsalou, 1999), action schemas (Glenberg, 1997), or the dynamic application of sensorimotor skills (van Elk, Slors, & Bekkering, 2010)—but there is a widespread recognition that such engagement is central to many of our concepts.

Few would deny that we often have related phenomenal experiences when employing physical concepts. Thinking about physical objects and events will often elicit mental imagery associated with those objects and events. Standard forms of the PCS generally presume that this phenomenal experience is in some significant sense external to the employment of the concept. An embodied perspective in which our concepts employ sensorimotor systems throws this presumption into question. After all, phenomenal experience is a fundamental feature of perception and action. The relevant multimodal imagery is therefore part of—not separate from—the exercise of the concepts. An embodied account thus connects the phenomenology associated with physical concepts to our ability to think with them.

4. An Elusive Distinction?

The upshot of the last section is that our physical concepts are likely to be at least partially dependent on experiential systems. This creates a problem for supporters of DIP: If the exercise of physical concepts generally involves these systems, then there may be no clear distinction between them and phenomenal concepts. In other words, the purported specialness of phenomenal concepts appears to vanish into thin air.

Recognizing this problem, Shea (2014) develops an argument against proponents of the PCS who employ the purported difference between the exercise of phenomenal and physical concepts in accounting for the appearance of consciousness' distinctness or apparent *sui generis* status. Objecting to DIP, Shea contends:

> This tactic fails because the phenomenological difference between exercise of phenomenal and physical-functional concepts relied on to date is empirically unsustainable; and there are reasons to doubt that there is any relevant difference in the phenomenology of the exercise of the two types of concepts that could do the required explanatory work. My objection has two strands. First, exercise of physical-functional concepts can carry perception-like phenomenological properties. Second, exercise of phenomenal concepts need not.
>
> (p. 559)

He then goes on to conclude:

> Caught between these two strands, it is hard to see that there could be a general phenomenological difference between the exercise of phenomenal and physical-functional concepts.
>
> (p. 560)

The thrust of the argument is clear, without a general phenomenological difference, one cannot explain consciousness' appearance as something other than physical in terms of phenomenological properties.

Given the potential importance of this argument, it should be examined carefully. According to Shea, research suggests that the employment of physical concepts may contain phenomenological properties (insofar as such an employment would give rise to a phenomenologically rich introspective state) and that the employment of so-called phenomenal concepts may not. We take the first claim to be a reasonable extension of an embodied approach to concepts. For it to be false, the experiential representations responsible for the processing of physical concepts would have to *never* be conscious. This strikes us as unlikely and unsupported by the relevant empirical findings. The second claim requires more discussion. The empirical evidence supports the notion that experiential systems are automatically engaged in conceptual tasks. Supporters of embodiment point to this automaticity as evidence that these representations are functionally relevant to conceptual processing and not epiphenomenal. Where is the empirical support for the claim that phenomenological properties are not required? That is, what is the evidence that supports the claim that the exercise of phenomenal concepts does not have to render *conscious* some of the experiential representations involved in these concepts? Shea does not cite any but, instead, seems to think that such a claim is uncontroversial. He holds that by entertaining thoughts such as "I am not currently having a red sensation", one deploys the phenomenal concept RED SENSATION[15] without at the same time instantiating the property to which the concept refers.[16] One might object to Shea's claim by insisting that no deployment of a phenomenal concept is such that it can occur without conscious access to the relevant experience. We are skeptical of the success of such a response, however, because it renders phenomenal concepts too special. Given that most researchers hold that concepts can be unconsciously exercised, the possible absence of perception-like phenomenological properties with phenomenal concepts follows almost by definition. Certainly, a fair amount of work would need to be done to justify the claim that a particular concept—let alone an entire class of concepts—must always be accompanied by specific mental imagery.[17]

We do not challenge either of Shea's central claims. Does this mean that we agree that a reformulated DIP cannot work? No. There are two weaknesses in Shea's argument. The first weakness is that, contrary to Shea's formulation of the DIP, one does not have to posit the existence of a *general* phenomenological difference between physical and phenomenal concepts. All that is needed is a specific phenomenological difference that emerges and plays a significant role in the context of the judgment of the appearance of distinctness. After all, the relevant explanandum of DIP is this judgment and not the general character of phenomenal concepts. The important question, then, is whether the exercise of the relevant concepts in the context of the contemplation of the nature of consciousness leads to a significant phenomenological difference or not.[18] Significantly, this contemplation is likely to involve a considerable amount of conscious reasoning. Thus, even if we accept that the employment of phenomenal concepts does not necessarily give rise to an associated introspective phenomenology, the employment of phenomenal concepts in the context of thinking about the physical place of consciousness will very likely yield an introspective phenomenology. The second weakness is that he assumes that the purported phenomenological difference is limited to the mere absence/presence of perception-like phenomenal properties. However, there may be alternative ways of making the relevant distinction. For instance, a quantitative or qualitative distinction defined over phenomenal properties may be possible. Next, we outline and defend such a distinction.

We imagine a reactionary objection to drawing any conclusions from the research outlined earlier. Someone could point to the defeasible nature of these empirical claims and suggest that they have no place in analytic metaphysics. The objector might press the point that the intuitive distinction at the heart of DIP is compatible with other theories of concepts. This may be the case, but notice that it fails to inoculate the PCS from empirical commitments because it is now dependent on the falsity of claims that enjoy the support of a diverse and robust body of evidence.

Furthermore, the claims are more flexible than they may seem at first glance. The challenge to DIP does not depend on a commitment to the more radical aspects of embodied cognition—nor does it require a commitment to enactive or extended cognition. It arises from the apparent involvement of sensorimotor systems in some non-phenomenal concepts. This involvement is compatible with a wide variety of theories, including pluralistic accounts that allow for amodal or disembodied representations (Dove, 2009, 2011; Louwerse, 2011; Lynott & Connell, 2010; Meteyard et al., 2012).

To recap, evidence of conceptual embodiment appears to throw into question the notion that there is a general phenomenological distinction between physical and phenomenal concepts. If such a distinction is unsustainable, then standard attempts to explain the appearance of consciousness' special status using DIP will not work. However, the situation is not as hopeless as it may seem at first. One can still provide an account that identifies an introspective phenomenal difference that emerges in the context of judgments about the physical nature of consciousness and involves more than the mere presence of experiential properties.

5. DIP Reformulated

If embodied theories of cognition are even partially correct, then the neural resources generally used for perception, action, and emotion can be recruited when we entertain thoughts about the world around us. As noted above, such embodiment would exclude any distinction between phenomenal and physical concepts that relies on the supposed absence of phenomenological properties during the employment of physical concepts. The question at hand is whether or not it is possible to draw a more sophisticated distinction between the introspective phenomenology that is associated with the employment of the two types of concepts—at least within the specific context of the sort of philosophical deliberation involved in generating contingency judgments. We think that such a distinction can be drawn.

A core idea of an embodied approach to cognition is that the employment of concepts typically involves the simultaneous engagement of multiple sensorimotor and affective neural systems. In other words, embodied cognition is committed to the de facto multimodality of our concepts. The following passage expresses a fairly standard embodied view of conceptual structure:

> A concept is an aggregated memory of aspects of experience that have repeatedly received attention in the past, and incorporates perceptual, motor, affective, introspective, social, linguistic and other information. For instance a concept of *dog* could potentially include a host of perceptual-motor information, possibly including visual information of the color and shape of a dog, tactile information regarding the feel of a dog's coat, olfactory information of the smell of a dog, auditory information of a dog's bark, motor information about patting a dog, social information about the status of dogs in human households, along with positive or negative affective valence depending on one's experience with dogs in the past. Any time the word "dog" is encountered, a subset of these aspects will be retrieved to suit the task at hand.
>
> (Lynott & Connell, 2010, p. 2)

From a general embodied perspective, the employment of a concept in a particular situation involves bringing experientially derived information that is stored offline to bear on a current, online cognitive task. What separates this approach from the traditional one (where online processing is handled by a functionally independent amodal symbol system) is the claim that the representations employed in our concepts are fundamentally grounded in our modality-specific interactions with the environment we inhabit.[19] Online cognitive processing involves the selective engagement of experiential states and which representations are employed at any given moment will depend in large part on the situated context and the relevant task. Thinking about dogs, for instance, can involve visual representations, olfactory representations, auditory representations, and even touch representations. On account of the different types of representations involved with the concept DOG, the concept DOG is said to be multimodal. Indeed, most of our concepts are multimodal in precisely this sense: Not only do they encode a rich array of experientially derived information (information that was derived from more than one sense modality), but also their employment involves the simultaneous and selective engagement of multiple sensorimotor and affective neural systems.[20] Physical concepts are particularly likely to be multimodal in their realization. After all, the presupposition is that they refer to external objects and events, which can be experienced in multiple ways. In fact, concepts that refer to external objects and events have to be multimodal. By their very nature, the referents of those concepts are ones that permit our multimodal interaction with them.

It is important to recognize that a commitment to conceptual embodiment does not require a commitment to the universally quantified claim that all realizations of our concepts are multimodal. Nothing in the theory excludes unimodal realizations. Indeed, even though concepts are *generally* multimodal, phenomenal concepts are likely to be an exception to this generalization. By definition, these concepts are about singular experiences such as seeing red and feeling pain. These experiences are in an important sense unimodal. In other words, unlike concepts that refer to external objects or events, which can be experienced in multiple ways, there is typically only one way to experience the referents of phenomenal concepts. The phenomenal concept RED SENSATION, for example, engages the visual system. Putting aside cases of synesthesia (which we discuss below in the objections and replies section), we neither touch, nor hear, nor smell, nor feel our red sensations. Unlike physical concepts, phenomenal concepts encode modality-specific information, and, crucially, their employment activates modality-specific neural systems.

One challenge faced by our approach is the existence of an ongoing controversy concerning how to properly individuate sensory modalities. Some philosophers defend a sparse, moderate view of the senses that lines up roughly with our folk psychological preconceptions and others defend a more fine-grained view that identifies a greater number of individual senses. In part, this debate is driven by the need to develop a neuroscientifically tractable conception that can be applied comparatively to non-human sensory systems (Keeley, 2002). It is also driven by a recognition that the various means by which scientists and philosophers attempt to individuate sensory modalities may not converge on a single solution to this problem (Macpherson, 2011). Our intention is to appeal to a notion of sensory modality that is tied to unified perceptual experiences while recognizing that other ways of individuating the senses may be useful and give different results. This potential mismatch has seemed problematic in two types of cases: instances where there are cross-modal illusions created by the influence of one modality on another (O'Callaghan, 2008) and instances where a unified experience seems to be the result of coordinated operations in multiple senses (Fulkerson, 2011). A good example of the latter is the experience of flavor when eating food (Fulkerson, 2014). This experience appears to depend on aroma, taste, texture, and even temperature; thus, it can be meaningfully described as multisensory. While the existence of cross-modal illusions and multisensory experiences poses important challenges for theories of the senses, our approach can handle both of these cases.

In developing the distinction between multimodal and unimodal concepts, what is crucial for our purposes is the fact that physical concepts display a kind of flexibility that phenomenal concepts lack. Thinking with physical concepts is flexible insofar as we can think of the referents of those concepts using a number of modally distinct representations. Furthermore, and rather importantly, no particular modality seems to enjoy an inherent privilege over the others: That is, there are a number of (modally) different ways of thinking about the referents of physical concepts. Such flexibility, however, seems to be absent in the case of phenomenal concepts for they do not permit us to think of their referents in modally distinct ways. We still have to think of the referents of phenomenal concepts in a particular way.

And that is the case, even if some experiences are multisensory. In the end, we are using the term "unimodal" as a shorthand for a kind of experiential specificity—one that can be associated either with phenomenologically unified experiences in one sensory modality (as in the case of seeing red or hearing middle C) or with phenomenologically unified "multisensory" experiences (as in the case of flavors).

Ultimately, what we want to suggest is that it is possible to offer an embodied version of DIP. Recall the fundamental idea behind DIP: "When we then bring phenomenal and physical-theoretical concepts together in our philosophical ruminations, those cognitive states are phenomenologically so different that the illusion may be created that their references must be different" (Loar, 1997, p. 302). Originally, Loar and others thought that the cognitive states involving phenomenal concepts were phenomenologically different from those involving physical concepts insofar as only the former involved a rich introspective phenomenology. As we have seen, evidence from cognitive science suggests that phenomenological properties may also be involved in the employment of physical concepts as well. However, this does not mean that there is not a significant phenomenological difference between the cognitive states associated with the employment of the two types of concepts. The difference lies in the fact that phenomenal concepts are phenomenologically circumscribed whereas physical concepts are phenomenologically open and flexible.

When we carefully consider a conscious experience, say, the experience of seeing red, we recognize that we need to think of it unimodally.[21] However, when we think of neural stimulation, we recognize that we are able to think of it multimodally. The employment of a physical concept has a potentially multimodal complexity that is lacking from the employment of a phenomenal concept. The appearance of consciousness' special and elusive status appears then to be a straightforward consequence of the phenomenological difference involved in the employment of the two types of concepts. The idea here is simple: We have come to associate multimodality with physical objects and events. When this multimodality is absent, however, from our employment of phenomenal concepts, it is natural for us to think that the referents of phenomenal concepts cannot be physical objects and events. Consequently, it is natural for us to think that phenomenal and physical concepts do not co-refer.

Our account builds upon a series of previous attempts to offer an explanation for the persistency of the appearance of contingency in mind-brain identity statements by utilizing features of the concepts involved in those statements. Although it is consistent with the overall approach of such attempts, what we offer here differs markedly from such accounts. First, our defense of a revised DIP is not tied to PCS. Neither do we make any claims about the metaphysical nature of consciousness nor do we demand that phenomenal concepts are conceptually isolated from physical concepts. All that our account utilizes is a psychological fact pertaining to the employment of those concepts. Second, we do not insist that the employment of physical concepts fails to have an associated phenomenology. In fact, we have shown that such a contention runs in the face of a robust and diverse body of evidence from the cognitive sciences. Third, we hold that even though it is possible for the employment of both types of concepts to have an associated phenomenology insofar as the employment of both activates sensorimotor neural mechanisms, there is still an important difference in their associated phenomenology. On account of this difference, it is tempting to think that the two types of concepts do not co-refer. Finally, previous attempts of accounting for the persistence of the appearance of contingency have excessively focused on the nature of phenomenal concepts. As a consequence, they failed to take sufficient notice of the multimodal representations that are associated with the deployment of physical concept. Such an oversight, we contend, misled theorists to think that only phenomenal concepts have an associated introspective phenomenology. Once we allow that physical concepts also have an associated introspective phenomenology, another way of accounting for the appearance of contingency makes itself evident. One can account for the appearance of contingency by noting the contrast between the multimodal character of physical concepts and the unimodal character of phenomenal concepts.

6. Objections and Replies

We anticipate four main objections to the provided account of the appearance of consciousness' uniqueness. In this section of the chapter, we present these objections and offer rejoinders.

Objection 1. The Unimodal-Multimodal Difference Does Nothing to Show That Phenomenal Concepts and Physical Concepts Co-Refer

Reply

Our account is not supposed to demonstrate that phenomenal concepts refer to physical properties: The aim of the chapter is neither to provide a positive argument for the veracity of physicalism nor to respond to conceivability arguments against physicalism. We have argued in detail that physicalism should be understood as a research program and thus the success of physicalism cannot be determined in advance and on the basis of theoretical grounds. Physicalism would be successful only if we are able to offer a compositional explanation of consciousness. Furthermore, we addressed conceivability arguments in Chapters 5 and 6 by exposing their fundamental assumptions and by showing how such assumptions do not arrest the research program. What we have offered in this chapter is something altogether different: We proposed an explanation of a purely psychological phenomenon, one that has been thought to constitute important difficulties for physicalist projects. All that we are offering, in other words, is a plausible and empirically informed explanation of the observation that consciousness appears to be distinct from its physical substratum.

Objection 2. Despite All That We Said, the Unimodal-Multimodal Difference Does Not Account for the Appearance That Consciousness Is Something Over and Above Its Physical Components

Reply

The objection aims to demonstrate that merely noting a contrast between the multimodal character of physical concepts and the unimodal character of phenomenal concepts does not amount to an explanation of the observation that consciousness appears to be over and above its physical components. The objection thus fits with a general criticism of PCS, which claims that the presence of a phenomenological distinction fails to adequately explain why consciousness should appear to be disconnected from its physical nature if consciousness is physical (Doggett & Stoljar, 2010). Before responding to this objection, it is important to clarify what it means to provide an explanation of this appearance. As mentioned above, explaining the appearance of consciousness' uniqueness is not tantamount to showing something about the ontological or metaphysical nature of consciousness. To explain the appearance of consciousness' uniqueness is to provide a purely psychological account that makes it *plausible* that one will think that consciousness is something other than physical when one entertains consciousness' ontological nature. But we have precisely offered such an account. When one thinks about how consciousness arises out of its physical components, one is employing, at the same time, both phenomenal concepts and physical concepts. The joint employment of these concepts leads to an introspectively "perceived" or "noticed" contrast between the characters of the two types of concepts. On account of this contrast, one finds it natural to conclude that consciousness cannot be captured by the physical.

It is crucial to note that our explanation does not amount *simply* to the claim that the appearance of consciousness' uniqueness is the result of the employment of two types of concepts. We also offer a reason why such a joint employment is responsible for such an appearance. A consequence of the multimodality of physical concepts is that no particular modality is essential to their realization. Indeed, a basic assumption among embodied theories of concepts is that sensorimotor systems are selectively engaged on any given occasion due to the context and the task involved. For instance, sound, shape, and movement but not color and touch might be engaged when trying to categorize something running across the yard. Phenomenal concepts do not enjoy this sensorimotor flexibility, particularly within the context of philosophical rumination. Indeed, they exhibit sensorimotor rigidity. We suggest then that the associated phenomenological difference—the ability to conceptualize physical categories in a flexible manner and the inability to conceptualize phenomenal concepts this way—gives rise to the appearance of consciousness' other-than-physical status. It is this phenomenological difference that leads one to conclude that consciousness cannot be fully captured by the referents of our physical concepts.

Objection 3. Isn't It Inconsistent to Hold, on the One Hand, That the Explanatory Gap Is Not Permanent and, on the Other Hand, That Consciousness' Appearance of Uniqueness May Persist?

The objection comes in two versions.

Objection 3.1

Either there is a physical explanation of consciousness that involves a priori entailment of phenomenal truths by physical truths or not. If the former, then consciousness will not appear to be other than physical. If the latter, then consciousness will appear to be other than physical, but such an appearance will be due to the fact that we have not offered a physical explanation of consciousness. Formulated this way, the objection is premised on an acceptance of the anti-physicalists' preferred account of explanation of consciousness, namely, one that holds that consciousness is explained only if truths about consciousness are a priori entailed by physical truths. If such a deductive model of explanation is accepted, then it is tempting to expect that a successful explanation should not be accompanied by the appearance that consciousness is other than physical (Chalmers, 1996, p. 42, 2010, p. 313; Chalmers & Jackson, 2001, p. 351). Indeed, why would consciousness appear to be other than physical if it is shown to be the logical consequence of physical truths?

REPLY

Part of our response to this objection should be by now familiar. We reject the dilemma as a false one: It rests on the problematic assumption that only a deductive model of explanation is an adequate model of explanation. As we argued in Chapter 4, such an assumption must be abandoned—in light both of our best scientific practices and of considerations stemming from philosophy of science. Thus, we do not take a priori entailment to be a necessary condition for explanation. Rather, research program physicalism demands only that consciousness is explained in terms of its (physical) components.

But there is more to our response than simply rejecting the deductive model of explanation. To see this, it is important to emphasize that even though the research program does not require the presence of a priori or conceptual connections between physical truths and phenomenal truths, it does not deny their existence either. According to the research program, whether such connections exist is irrelevant—explanation does not depend on them. So, it could turn out that there are conceptual connections between physical and phenomenal truths. Still, the possibility of such connections does not guarantee that consciousness will cease to appear to be unique, special, or other than physical. When the a priori entailment of phenomenal truths from physical truths is discussed in the literature, it is assumed that such an entailment can be carried out *only* by an ideal reasoner. Indeed, the required entailment *has* to be ideal—it is simply not possible for an ordinary subject to entertain the totality of all relevant physical facts. Thus, even if physical truths were to a priori entail all truths about consciousness, the entailment is not one that can be performed by us—regular, fallible, and cognitively limited subjects. As such, the availability of the relevant entailment or deduction is irrelevant to the issue of the appearance of consciousness' uniqueness. The latter is a fact (or a presumed fact) of human psychology—a fact about what *we*, as ordinary human beings, experience when we think of consciousness' relationship to the brain, body, and even to the environment. The former is what can be performed under ideal—and thus psychologically unrealistic—conditions. Whether Jackson's Mary or Laplace's demon—both fictional entities—experience no ambivalence about consciousness' ontological nature is inconsequential. In sum, even if we assume the availability of a deduction of phenomenal truths from physical truths, this does not show that regular humans, when thinking about the problem of consciousness, will *not* think of consciousness as being other than physical.

Objection 3.2

Whereas the first version of the objection insists that physicalism requires a deductive model of explanation, there is another version that does not place such a demand. Instead, it holds that no adequate physical explanation of consciousness should give rise to a perplexity or ambivalence about consciousness' ontological status. In other words, whatever model of explanation we take to be the right or appropriate one, it should be one that leaves us with no ambiguity about the character of the explained phenomenon.

REPLY

The second version of the objection rests on an overly demanding notion of what is necessary in order to have an adequate explanation. And we reject the claim that adequate scientific explanations are always ones that leave no residual feelings of puzzlement. (We also deny that a feeling of satisfaction when considering a provided explanation is a sufficient condition of an adequate explanation.)[22] There are at least two reasons in support of our contention: The first is drawn from explanations found in physical sciences; the second is specific to consciousness.

FIRST REASON

It appears that there are all sorts of puzzling explanations in science—that is, explanations that we take to be correct or adequate even if they do not entirely dispel the mystery surrounding the explained phenomena. One such example is quantum tunneling. In quantum tunneling, the wave function of a particle can go through ("tunnel") a narrow energy barrier thereby permitting a proportion of its amplitude to be found on the other side of the barrier. Tunneling is a wave phenomenon that is exhibited by classical waves (for example, sound waves propagate through all sorts of barriers—walls, doors, etc.). However, when the wave amplitude is used in order to measure the probability of the location of a particle, difficulties in our comprehension of this phenomenon arise. The use of the wave amplitude predicts that the particle (e.g., an electron) has a finite probability of being on the other side of a barrier that classically would be impossible for it to cross. In other words, a particle with energy smaller than that of the surrounding barrier can go through the barrier. Although tunneling has been both adequately explained and utilized successfully in numerous real-life applications, the phenomenon itself has not been rendered entirely non-mysterious or mundane. Electrons, after all, can be found where they are not supposed to be.

The offered example could be met with skepticism. First, one could hold that quantum tunneling is not mysterious. But even if quantum tunneling is not mysterious, plenty of other phenomena are. Albert Einstein famously stated that quantum entanglement involves "*spukhafte Fernwirkung*" ("spooky action at a distance"). Richard Feynman, in discussing the behavior of particles in double slit experiments, wrote: "We cannot make the mystery go away by 'explaining' how it works. We will just *tell* you how it works" (Feynman, Leighton, & Sands, 2010, pp. 1–2). If Einstein and Feynman thought that quantum mechanics is mysterious, then we should accept that it is.

Second, one could hold that even though quantum tunneling (entanglement, or some other phenomenon) seems mysterious to us, that is because we do not yet have an adequate explanation for it. Such a view, however, would make explanations too hard to come by—if we do not have an explanation for quantum tunneling, then we do not have an explanation for many (if not for most) quantum phenomena. The view is also anathema to received scientific opinion. Quantum mechanics is remarkably successful—"perhaps the most successful theory in the history of science" (Faye, 2014)—in terms of both its accuracy in its predictions and its resilience to tests. As such, it is hard to deny that the explanations offered by quantum mechanics are not adequate.

Third, one could argue that, even if they are in some sense mysterious or not fully satisfying, quantum mechanical explanations are inconsequential for present purposes because they are not *compositional* explanations. The objection, however, is unconvincing. It is not entirely clear that quantum mechanical explanations are not compositional *in some sense* (see Healey, 2013). Furthermore, even if we assume that quantum mechanical explanations are not compositional, it is not obvious that such a fact is pertinent in this context. What the example of quantum tunneling demonstrates is that we have an explanation of a *physical* phenomenon that is both adequate and puzzling in some respects. Thus, the example demonstrates that the presence of our puzzlement about an explained phenomenon does not mean that the phenomenon has not been explained.

In turn, it is important to underline that explanations of quantum mechanical phenomena are not the only type of explanations that appear to be puzzling. Consider, for instance, the fact that a macroscopic object, such as a diamond, is hard. As we discussed before, we have an adequate and widely accepted compositional explanation of this property of the diamond (Chapter 4). Yet, despite its adequacy, the explanation is still one that appears to us to be perplexing in some respects. The explanation of the diamond's hardness requires us to make sense of how an object that is composed of mostly empty space can be such that it retains its space and volume and resists penetration. (For a development of this point, see Rowlands, 2001). Or consider a different example given by Wayne Wright (2007). By focusing on mechanistic explanations, Wright argues that we will have a satisfactory explanation of a phenomenon when we have "identified a mechanism that enables manipulations and interventions that bring about non-accidental, fine-grained changes in the behavior of the phenomenon, or that allows us to answer a range of questions about how the phenomenon would behave if things were different" (p. 310). Still, such an explanation with a focus on manipulability might not be necessarily associated with a sense of satisfaction or even transparency, for we might fail to "'see' the relation between a mechanism and the target phenomenon" (p. 313). Nevertheless, this failure of satisfaction is not a reason to deny the adequacy of the explanation. The explanation after all allows scientists to meet their goals.

> [I]t is unclear what further "mystery removal" scientists have to do. With a good control explanation in hand, scientists are equipped to meet various practical goals associated with their disciplines (e.g., correcting malfunctions, improving normal function, earlier and more precise diagnosis of malfunction) and to make strides forward in their investigation of phenomena related to the explained phenomenon. Considering all the virtues that explanations can have without it, intelligibility of the kind connected to the hard problem seems ill-suited as a requirement on scientific explanation.
>
> (ibid.)

Thus, the subjective feeling of satisfaction or intelligibility that we have when we consider an explanation for a phenomenon is not a necessary condition for explanatory adequacy (see also Trout, 2002).

SECOND REASON

But let us assume, contrary to what we have been arguing so far, that there is an intimate connection between subjective feelings of satisfaction and explanatory adequacy. Even this view of explanation does not raise trouble for the claims of the research program. That is because we can still maintain that a physical explanation of consciousness should be excluded from this requirement about explanations. In fact, our account both predicts and explains why a physical explanation of consciousness would be perplexing. Unlike ordinary scientific explanations, an explanation of consciousness would require the employment of both physical and phenomenal concepts and on the basis of this joint employment of concepts, consciousness would appear to be something other than physical.

Objection 4. Phenomenal Concepts Are Not Unimodal

Our explanation of the appearance of consciousness' other-than-physical status is premised on the claim that phenomenal concepts are unimodal. But are they? There are different ways in which one can try to motivate the claim that phenomenal concepts are not unimodal. Before we consider some of those ways, it is important to clarify two views of phenomenal concepts, both of which are congenial to our purposes. The first view treats phenomenal concepts as *essentially* unimodal concepts. Accordingly, the employment of a phenomenal concept is such that necessarily includes only representations that are of the same sensory modality to that of the referent of the concept. For example, the employment of the phenomenal concept RED SENSATION is such that necessarily invokes (consciously or unconsciously) a set of visual representations that are related to the experience of seeing red. The second view of phenomenal concepts does not treat phenomenal as essentially unimodal. Rather, it allows that phenomenal concepts, just like the majority of our concepts, are multimodal. Still, the view insists that (a) the nature of the representations invoked by the employment of phenomenal concepts is context-specific and (b) within the context of consciously thinking about the "hard" problem of consciousness, the employment of a phenomenal concept becomes unimodal. For instance, when thinking about whether red sensations are nothing over and above a set of neural processes, one employs the phenomenal concept RED SENSATION in a unimodal way. To employ the concept in this context is to filter out everything that is *not* the sensation of seeing red. This "filtering out" process is one that we often and unconsciously do. For instance, thinking about dogs in contexts that we are interested in their smell, we employ the concept DOG in a way that filters out many of our associated representations of that concept that are not olfactory representations. Thus, this second view of phenomenal concepts holds that even if phenomenal concepts are not essentially unimodal, they are *contingently* unimodal: In the context of conscious contemplation regarding the problem of consciousness, phenomenal concepts act as filters that allow us to focus on specific qualitative features of our experiences.

For current purposes, we wish to remain neutral on whether phenomenal concepts are essentially or only contingently unimodal. Although we are inclined to accept the view that phenomenal concepts are only contingently unimodal, there is no need to adjudicate this difficult issue here. Recall that the relevant explanandum of our account is the psychological observation that consciousness appears to be other-than-physical *when we consciously deliberate about the ontological status of consciousness*. In the specific context of thinking about the ontological character of consciousness, both views of phenomenal concepts predict that their employment will be unimodal.

In what follows, we consider reasons against the claim that phenomenal concepts are unimodal. We show that even if those reasons can be taken to suggest that phenomenal concepts are not essentially multimodal, they do nothing to undermine the weaker claim that they are contingently unimodal.

Objection 4.1. The Case of Synesthesia

"Synesthesia" refers to the statistically rare capacity to experience the merge of different sense modalities. Synesthetes, for instance, feel voices, see music, smell colors, and even taste shapes. Consider the following reports of such experiences (all quoted from Cytowic, 2002, p. 1):

> What first strikes me is the color of someone's voice. [V—] has a crumbly, yellow voice, like a flame with protruding fibers. Sometimes I get so interested in the voice, I can't understand what's being said.

> Spearmint tastes like cool, glass columns. Lemon is a pointed shape, pressed into my face and hands. It's like laying my hands on a bed of nails.

> I enjoy music that has wavy metallic lines, like oscilloscope tracings. My favorite music has movement that extends beyond my peripheral vision. I really like music that makes the lines go up.

Phenomenal concepts, we claimed above, are unimodal insofar as their employment (at least in the context of thinking about the ontological status of consciousness) gives rise to the activation of neural mechanisms that match the sensory modality of the manner in which we come to experience their referents.[23] The case of synesthesia, one might suggest, speaks against the claim that the referents of phenomenal concepts are experienced only via one sense modality. If a synesthete both hears and sees sounds, then not only the information encoded by the phenomenal concept of a specific sound will be multimodal but also the employment of that concept will very likely activate neural mechanisms related to distinct sense modalities.

REPLY

The problem that synesthesia raises for our account is more apparent than real. Granted, synesthetes have modally fused experiences that appear to involve multiple perceptual systems. Functional neuroimaging studies have observed activation of color processing areas of the visual cortex with the auditory presentation of spoken number words (Nunn et al., 2002) and the visual presentation of achromatic number graphemes (Hubbard, Arman, Ramachandran, & Boynton, 2005). Other studies detect activation of somatosensory areas with synesthetic auditory-tactile experiences (e.g., Beauchamp & Ro, 2008). In keeping with an embodied and grounded perspective, there is also behavioral and neural evidence that synesthetic experiences can be generated by some synesthetes performing mental imagery tasks (Aleman, Rutten, Sitskoorn, Dautzenberg, & Ramsey, 2001; Grossenbacher & Lovelace, 2001; Spiller & Jansari, 2008). Yet, conceding modally fused experiences does nothing to show that they are incapable of isolating the two modally distinct aspects of their experiences. Indeed, synesthetes's own descriptions of their experiences strongly suggest that they are able to discern these modally distinct features of their experiences. They *hear* music and at the same time they *see* colors or shapes. This point holds even though there are some individual differences with respect to how synesthetes describe their phenomenological experience (Ward & Mattingly, 2006). Regardless of how intimately connected or fused the two modally distinct aspects of their experiences are, synesthetes still recognize them as being modally *distinct*. As long as synesthetes can isolate aspects of their experience as properly belonging to their respective sense modalities, then it is enough to show that phenomenal concepts can be (at least *contingently*) unimodal. One employs a phenomenal concept when one thinks about one's experiences. Thus, when synesthetes think about one modal aspect of their experiences, then they think of that aspect by employing a unimodal phenomenal concept.[24]

Objection 4.2. Phenomenal Concepts Are Not Perspectival

If phenomenal concepts are unimodal, then it seems plausible to suggest that phenomenal concepts are *perspectival* (Tye, 1995, Ch. 6). That is, phenomenal concepts are perspectival insofar as one can come to possess a phenomenal concept only if one experiences that to which the concept refers. For instance, one is said to be in possession of the phenomenal concept RED SENSATION, only if one has had a red experience. Although the claim that phenomenal concepts are perspectival is widely accepted (see, e.g., Papineau, 2007; Block, 2006) and has been utilized in providing a response to Jackson's knowledge argument (Loar, 1997; Tye, 2003), recently such a claim has been met with resistance (see, e.g., Stoljar, 2000, 41 n.15; MacDonald, 2004; Ball, 2009; Tye, 2009). If it turns out that phenomenal concepts are not perspectival, then the claim that phenomenal concepts are unimodal is threatened.

REPLY

It is not our aim to explicate the possession conditions of phenomenal concepts. Nor do we wish to critically assess arguments in support of the claim that phenomenal concepts are not perspectival (see instead Alter, 2013; Elpidorou, 2012; Veillet, 2012). Instead, we shall grant that phenomenal concepts are not perspectival. Consequently, we accept that one can come to possess them even if one did not have the relevant experience. Still, accepting that phenomenal concepts are not perspectival only militates against the claim that phenomenal concepts are essentially unimodal. The concession that phenomenal concepts are not perspectival does nothing to undermine that phenomenal concepts are *contingently* unimodal. And this weaker claim is all that we need.

7. Wonders May Never Cease

Consciousness' appearance of uniqueness may persist, even as our scientific understanding of consciousness progresses. This, however, should not be taken to be an indication of a problem with our explanatory practices and in this chapter we offered an attempt to account for this appearance by appealing to our psychological sciences. Specifically, we have shown that one can offer a novel version of DIP that is thoroughly in keeping with embodied cognition and which successfully succeeds in explaining why consciousness appears to be other than physical. Phenomenal concepts, at least when deployed within the context of philosophical ruminations regarding the mind-body problem, are unimodal. On account of this unimodality, the deployment of phenomenal concepts exhibits both a type of simplicity and sensorimotor rigidity. From an introspective perspective, the deployment of physical concepts appears very different from that of phenomenal concepts. It is on account of such a difference that one is misled to conclude that consciousness should be something over and above its physical components.

The problem of consciousness might appear to be hard or even unsolvable, but such an appearance is no indication that the explanatory gap cannot be bridged. In fact, given our discussion of the psychology of a physical explanation of consciousness, the research program should persist in the face of such an appearance.

Notes

1. A compelling argument could be made that the appearance of uniqueness associated with life has not disappeared in the face of advances in biology. To be

more specific, although vitalism has failed as a scientific research program, it retains a kind of persistent intuitive plausibility.

2. The label "phenomenal concept strategy" comes from Stoljar (2005). Proponents of the phenomenal concept strategy are physicalists who respond to epistemic arguments against physicalism by maintaining (i) that the existence of an epistemic (or explanatory) gap between phenomenal truths and physical truths is consistent with the truth of physicalism—they are thus proponents of what David Chalmers (1999) calls "Type-B Materialism"– and (ii) that the existence of such a gap admits of a purely physical explanation insofar as it is the product of certain features of our phenomenal concepts. Authors who defend physicalism from epistemic arguments by citing the nature of phenomenal concepts include: Loar (1990, 1997, and 2003); Hill (1997); Hill and McLaughlin (1999); Tye (1995, 1999, 2000, and 2003); Perry (2001); Papineau (2002 and 2007); Levin (2007a); Balog (2012); Diaz-Leon (2008 and 2010); Elpidorou (2013 and 2016).
3. Proponents of PCS maintain that the explanatory gap is permanent and explain the permanence of the gap in virtue of certain features of our conceptual repertoire. Specifically, they hold that phenomenal concepts are conceptually isolated or disconnected from physical concepts insofar as one cannot deduce on the basis of reasoning alone whether physical truths about the workings of our mind and phenomenal truths co-refer.
4. Many philosophers use the identity statement "pain is C-fiber firing" as shorthand for the more general claim that pain is identical to some brain state or process. We avoid this locution here because it is misleading. Not only is C-fiber firing neither necessary nor sufficient for pain experience, but this formulation suggests without argument that both pain (which is associated with different phenomenal properties such as stabbing, dull, etc., and comes in different varieties such as acute, chronic, neuropathic, psychogenic, etc.) and the relevant brain states or processes (which involve multiple cortical and subcortical systems) are inherently simple and one-dimensional. Our formulation is compatible with the likely complexity of both sides of the identity.
5. Our use of possible-worlds discourse leaves undecided many contentious philosophical issues including the semantic and logical structure of possible-worlds sentences and the ontological commitments of such a discourse. Such neutrality is intentional. Not only are our findings independent of how one interprets possible-worlds discourse, but we also wish to reap the benefits of such discourse without incurring, at least at this point, any ontological costs. Our use of possible worlds is thus similar to everyday use of mathematical, moral, or color discourse: more often than not, one employs such a discourse both effectively and profitably, without having to accept either a particular interpretation of such discourse or its ontological commitments.
6. In the quoted passage, Kripke uses "A" as the name for a *specific* sensation of pain, and not, as we do, as a name for a type of sensation.
7. Although Kripke's argument was intended as an argument against identity theory, it can be easily turned into an argument against supervenience or metaphysical necessitation physicalism. Suppose that "P" stands for the conjunction of all physical facts and laws about the world expressed in the fundamental vocabulary of a true and complete physical theory; "T" stands for a "that's all" claim stating that what is expressed in *P* is the complete description of our world; "I" stands for basic indexical information of the sort, "I am here" and "It is now;" and "Q'" stands for any true claim about phenomenal states. If either supervenience or metaphysical necessitation physicalism is true, then the conditional $PIT \supset Q$ must be necessarily true. But the conditional appears to be contingent: one can imagine a possible world in which *PIT* holds, but in which *Q* (say, "I

am now in pain") does not. If the conditional appears to be contingent, then proponents of supervenience or metaphysical necessitation physicalism, just like those of identity theory, need to respond to Kripke's argument.

8. For our purposes, what is crucial to note about physical concepts is that they permit us to conceptualize physical categories in a manner that is not restricted to one particular sensorimotor modality. The fact that physical concepts are such that they permit us to apprehend their referents from a multiplicity of modally distinct points of view underlies (at least partly) the claim that the referents of physical concepts are external or third-personal entities or properties. In other words, physical concepts, in light of the fact that they multimodal (in the sense just specified), are prime candidates of concepts that ought to figure in descriptions of how things objectively are (see Nagel, 1974, p. 442f.) A more detailed explication of physical concepts is given in sections 5 and 6.
9. Some hold that phenomenal concepts are recognitional concepts that pick out their referents directly and that are individuated in terms of the possession of certain recognitional capacities (Loar, 1997; Tye, 2000; Carruthers, 2003). Others claim that phenomenal concepts are such that either they are partly constituted by the very phenomenological experience to which they refer, or their use involves versions of their referents (Papineau, 2002 and 2007; Chalmers, 2003; Block, 2006; Balog, 2012). Others argue that phenomenal concepts are indexical or demonstrative concepts and hold that their use involves something akin to an introspective "pointing" ("this [kind of experience]") (Tye, 1995; Ismael, 1999; Perry, 2001; Levin, 2007a; Stalnaker, 2008; Schroer, 2010). Additional characterizations of the nature of phenomenal concepts, can be found in Sturgeon (1994); Hill and McLaughlin (1999); Hawthorne (2002); Braddon-Mitchell (2003); and Aydede and Güzeldere (2005). For an account of the involvement of phenomenal concepts in introspective knowledge, see Gertler (2001). And for an overview of phenomenal concepts, see Elpidorou (2015).
10. A very similar passage can be found in the 1990 version of Loar's essay, see p. 90. The main difference between the two passages is that in the 1990 version Loar states that the respective deployment of the two types of concepts brings about two different psychological states without specifying that the main difference between them is one of phenomenology. Even so, the ensuing statement makes it clear that even in 1990 Loar had in mind a model that accounts for the appearance of contingency that is pretty close (if not identical) to DIP.
11. In the quotes from Loar and Papineau one could perhaps discern two distinct explanations of the appearance of contingency. One is simply DIP; the other is DIP *plus* the claim that only the employment of phenomenal concepts bears a certain resemblance to their referents. In what follows, we do not address the second, extended version of DIP for two reasons. First, we are skeptical that the appearance of contingency can be accounted in terms of resemblance. Second, we do not think that an appeal to resemblance is necessary. We shall demonstrate how a revised account of DIP can explain the persistency of the intuition that phenomenal concepts and physical concepts do not co-refer.
12. One might wonder whether the demonstrative account of phenomenal concepts is also compatible with DIP. The answer to that question depends on how one characterizes demonstrative phenomenal concepts. It is customary to draw a distinction between two different characterizations of demonstrative phenomenal concepts: thin vs. thick (see, e.g., Levine, 2001, p. 82ff.; Levin, 2007a; Schroer, 2010; cf. Chalmers, 2007, p. 178; Levine, 2007). According to the thin characterization, phenomenal concepts do not furnish us with a substantial grasp of their referents. As Joseph Levine puts it: such concepts "are pointers we aim at our internal states with very little substantive conception of what sort of thing we're pointing at—demonstrative arrows shot blindly that refer to whatever they hit" (Levine,

2001, p. 84). On the contrary, a thick characterization of phenomenal concepts holds that the use of phenomenal concepts does provide us with a fairly good grasp of what it is like to have certain experiences. Such a grasp is intimately tied to an introspective phenomenology: We are able to form a substantive conception of those experiences because those experiences are introspectively presented to us. Consequently, a thick characterization is compatible with DIP and proponents of this account can make use of DIP in an attempt to explain the appearance of contingency. However, a thin characterization does not appear to be compatible with DIP. If demonstrative phenomenal concepts are taken to be empty pointers, then the introspective phenomenology required by DIP would be absent. In this chapter, we will not be concerned with a thin demonstrative account of phenomenal concepts. Such an account has been met—rightly so, we believe—with resistance. Indeed, it has been argued that such an account cannot be a characterization of phenomenal concepts, for it fails to account for the distinctive nature of phenomenal concepts. See, e.g., Levine (2007b), Chalmers (2003 and 2007), and Levin (2007a, p. 91). We are grateful to an anonymous referee for *Mind and Language* for pressing us to address the relationship between DIP and the demonstrative account of phenomenal concepts.

13. Edouard Machery (2009) points out that, although philosophers and psychologists generally assume that they are talking about the same thing when they use "concepts," it may very well be the case that they are talking past each other. There is good reason to think that they asking different questions and seeking to explain different phenomena. We are not going to take a stand on this issue. Our contention is merely that some of the empirical research on this subject excludes standard versions of DIP but also supports a new embodied version.
14. Following a convention of the embodied cognition literature, we are going to use the term *experiential systems* as shorthand for the action, emotion, and perceptual systems associated with our experience of the world. *Experiential representations* and *experiential processes* are elements of these systems. Some of these will have associated phenomenal properties but some will not. Roughly put, we are leaving room for unconscious aspects of experience.
15. Phenomenal concepts are about conscious states. Given that realism and externalism are active topics in the philosophy of color (for a thorough discussion of the theoretical terrain, see Cohen, 2009), it would be presumptuous to claim that red is a phenomenal concept. For that reason, we will discuss the phenomenal concept, RED SENSATION.
16. The thought, and ultimately objection to the PCS, that phenomenal concepts can be deployed without instantiating the properties to which they refer does not originate in Shea (2014). Papineau (2007) discusses this objection and attributes it to Tim Crane and Scott Sturgeon. Ned Block (2006) attributes the same objection to Kirk Ludwig.
17. For additional reasons against the contention that the exercise of phenomenal concepts necessarily involves conscious awareness of the experience of their referents, see MacDonald (2004), Ball (2009), and Tye (2009).
18. A close examination of the Loar and Papineau quotes provided previously as examples of DIP reveals that both restrict their claims to circumscribed applications of the relevant concepts. Loar explicitly limits his claims to the context of "philosophical ruminations" and Papineau limits his claims to the context of thinking "imaginatively."
19. Admittedly, all of the information outlined earlier could be encoded in an amodal representational system. This means that we cannot categorically rule out a traditional symbolic account (Machery, 2007). We believe, though, that the brain imaging and neuropsychological evidence outlined previously favors the

view that much of this information is encoded in representations that are indigenous to specific sensorimotor and affective neural systems.

20. Within the embodied cognition literature, there is an active debate concerning the status of abstract concepts such as JUSTICE, ODD NUMBER, and ELECTRON. Some contend that these are fully embodied (Gallese & Lakoff, 2005; Prinz, 2002; Wilson-Mendenhall, Simmons, Martin, & Barsalou, 2013) and others suggest that they may require multiple types of representations (Borghi & Cimatti, 2009; Dove, 2009; Louwerse, 2011). Both of these responses are compatible with our embodied version of DIP, which focuses on phenomenological flexibility.
21. Even if our natural tendency is to think of the experience of seeing red in a multimodal fashion (including, perhaps, an affective dimension), the particular task of judging the ontological status of the experience of seeing red requires filtering out these factors just as thinking about the shape of a pug requires filtering out texture, color, smell, and sound. In other words, this selectivity is entirely consistent with an embodied approach to concepts. For a further discussion of these issues, see our discussion of objections and replies as follows.
22. Ptolemy is often provided as an example of someone who had no ambivalence toward his theory—in fact, he was unable to see how his theory could be false (see Trout, 2002, p. 231)—and yet he believed in a false theory. By citing empirical literature on hindsight and overconfidence biases, J. D. Trout (2002 and 2007) has argued that satisfaction or intelligibility in a given explanation is not an indication that such an explanation is adequate. See also Wright (2007) for a defense and an elaboration of the view that intelligibility is neither a necessary nor a sufficient condition of an adequate explanation.
23. In light of our previous discussion regarding the vexing issue of individuating the senses, it is worth emphasizing that our use of the term "unimodal" permits the possibility that certain phenomenologically unified experiences are inherently multisensory. Therefore, even if some phenomenal concepts turn out to be multisensory (e.g., the ones that we use to introspectively examine the phenomenal character of flavors), they are still meaningfully unimodal insofar as their employment involves an experiential specificity and inflexibility that is absent from paradigmatic multimodal concepts such as physical concepts. Synesthesia seems to be a more problematic kind of multisensory experience than these examples because of its phenomenological complexity.
24. The case of synesthesia does not differ *radically*, one might even suggest, from the manner in which we experience our environment. Our experiences are modally complex: they typically involve the objects of more than one sense modality. Still, we are capable, at least most of the time, of isolating and focusing on the contributions of each modality.

References

Adolphs, R., Damasio, H., Tranel, D., Cooper, G., & Damasio, A. R. (2000). A role for somatosensory cortices in the visual recognition of emotion as revealed by three-dimensional lesion mapping. *Journal of Neuroscience*, *20*, 2683–2690.

Aleman, A., Rutten, G. M., Sitskoorn, M. M., Dautzenberg, G., & Ramsey, N. F. (2001). Activation of the striate cortex in the absence of visual stimulation: An fMRI study of synesthesia. *NeuroReport*, *12*(13), 2827–2830.

Alter, T. (2013). Social externalism and the knowledge argument. *Mind*, *122*(486), 481–496.

Anderson, J. R. (1983). *The architecture of cognition*. Hillsdale, NJ: Erlbaum.

Aydede, M., & Güzeldere, G. (2005). Cognitive architecture, concepts, and introspection: An information-theoretic solution to the problem of phenomenal consciousness. *Noûs*, *39*(2), 197–255.

Ball, D. (2009). There are no phenomenal concepts. *Mind*, *118*(472), 935–962.

Balog, K. (2012). Acquaintance and the mind-body problem. In C. S. Hill & S. Gozzano (eds.), *New perspectives on type identity: The mental and the physical* (pp. 16–42). Cambridge, UK: Cambridge University Press.

Barsalou, L. W. (1999). Perceptual symbol systems. *Behavioral and Brain Sciences*, *22*, 577–609.

Barsalou, L. W. (2008). Grounded cognition. *Annual Review of Psychology*, *59*, 617–645.

Beauchamp, M. S., & Ro, T. (2008). Neural substrates of sound-touch synesthesia after a thalamic lesion. *The Journal of Neuroscience*, *28*(50), 13696–13702.

Bergen, B. K. (2012). *Louder than words: The new science of how the mind makes meaning*. Philadelphia, PA: Perseus Books Group.

Block, N. (2006). Max Black's objection to mind-body identity. *Oxford Studies in Metaphysics*, 2, 3–78.

Borghi, A. M., & Cimatti, F. (2009). Words as tools and the problem of abstract words meanings. In N. Taatgen & H. van Rijn (eds.), *Proceedings of the 31st annual conference of the cognitive science society* (pp. 2304–2309). Amsterdam: Cognitive Science Society.

Borghi, A. M., Glenberg, A. M., & Kaschak, M. P. (2004). Putting words in perspective. *Memory and Cognition*, *32*, 863–873.

Braddon-Mitchell, D. (2003). Qualia and analytical conditionals. *The Journal of Philosophy*, *100*(3), 111–135.

Buccino, G., Riggio, L., Melli, G., Binkofski, F., Gallese, V., & Rizzolatti, G. (2005). Listening to action-related sentences modulates the activity of the motor system: A combined TMS and behavioral study. *Cognitive Brain Research*, *24*, 355–363.

Carruthers, P. (2003). Phenomenal concepts and higher-order experiences. *Philosophy and Phenomenological Research*, *68*(2), 316–336.

Chalmers, D. J. (1996). *The conscious mind: In search of a fundamental theory*. New York: Oxford University Press.

Chalmers, D. J. (1999). Materialism and the metaphysics of modality. *Philosophy and Phenomenological Research*, *59*, 473–496.

Chalmers, D. J. (2003). The content and epistemology of phenomenal belief. In Q. Smith & A. Jokić (eds.), *Consciousness: New philosophical perspectives* (pp. 220–272). Oxford, UK: Clarendon Press.

Chalmers, D. J. (2007). Phenomenal concepts and the explanatory gap. In T. Alter & S. Walter (eds.), *Phenomenal concepts and phenomenal knowledge: New essays on consciousness and physicalism* (pp. 167–194). Oxford, UK: Oxford University Press.

Chalmers, D. J. (2010). *The character of consciousness*. New York, NY: Oxford University Press.

Chalmers, D. J., & Jackson, F. (2001). Conceptual analysis and reductive explanation. *Philosophical Review*, 315–360.

Chatterjee, A. (2010). Disembodying cognition. *Language and Cognition*, 2, 79–116.

Churchland, P. S. (1986). *Neurophilosophy*. Cambridge, MA: MIT Press.

Cohen, J. (2009). *The red and the real: An essay on color ontology*. New York, NY: Oxford University Press.

Cytowic, R. E. (2002). *Synesthesia: A union of the senses*. Cambridge, MA: MIT Press.

Daniel, D. (1991). *Consciousness explained*. New York: Little Brown & Co.

de Regt, H. W. (2009). The epistemic value of understanding. *Philosophy of Science, 76*(5), 585–597.

Diaz-Leon, E. (2008). Defending the phenomenal concept strategy. *Australasian Journal of Philosophy, 86*(4), 597–610.

Diaz-Leon, E. (2010). Can phenomenal concepts explain the epistemic gap? *Mind, 119*(476), 933–951.

Doggett, T., & Stoljar, D. (2010). Does Nagel's footnote even solve the mind-body problem? *Philosophical Issues, 20*(1), 125–143.

Dove, G. (2009). Beyond perceptual symbols: A call for representational pluralism. *Cognition, 110*, 412–431.

Dove, G. (2011). On the need for embodied and dis-embodied cognition. *Frontiers in Cognition, 1*, Article 242.

Elpidorou, A. (2012). Are phenomenal concepts perspectival? *Southwest Philosophy Review, 28*(1), 43–53.

Elpidorou, A. (2013). Having it both ways: Consciousness, unique not otherworldly. *Philosophia, 41*(4), 1181–1203.

Elpidorou, A. (2015). Phenomenal concepts. In D. Pritchard (ed.), *Oxford bibliographies in philosophy*. New York: Oxford University Press.

Elpidorou, A. (2016). A posteriori physicalism and introspection. *Pacific Philosophical Quarterly, 97*(4), 474–500.

Faye, J. (2014). Copenhagen interpretation of quantum mechanics. In E. N. Zalta (ed.), *The Stanford encyclopedia of philosophy*. https://plato.stanford.edu/archives/fall2014/entries/qm-copenhagen/

Feynman, R. P., Leighton, R. B., & Sands, M. (2010). *The Feynman lectures on physics, Vol. II: The new millennium edition*. New York, NY: Basic books.

Fischer, M. H., & Zwaan, R. A. (2008). Embodied language: A review of the motor system in language comprehension. *The Quarterly Journal of Experimental Psychology, 6*, 825–850.

Fulkerson, M. (2011). The unity of haptic touch. *Philosophical Psychology, 24*(4), 493–516.

Fulkerson, M. (2014). Explaining multisensory experience. In R. Brown (ed.), *Consciousness inside and out: Phenomenology, neuroscience, and the nature of experience* (pp. 365–373). Netherlands: Springer.

Gallese, V., & Lakoff, G. (2005). The brain's concepts: The role of the sensory-motor system in reason and language. *Cognitive Neuropsychology, 22*, 455–479.

Gerlach, C. (2007). A review of functional imaging studies on category specificity. *Journal of Cognitive Neuroscience, 19*(2), 296–314.

Gertler, B. (2001). Introspecting phenomenal states. *Philosophy and Phenomenological Research, 63*(2), 305–328.

Glenberg, A. M. (1997). What memory is for. *Behavioral and Brain Sciences, 20*, 1–55.

Glenberg, A. M., & Kaschak, M. P. (2002). Grounding language in action. *Psychonomic Bulletin and Review, 9*, 558–565.

Gonzalez, J., Barros-Loscertales, A., Pulvermüller, F., Meseguer, V., Sanjuan, A., Belloch, V., & Avil, C. (2006). Reading *cinnamon* activates olfactory brain regions. *Neuroimage, 32*, 906–912.

Grossenbacher, P. G., & Lovelace, C. T. (2001). Mechanisms of synesthesia: Cognitive and physiological constraints. *Trends in Cognitive Sciences*, *5*(1), 36–41.
Hauk, O., Johnsrude, I., & Pulvermüller, F. (2004). Somatotopic representation of action words in human motor and premotor cortex. *Neuron*, *41*, 301–307.
Hawthorne, J. (2002). Advice for physicalists. *Philosophical Studies*, *109*(1), 17–52.
Healey, R. (2013). Physical composition. *Studies in History and Philosophy of Science Part B: Studies in History and Philosophy of Modern Physics*, *44*(1), 48–62.
Hesslow, G. (2012). Current status of the simulation theory of cognition. *Brain Research*, *1428*, 71–79.
Hill, C. S. (1984). In defense of type materialism. *Synthese*, *59*(3), 295–320.
Hill, C. S. (1997). Imaginability, conceivability, possibility and the mind-body problem. *Philosophical Studies*, *87*, 61–85.
Hill, C. S., & McLaughlin, B. (1999). There are fewer things in reality than are dreamt of in Chalmers's philosophy. *Philosophy and Phenomenological Research*, *59*, 445–454.
Hubbard, E. M., Arman, A. C., Ramachandran, V. S., & Boynton, G. M. (2005). Individual differences among grapheme-color synesthetes: brain-behavior correlations. *Neuron*, *45*(6), 975–985.
Ismael, J. (1999). Science and the phenomenal. *Philosophy of Science*, *66*(3), 351–369.
Jackson, F. (1980). A note on physicalism and heat. *Australasian Journal of Philosophy*, *58*(1), 26–34.
Keeley, B. L. (2002). Making sense of the senses. *The Journal of Philosophy*, *99*(1), 5–28.
Kemmerer, D. (2010). How words capture visual experience: The perspective from cognitive neuroscience. In B. Malt & P. Wolff (eds.), *Words and the world: How words capture human experience* (pp. 289–329). Oxford, UK: Oxford University Press.
Kiefer, M., & Pulvermüller, F. (2012). Conceptual representations in mind and brain: Theoretical developments, current evidence, and future directions. *Cortex*, *48*, 805–825.
Kiefer, M., Sim, E., Herrnberger, B., Grothe, J., & Hoenig, K. (2008). The sound of concepts: Four markers for a link between auditory and conceptual systems. *The Journal of Neuroscience*, *28*(47), 12224–12230.
Kripke, S. (1971). Identity and necessity. In M. K. Munitz (ed.), *Identity and individuation* (pp. 135–164). New York, NY: New York University Press.
Kripke, S. (1980). *Naming and necessity*. Cambridge, MA: Harvard University Press.
Levin, J. (2007a). What is a phenomenal concept? In T. Alter & S. Walter (eds.), *Phenomenal concepts and phenomenal knowledge: New essays on consciousness and physicalism* (pp. 87–110). New York, NY: Oxford University Press.
Levin, J. (2007b). Nagel vs. Nagel on the nature of phenomenal concepts. *Ratio*, *20*(3), 293–307.
Levine, J. (2001). *Purple haze: The puzzle of consciousness*. Oxford, UK: Oxford University Press.
Levine, J. (2007). Phenomenal concepts and the materialist constraint. In T. Alter & S. Walter (eds.), *Phenomenal concepts and phenomenal knowledge: New essays on consciousness and physicalism* (pp. 81–108). New York, NY: Oxford University Press.
Loar, B. (1990). Phenomenal states. *Philosophical Perspectives*, *4*, 81–108.

Loar, B. (1997). Phenomenal states. In N. Block, O. Flanagan, & G. Güzeldere (eds.), *The nature of consciousness: Philosophical debates* (pp. 597–616). Cambridge, MA: MIT Press.

Loar, B. (2003). Qualia, properties, and modality. *Philosophical Issues*, *13*(1), 113–129.

Louwerse, M. (2011). Symbol interdependency in symbolic and embodied cognition. *Topics in Cognitive Science*, *3*, 273–302.

Louwerse, M., & Connell, L. (2011). A taste of words: Linguistic context and perceptual simulation predict the modality of words. *Cognitive Science*, *35*, 381–398.

Lycan, W. G. (1987). *Consciousness*. Cambridge, MA: MIT Press.

Lynott, D., & Connell, L. (2010). Embodied conceptual combination. *Frontiers in Psychology*, *1*, Article 212.

Macdonald, C. (2004). Mary meets Molyneux: The explanatory gap and the individuation of phenomenal concepts. *Noûs*, *38*(3), 503–524.

Machery, E. (2007). Concept empiricism: A methodological critique. *Cognition*, *104*, 19–46.

Machery, E. (2009). *Doing without concepts*. New York, NY: Oxford University Press.

Macpherson, F. (2011). Taxonomising the senses. *Philosophical Studies*, *153*(1), 123–142.

Mahon, B. Z. (2015). What is embodied about cognition. *Language, Cognition, and Neuroscience*, *30*(4), 420–429.

Mahon, B. Z., & Caramazza, A. (2008). A critical look at the embodied cognition hypothesis and a new proposal for grounding conceptual content. *Journal of Physiology—Paris*, *102*(1), 59–70.

Markman, A. B., & Brendl, C. M. (2005). Constraining theories of embodied cognition. *Psychological Science*, *16*, 6–10.

Martin, A., Wiggs, C. L., Ungerleider, L. G., & Haxby, J. V. (1996). Neural correlates of category-specific knowledge. *Nature*, *379*, 649–652.

Meteyard, L., Cuadrado, S. R., Bahrami, B., & Vigliocco, G. (2012). Coming of age: A review of embodiment and the neuroscience of semantics. *Cortex*, *48*, 788–804.

Nagel, T. (1974). What is it like to be a bat? *The Philosophical Review*, *83*(4), 435–450.

Nunn, J. A., Gregory, L. J., Brammer, M., Williams, S. C., Parslow, D. M., Morgan, M.J., et al. (2002). Functional magnetic resonance imaging of synesthesia: activation of V4/V8 by spoken words. *Nature Neuroscience*, *5*(4), 371–375.

O'Callaghan, C. (2008). Seeing what you hear: Cross-modal illusions and perception. *Philosophical Issues*, *18*(1), 316–338.

Papineau, D. (1993). Physicalism, consciousness and the antipathetic fallacy. *Australasian Journal of Philosophy*, *71*(2), 169–183.

Papineau, D. (2002). *Thinking about consciousness*. Oxford, UK: Oxford University Press.

Papineau, D. (2007). Phenomenal and perceptual concepts. In T. Alter & S. Walter (eds.), *Phenomenal concepts and phenomenal knowledge: New essays on consciousness and physicalism* (pp. 111–144). Oxford, UK: Oxford University Press.

Pecher, D., Zeelenberg, R., & Barsalou, L. W. (2003). Verifying properties from different modalities for concepts produces switching costs. *Psychological Science*, *14*, 119–124.

Perry, J. (2001). *Knowledge, possibility and consciousness*. Cambridge, MA: MIT Press.
Prinz, J. J. (2002). *Furnishing the mind: Concepts and their perceptual basis*. Cambridge, MA: MIT Press.
Pulvermüller, F., Hauk, O., Nikulin, V. V., & Ilmonlemi, R. J. (2005). Functional links between motor and language systems. *European Journal of Neuroscience*, *21*, 793–797.
Rowlands, M. (2001). *The nature of consciousness*. Cambridge, UK: Cambridge University Press.
Schroer, R. (2010). Where's the beef? Phenomenal concepts as both demonstrative and substantial. *Australasian Journal of Philosophy*, *88*(3), 505–522.
Scorolli, C., & Borghi, A. M. (2007). Sentence comprehension and action: Effector specific modulation of the motor system. *Brain Research*, *1130*, 119–124.
Shapiro, L. (2011). *Embodied cognition*. New York, NY: Routledge.
Shea, N. (2014). Using phenomenal concepts to explain away the intuition of contingency. *Philosophical Psychology*, *27*(4), 553–570.
Simmons, K. W., & Barsalou, L. W. (2003). The similarity-in-topography principle: Reconciling theories of conceptual deficits. *Cognitive Neuropsychology*, *20*, 451–486.
Spiller, M. J., & Jansari, A. S. (2008). Mental imagery and synaesthesia: Is synaesthesia from internally-generated stimuli possible? *Cognition*, *109*, 143–151.
Stalnaker, R. (2008). *Our knowledge of the internal world*. Oxford, UK: Oxford University Press.
Stoljar, D. (2000). Physicalism and the necessary a posteriori. *The Journal of Philosophy*, *97*(1), 33–54.
Stoljar, D. (2005). Physicalism and phenomenal concepts. *Mind & Language*, *20*(5), 469–495.
Sturgeon, S. (1994). The epistemic view of subjectivity. *The Journal of Philosophy*, *91*(5), 221–235.
Tettamanti, M., Buccino, G., Saccuman, M., Gallese, V., Danna, M., Scifo, P., . . . Perani, D. (2005). Listening to action-related sentences activates fronto-parietal motor circuits. *Journal of Cognitive Neuroscience*, *17*, 273–281.
Trout, J. D. (2002). Scientific explanation and the sense of understanding. *Philosophy of Science*, *69*(2), 212–233.
Trout, J. D. (2007). The psychology of scientific explanation. *Philosophy Compass*, *2*(3), 564–591.
Trumpp, N. M., Kliese, D., Hoenig, K., Haarmeier, T., & Kiefer, M. (2013). Losing the sound of concepts: Damage to auditory association cortex impairs the processing of sound-related concepts. *Cortex*, *49*, 474–486.
Tye, M. (1995). *Ten Problems of consciousness: A representational theory of the phenomenal mind*. Cambridge, MA: MIT Press.
Tye, M. (1999). Phenomenal consciousness: The explanatory gap as a cognitive illusion. *Mind*, *108*(432), 705–725.
Tye, M. (2000). *Consciousness, colour and content*. Cambridge, MA: MIT Press.
Tye, M. (2003). A theory of phenomenal concepts. *Royal Institute of Philosophy Supplement*, *53*, 91–105.
Tye, M. (2009). *Consciousness revisited: Materialism without phenomenal concepts*. Cambridge, MA: MIT Press.

van Dantzig, S., Pecher, D., Zeelenberg, R., & Barsalou, L. W. (2008). Perceptual processing affects conceptual processing. *Cognitive Science*, *32*, 579–590.
van Elk, M., Slors, M., & Bekkering, H. (2010). Embodied language comprehension requires an enactivist paradigm of cognition. *Frontiers in Psychology*, *1*, Article 234.
Veillet, B. (2012). In defense of phenomenal concepts. *Philosophical Papers*, *41*(1), 97–127.
Ward, J., & Mattingly, J. B. (2006). Synaesthesia: An overview of contemporary findings and controversies. *Cortex*, *42*, 129–136.
Weiskopf, D. (2007). Concept empiricism and the vehicles of thought. *Journal of Consciousness Studies*, *14*(9–10), 156–183.
Willems, R. M., & Casasanto, D. (2011). Flexibility in embodied understanding. *Frontiers in Psychology*, *2*, Article 116.
Willems, R. M., Hagoort, P., & Casasanto, D. (2010). Body-specific representation of action words: Neural evidence from right- and left-handers. *Psychological Science*, *21*, 67–74.
Wilson-Mendenhall, C. D., Simmons, W. K., Martin, A., & Barsalou, L. W. (2013). Contextual processing of abstract concepts reveals neural representations of nonlinguistic semantic content. *Journal of Cognitive Neuroscience*, *25*, 920–935.
Wright, W. (2007). Explanation and the hard problem. *Philosophical Studies*, *132*(2), 301–330.

8 Conclusion

Our preferred version of physicalism is unlike others in the literature—although it contains insights from various and differing attempts to explicate the character of physicalism, the resulting position has no exact precedent in the literature. First, we hold that physicalism should not be understood as a metaphysical thesis: According to our view, physicalism is neither a thesis nor is it primarily about metaphysics. Instead, we treat physicalism as an ongoing interdisciplinary project that strives to explain natural phenomena in a manner that makes explicit how they arise out of and are nothing over and above physical entities. It is through this explanatory project that physicalism would be vindicated. Second, we do not assume the success of research program physicalism. Rather, we have argued that there are no good theoretical reasons to think that it cannot be successful. And given our progress in the sciences of the mind, we contend that the eventual success of research program physicalism is probable. Third, although our version of physicalism is explanatory at heart, we reject the use of a deductive-nomological model of explanation in favor of a compositional account of explanation. Contrary to received opinion within the metaphysics of consciousness literature, the deductive-nomological model is doubly unfit: it fails to accurately capture our best explanations in science and is not necessary for physicalism. Compositional explanation liberates physicalism from its metaphysical and epistemological shackles and renders it continuous with scientific practice. Physicalism—*our* physicalism—is neither "outside" of nor "above" science. It is instead scientific practice in action.

1. Neither Type-A nor Type-B nor Type-C

How does our view of physicalism compare to other existing formulations of physicalism? Although we have touched upon this question in various places throughout the book, we would be remiss if we were not to discuss how our position fits in the existing taxonomy. Following David Chalmers's (2003/2010) essay, "Consciousness and its Place in Nature," it is customary to divide (unambiguously) physicalist positions into three categories: type-A materialism, type-B materialism, and type-C materialism.

(i) Type-A materialism holds that there is no epistemic (and thus no explanatory) gap between truths about (phenomenal) consciousness and physical truths. If an explanatory gap appears, its appearance is illusory. Most type-A materialists hold that an explanation of consciousness will be exhausted by an explanation of consciousness' function and all hold that truths about consciousness are a priori entailed by the totality of physical truths.

(ii) Type-B materialism holds that there is an epistemic (and thus a permanent explanatory) gap between truths about (phenomenal) consciousness and physical truths. Still, it denies that there exists a corresponding ontological gap: Although we might be incapable of offering a physicalist explanation of consciousness, consciousness is still physical. The phenomenal concept strategy (PCS) discussed in the previous chapter is an example of a view that espouses type-B materialism.

(iii) Type-C materialism accepts that the complete physical description of the world a priori entails truths about phenomenal consciousness while maintaining that we cannot "see" how this entailment thesis can be true.[1] As Chalmers puts it: "while we cannot see now how to solve the hard problem in physical terms, the problem is solvable in principle."[2]

We fall in none of the categories. As we discussed in the previous chapter, we reject the PCS and all versions of type-B materialism. We think that any physicalist position should offer an explanation of consciousness' place in the world in a manner that shows how consciousness arises out of the physical. Without such a requirement in place, type-B materialism remains, in our eyes, a problematic version of physicalism: It is too weak to ground an acceptable form of physicalism because the connection between physical processes and consciousness remains brute. To put this contention in another way, type-B materialism is compatible with the failure of research program physicalism. Clearly then, we are not type-B materialist.

Both type-A and type-C hold that there is no explanatory gap between phenomenal truths and physical truths and justify this claim by maintaining that there is no epistemic gap between the two—the former truths are a priori entailed by the latter. Research program physicalism differs from type-A and type-C in two important respects. First, we reject the model of explanation assumed by both type-A and type-C. We do not accept that a priori entailment of phenomenal truths from physical truths is a necessary condition for an adequate physical explanation. Thus, research program physicalism can focus on the explanatory gap without having to decide on the fate of the epistemic gap. The research program is an explanatory project and not a metaphysical thesis. It strives to offer a compositional explanation of consciousness and if such an explanation were to be provided, it would mark the success of the program. The question as to whether in addition to such a compositional explanation there are also logical connections between physical and phenomenal truths, is beside the point. Second, just like type-A and type-C materialism, the research program denies that there are a priori reasons that demonstrate that the explanatory gap is permanent. However, it does not assume that there is no explanatory gap. Unlike type-A and type-B, our version of physicalism is an a posteriori explanatory project. As such, it cannot assume its success from the start. Whether the research program succeeds or not in offering a compositional explanation of consciousness is an open, empirical question.

If we are neither type-A, nor type-B, nor type-C, then what type of physicalists are we? We do not particularly care about categories. But if one must think of our view in terms of Chalmers' categories, then we are closest to type-Q materialism than any other type of physicalism. Chalmers describes type-Q materialism in the following way:

> Are there any other options for the materialist? One further option is to reject the distinctions on which this taxonomy rests. For example, some philosophers, especially followers of Quine (1951), reject any distinction between conceptual truth and empirical truth, or between the a priori and the a posteriori, or between the contingent and the necessary. One who is sufficiently Quinean might therefore reject the distinction between type-A and type-B materialism, holding that talk of epistemic implication and/or modal entailment is ungrounded, but that materialism is true nevertheless. We might call such a view type-Q materialism.
>
> (Chalmers, 2010, pp. 123–124)

Our view is not in any substantial sense Quinean. Nothing of what we have claimed relies on the rejection of the listed distinctions. Nonetheless, we do reject the terms on which the standard physicalist/anti-physicalist debate stands. In particular, we have argued that physicalism should be conceived of as an explanatory project that aims to offer compositional explanations of natural phenomena. If a type-Q materialist is merely someone who rejects the relevance of epistemic implication, then we are type-Q materialists.

Chalmers does not examine in detail the prospects of type-Q materialism (for recent defenses, see Mandik & Weisberg, 2008; Weisberg, 2011). But he does think that it is not a viable option. He writes:

> Still, even on this view, similar issues arise. Some Quineans hold that explaining the functions explain everything (Dennett may be an example); if so, all the problems of type-A materialism arise. Others hold that we can postulate identities between physical states and conscious states in virtue of the strong isomorphic connections between them in nature (Paul Churchland may be an example); if so, the problems of type-B materialism arise. Others may appeal to novel future sorts of explanation; if so, the problems of type-C materialism arise. So the Quinean approach cannot avoid the relevant problems.
>
> (Chalmers, 2010, p. 124)

We have no interest in defending type-Q materialism as such. We do wish, however, to defend our position. Compositional explanation is neither functional explanation nor identity. Compositional explanation is stronger than a type of explanation based on isomorphic connections. And compositional explanation is not a novel type of explanation, but rather one that figures prominently in successful scientific practice. What is more, in Chapters 5–7 we discussed in detail why our version of physicalism does not face the problems of type-A, type-B, and type-C materialism. Whatever Chalmers lists as issues for other versions of type-Q materialism, they do not apply to the research program. Thus, even if research program physicalism is a version of type-Q materialism, it is not one that has been given the attention that it deserves in the literature.

2. Still, It Is Physicalism and Not Physicalism*

We have called for a reconceptualization of physicalism. But reconstructive projects like ours are often met with incredulity. One could ask: "Is research program physicalism really physicalism?"; "Don't you need to assert the existence of conceptual or metaphysical connections (or necessities) between the physical and the non-physical (mental, social, biological, etc.) in order for your view to be physicalist?"; or "Shouldn't you have called your position 'physicalism*' in order to distinguish it from real physicalism?" Our answers: "No," "No," and "No." Research program physicalism is a real form of physicalism and not a physicalism in name only.

Attempts to delineate genuine versions of physicalism from ersatz or imitation ones often fail to acknowledge the variety of views that have been presented as physicalist. There are identity, supervenience, a priori entailment, realization, Grounding, truthmaking, and part-whole definitions of physicalism. There are characterizations of physicalism that involve fundamental properties and others that reject that physicalism is committed to the existence of a fundamental level. There are views of physicalism that understand physicalism to be a metaphysical thesis and others that take physicalism to be an attitude. And there are even those who do not think that there is such a thing as physicalism. There is no uncontroversial dictionary definition of "physicalism." Nor is there an agreed-upon definition of the term within philosophical discourse. Rather, "physicalism" refers to a family of positions that aim to articulate the nature of our world in a manner that assigns some kind of priority (ontological, metaphysical, or explanatory) to its physical nature. To explicate this account further is already to take a position as to how physicalism ought to be understood. A sober look at the vast and variegated literature on physicalism reveals that "physicalism" is said in many ways. To demand that "physicalism" applies only to positions that meet certain predetermined criteria is both to overlook the complexities of the literature on physicalism and to fail to acknowledge that physicalism is still a moving target.

We suspect that some would remain unmoved by our call to be permissive and open about the meaning of the term "physicalism." Instead, they would argue that regardless of how physicalism has been used, there is a way to separate legitimate articulations of physicalism from ones that are physicalist in name only. The driving contention behind this distinction is two-fold: Any form of physicalism that does not demand the existence of either conceptual or metaphysical connections between the physical and the non-physical fails (a) to show how the non-physical is nothing over and above the physical and (b) to distinguish itself from non-physicalist alternatives. We reject both parts of this criticism.

On the one hand, the demand that conceptual or metaphysical connections are necessary in order for the non-physical to be nothing over and above the physical is misplaced. First, there are proponents of physicalism who deny the existence of conceptual connections between the physical and the non-physical and still maintain that the latter is nothing over and above the former. In fact, the very distinction between *a priori* and *a posteriori* physicalism is premised on the viability of such versions of physicalism. Hence, the existence of conceptual connections is not a necessary condition for physicalism. Second, proponents of physicalism can choose to explicate the notion of nothing-over-and-aboveness in metaphysical terms. Indeed, many of them have done precisely that. However, as we have argued in Chapter 2, such attempts face important difficulties. Still, the respective positions are physicalist, and recognizably so. Thus, one need not offer a fully articulated account of the presumed metaphysical connections between the physical and the non-physical in order to present a physicalist view. What this suggests is that the notion of nothing-over-and-aboveness is prior to the various metaphysical notions (supervenience, Grounding, realization, etc.) that are enlisted in attempts to make it explicit. Third and most important, we have argued that there is an alternative (i.e., a non-conceptual and non-metaphysical) account of the notion of over-and-aboveness that does justice to physcialism's contention that the non-physical is nothing over and above the physical. Demanding that non-physical (but natural) phenomena are compositionally explained in terms of their physical components is a way of showing that the non-physical is nothing and over above the physical. The existence of compositional explanations of this type would not only establish a hierarchical relationship between the non-physical and the physical, but it would also offer a clear account of how the various non-physical (but natural) phenomena arise *solely* out of their physical components.

On the other hand, research program physicalism does not require the presence of either conceptual or metaphysical connections in order to distinguish itself from its non-physicalist competitors. To see this we must emphasize that our proposed take on physicalism does not merely call for a reconceptualization of physicalism itself but also of its relationship to other positions. In fact, if physicalism is no longer understood as a thesis, then its competitors will not be *theses* either. As such, research program physicalism is not distinguished from its competitors in virtue of the fact that it accepts certain metaphysical theses that other positions deny. Rather, research program physicalism is distinguished from its competitors in virtue of its explanatory commitments as a research program.

Once both physicalism and its competitors are conceived of as research programs, there is no difficulty in distinguishing between research program physicalism, (research program) dualism, (research program) Russellian monism, and (research program) emergentism. Indeed, all of these competing programs are competitors because they are not committed to offering compositional explanations of all natural phenomena. For (research program) dualism, consciousness will never be *physically* explained. For (research program) Russellian monism, consciousness will not be *compositionally* explained in terms of its physical parts. And for (research program) emergentism, not *all* phenomena will be compositionally explained—some will and some will be not. It should be clear that our demand that all natural phenomena ought to be compositionally explained is a strong one: Not only does it solve various location problems insofar as it shows how natural phenomena arise out of their physical components, it also readily distinguishes our position from non-physicalist alternatives. Naturally, we think that the prospects of research program physicalism are much better than any of these.

3. Consciousness, Again

One should not exaggerate consciousness' complexity and apparent *sui generis* status. It is fine to take consciousness seriously; one, however, should not take it too seriously. The fact that consciousness appears to us to be different than the physical entities that surround us does not mean that it is in fact different. Likewise, the fact that it is hard to understand how collections of interacting neurons can give rise to conscious phenomena does not mean that they do not. Non-Euclidean structures were taken to be impossible and the relativity of mass seemed unimaginable. But now we know that such phenomena are not only possible but are likely to be actual. And we have adequate explanations or accounts for them. Failure of imagination is neither an accurate ontological guide nor a reliable predictor of the demise of a research program.

What is more, the problem of consciousness as a *problem* should also not be exaggerated. Claims to the contrary notwithstanding, consciousness is not the only scientific problem that we currently have little idea of how to solve. In Chapter 3, we mentioned in passing the problem of baryogenesis, namely, the fact that we are not currently in a position to explain why there is more (observed) matter than antimatter in the universe. And there are more. We do not understand dark energy, the arrow of time, how measurements collapse quantum wavefunctions, why charge-parity violations happen, and why fundamental constants have the values that they do. Even more down-to-earth phenomena have proven resilient to our persistent attempts to explain them. The exact beginnings of life still remain a mystery, the phenomenon of protein folding is not well understood, and currently we have no theory of turbulence. The list goes on and on. Most of these problems do not call for a rejection of a physicalist ontology, so why should the problem of consciousness get special treatment? There are, of course, philosophical reasons in support of the claim that consciousness is indeed special and thus our inability to explain it is not temporary and ontologically revealing. Yet, as we have already seen (Chapters 5–7), a close examination of these reasons does not yield the desired anti-physicalist conclusion.

The litmus test of the research program is consciousness. Will we be able to explain it compositionally or not? We do not think that this question is going to be settled any time soon. And although we consider the success of research program physicalism probable, we cannot guarantee it. All the same, we are confident in the value of treating consciousness not as an insuperable obstacle for physicalism but as a phenomenon that calls for explanation. This is how neuroscientists and other practicing physicalists view consciousness. We will be well served if we do the same. Faced with the problem of consciousness, one needs both patience and perseverance.

Notes

1. Even if we cannot "see" how the entailment can be carried out, some have argued that we can still "see" *why* the entailment thesis has to be true: Jackson (1998), Chalmers and Jackson (2001) and Boutel (2013).
2. Chalmers does not think that type-C materialism is a stable position: He argues that it ultimately collapses into a type of physicalism (type-A or type-B materialism), Russellian Monism (type-F monism), or dualism (type-D dualism). Not everyone agrees with Chalmers's assessment. See, for example, Dowell (2008) and Boutel (2013).

References

Boutel, A. (2013). How to be a type-C physicalist. *Philosophical Studies*, *164*, 301–320.

Chalmers, D. J. (2003). Consciousness and its place in nature. In S. P. Stich & T. A. Warfield (eds.), *The Blackwell guide to philosophy of mind* (pp. 102–142). Malden, MA: Blackwell Publishing. Revised version in Chalmers, 2010, pp. 103–140.

Chalmers, D. J. (2010). *The character of consciousness*. New York, NY: Oxford University Press.

Chalmers, D. J., & Jackson, F. (2001). Conceptual analysis and reductive explanation. *Philosophical Review*, *110*, 315–361.

Dowell, J. L. (2008). A priori entailment and conceptual analysis: Making room for type-C physicalism. *Australasian Journal of Philosophy*, *86*, 93–111.

Jackson, F. (1998). *From metaphysics to ethics: A defence of conceptual analysis.* Oxford, UK: Oxford University Press.

Mandik, P., & Weisberg, J. (2008). Type-Q materialism. In C. Wrenn (ed.), *Naturalism, reference, and ontology: Essays in honor of Roger F. Gibson* (pp. 223–246). New York, NY: Peter Lang Publishing.

Weisberg, J. (2011). The zombie's cogito: Meditations on type-Q materialism. *Philosophical Psychology, 24*(5), 585–605. doi:10.1080/09515089.2011.562646

Index